THE POETRY OF HISTORY

... THE POETRY OF HISTORY DOES NOT CONSIST OF IMAGINATION ROAMING AT LARGE, BUT OF IMAGINATION PURSUING THE FACT AND FASTENING UPON IT. ... JUST BECAUSE IT REALLY HAPPENED, IT GATHERS ROUND IT ALL THE INSCRUTABLE MYSTERY OF LIFE AND DEATH AND TIME. LET THE SCIENCE AND RESEARCH OF THE HISTORIAN FIND THE FACT, AND LET HIS IMAGINATION AND ART MAKE CLEAR ITS SIGNIFICANCE.

George Macaulay Trevelyan

THE POETRY OF HISTORY

THE CONTRIBUTION OF
LITERATURE AND LITERARY SCHOLARSHIP
TO THE WRITING OF HISTORY
SINCE VOLTAIRE

Emery Neff

NEW YORK AND LONDON
COLUMBIA UNIVERSITY PRESS

D
13
.N35

COPYRIGHT © 1947 COLUMBIA UNIVERSITY PRESS, NEW YORK
COLUMBIA PAPERBACK EDITION 1961
MANUFACTURED IN THE UNITED STATES OF AMERICA

*TO THOSE WHO BELIEVE THAT
KNOWLEDGE IS ONE AND
INDIVISIBLE*

FOREWORD

The Poetry of History is the fourth in a series of books breaking down the compartments of literature, history, science, social studies and philosophy, to exhibit the interdependence of ideas, events, and art. The first, *Carlyle and Mill* (1924, 1926), uses the personal and intellectual relations of those contrasting figures as an introduction to the complex pattern of Victorian thought and society. *Carlyle* (1932) is a critical biography of the versatile historian and man of letters. *A Revolution in European Poetry* (1940) relates the major changes in literary taste and creation in France, England, Germany, and Italy since the seventeenth century to corresponding revolutions in science, politics, and economics. The present book, resting on this previous work, will show how literature and literary scholarship, in conjunction with political events and with developments in science and industry, have affected the spirit, form, and content of historical writing since Voltaire. It will confine itself to Europe, since there alone have historical writing, literature, and science had parallel development in a changing but fairly homogeneous society for the past two hundred years.

The common purpose of these books is to clarify the picture of the modern world and to present a basis for intelligent action in this period of crisis. For readers with an appetite for ideas without technical husks, *The Poetry of History* is offered in the form of narrative that represents the flow of history, mingling ideas, events, and artistic creations.

To Jacques Barzun, who advised concerning the plan of the book and encouraged its progress with stimulating suggestions, the author is deeply indebted. Lionel Trilling, Irwin Edman,

Elliott V. K. Dobbie and Alan Brown gave without stint from their special knowledge. For errors of fact and judgment that remain, the author is alone responsible.

Acknowledgment is gratefully made Alfred A. Knopf, Inc. for permission to quote from the authorized translation of *The Decline of the West*, by Oswald Spengler; to Harcourt, Brace and Company for permission to quote from the authorized translation of *History: Its Theory and Practice* by Benedetto Croce; to the Cambridge University Press for permission to quote from *A History of Classical Scholarship*, by Sir John Sandys; to the Oxford University Press for permission to quote from *A Study of History*, by Arnold J. Toynbee; to Longmans, Green and Company for permission to quote passages from *Clio, A Muse and Other Essays*, by George Macaulay Trevelyan, including the motto for this study; to Charles Scribner's Sons for permission to quote from Edmund Gosse's *Father and Son;* and to Mr. Oskar Piest for permission to quote from J. G. Herder's *God: Some Conversations*, translated by Frederick Burckhardt.

E. N.

New York
February, 1947

CONTENTS

Part One: Perspectives Open

I. VOLTAIRE SHATTERS TRADITION	3
II. HERDER AND GOETHE: THE LIVING PAST	21
III. GIBBON, VICO, AND THE MASSES	79

Part Two: The Fulfillment

IV. THE FASCINATION OF ORIGINS: NIEBUHR, OTFRIED MÜLLER	93
V. THE ROMANTIC GARB: CHATEAUBRIAND, SCOTT, THIERRY, CARLYLE	116
VI. RESURRECTION OF THE PAST: MICHELET	129
VII. HISTORY AS ART: RENAN, BURCKHARDT, GREEN	150

Part Three: Toward a New Synthesis

VIII. HISTORY AS SCIENCE	189
IX. TWENTIETH-CENTURY THOUGHT IN SEARCH OF A HISTORIAN	203
Notes	225
Selected References	241
Index	249

PART ONE

PERSPECTIVES OPEN

I

VOLTAIRE SHATTERS TRADITION

"WHEN a historian is reviving former times, the interest in them and sympathy with them will be the deeper, the greater the events he has witnessed with a bleeding or a rejoicing heart. His feelings are moved by justice and injustice, by wisdom or folly, by coming or departing greatness, as if all were going on before his eyes; and when he is thus moved his lips speak, although Hecuba is nothing to the player." This eloquent testimony of Niebuhr to the vibrating effect of the Napoleonic struggle upon his study of ancient Rome needs no underlining for the twentieth century. We know it was not chance which made the golden age of historical writing open with the great upheavals of the eighteenth century, the American, French, and Industrial Revolutions, and continue into our own disturbed time. But political, economic and scientific change alone could not have produced the distinctive quality of this golden age: intimate, sympathetic and unreserved participation in the life of the past such as warms Niebuhr's words. This was the gift of still another revolution begun in the eighteenth century, a revolution in taste and in literary creation.

The highest step in human culture will be to comprehend humanity. To that end, history has been breaking its traditional bounds of public affairs, wars, and religion to record every manifestation of the human spirit. Literature—the expression of man's desires and aspirations, imagination and taste—has furthered this advance as much as science, the austere expression of his will to know. The aid of letters has gone far beyond form and style, described in books on "history as literature."

It has given historians their subtlest and profoundest insight into the human spirit. But where literature dominates the historian to his neglect of science, or science to his neglect of literature, the picture of humanity is distorted. History nears perfection in so far as knowledge and art work in harmony. The approaches to that harmony will be my theme.

I have called the book "The Poetry of History," because poetry seems the most adequate symbol for the quintessence of the human spirit. I might have named it "The Artistry of Knowledge," to describe the means historians have chosen to win humanity to recognize its own likeness, to understand itself. From an era fertile in historians, I have selected those who represent the highest synthesis of literature with science and social consciousness. As a French writer has said: "Truth is not always beautiful; beauty is not always true. But truth and beauty have their points of meeting. I seek them out."

History of this superlative quality emerges when Voltaire, armed with the results of physical science, assaults the theological version of history dominant in Europe for the fourteen centuries since Saint Augustine's *City of God*, and the more recent Humanist reverence for the literal text of the great Greek and Latin historians. But the view of Voltaire and his generation of "philosophical" historians was still narrow and distorted. The account of its correction and broadening by a revolution in literary taste, supported by new sciences, will bring us to our theme.

"You wish that philosophers had written ancient history, because you want to read it as a philosopher," Voltaire addressed the reader of his *Essay on the Manners and Character of the Nations:* "You are looking for useful truths and have

VOLTAIRE SHATTERS TRADITION

found, you say, scarcely anything but useless errors. Let us try to enlighten ourselves together; let us try to disinter some precious monuments from the ruins of centuries." This boldly confident proposal rested upon the special meaning of the word philosopher for eighteenth-century Europe. The Dictionary of the French Academy (1694) had defined *philosophe* (philosopher) as "one who applies himself to the study of the sciences, and in them seeks to recognize effects by their causes and principles.... Sometimes arbitrarily used to denote a man who, by free thought, puts himself above the duties and obligations of civil life." When Voltaire wrote his *Essay* half a century later, the secondary meaning of "free-thinker" had lost its derogatory flavor among most educated men, who prided themselves upon emancipation from the "prejudices" which had hitherto clouded the human mind. The entirely favorable use of "philosopher" in both senses is familiar to readers of Gibbon.

The triumphs of science since the seventeenth century had filled Voltaire's public with a vertiginous sense of man's power to know all things and by knowledge to control his future. Not long after the globe, the theater of history, had been circumnavigated, Galileo's telescope opened infinite stellar space and the microscope revealed a corresponding universe of the infinitely small. Man's mind proved capable of understanding both infinities. By algebra, an abstract construction of the intellect, Descartes solved problems of real and solid space. Newton in 1687 demonstrated that the solar system behaves according to mathematical principles. Nothing was found too subtle or too fleet for mathematical measurement. The pendulum clock recorded accurately the passage of time, the barometer the pressure of the atmosphere, the thermometer heat and cold. In 1675 Roemer calculated the speed of light.

The greatest poet of the early eighteenth century was moved to say:

> Nature, and Nature's laws, lay hid in night:
> God said, Let Newton be, and all was light.

Light, Enlightenment became the pride of the eighteenth century. Never had so many shared confidence in the human intellect, in its powers of analysis, abstraction, and logical construction. Comparing the extraordinary advances of mathematics, astronomy, and physics with the inertia in other sorts of knowledge, Descartes concluded, as early as 1637, that their advantage lay in their method, and that its application elsewhere would bring comparable progress. His disciple Fontenelle urged: "A work of politics, of morality, of criticism, perhaps even of literature, will be finer, all things considered, if made by the hands of a geometer. The order, the clarity, the precision which have reigned for some time in good books may indeed have their primary source in this geometric spirit, which, more or less diffused, somehow communicates itself even to those who know no geometry." Although the deductive method of geometry achieved the more spectacular triumphs, another scientific method was growing in favor: the induction from concrete facts of experience acclaimed by Bacon, encouraged by the British Royal Society, and fruitfully applied to psychology in Locke's *Essay on the Human Understanding* (1696). Proponents of both methods agreed that knowledge of every sort was sorely in need of reexamination by the critical intellect, unawed by tradition and authority, even by unanimity of opinion. Already in the third quarter of the seventeenth century, the universal genius Leibnitz boasted: "We have raised up a truly philosophical age, in which the deepest recesses of nature are laid open, in which splendid arts, noble aids to convenient living, a supply of innumerable instruments and machines, even the hidden secrets of our bodies are discovered; not to mention the new light daily thrown upon antiquity."

New light on antiquity did not often inspire the reverence which the Humanist of the fifteenth or sixteenth centuries had felt before a rediscovered Greek manuscript, with its evidence of a greater culture. The moderns at last had their turn to feel superior. Descartes pointed out that his invention of analytical geometry solved problems beyond the best Greek and Roman minds. The educated layman remarked upon the pygmy universe of Ptolemy's astronomy, the provincial geography of Herodotus and Orosius, Galen's mistakes in anatomy and physiology, upon the ignorance of natural law which permitted signs and portents to sway public policy in Sparta and Rome as well as in what had been recently named the Middle Ages. Even inferiority to classical antiquity in literary art and in the fine art of urbane living was being overcome. If Virgil remained supreme in epic majesty and grace, Aristotle in literary criticism, already Racine seemed to rival Sophocles in tragedy, Molière to surpass the comedies of Aristophanes and Menander. Homer, the father of poetry, was beginning to offend refined taste. In 1714 Houdar de la Motte offered a translation of the *Iliad* suited to Parisian salons by elevating its "low" vocabulary, by eliminating repetitions, digressions, prolix description, and the unseemly, often barbarous behavior of gods and heroes. Alexander Pope followed with similar, though less drastic, versions of the *Iliad* and the *Odyssey*. Minds not so bold tried to save Homer's reputation by interpreting his works as allegories, designed to teach the rude Greek people profound political truths and the hoary wisdom of Egypt. The critic Le Bossu defined the epic as a "discourse invented with art to form manners by instructions concealed under the allegories of an important action, versified in a plausible, diverting and marvellous manner."

Over all previous historians, Voltaire and his contemporaries felt an advantage, not only in scientific knowledge but also in perspective of time and space. The greatest of the ancients, Herodotus, Thucydides, Polybius, Tacitus, though often admirable in critical detachment, had been too close to the events they recounted and analyzed. Essentially, they were writers of modern history, Thucydides indeed of contemporary history. Events in antiquity seemed to repeat monotonously a single pattern, while those thereafter showed the more varied forms and colors of Christian feudalism and the recent age of exploration, commerce, and science. The classical historians had rarely looked beyond the borders of the Mediterranean, or at most of the Roman Empire. Now the stage of events was the entire globe, with a background of countless worlds, possibly inhabited.

Man, too, had become a far more complex subject. Discovery of the Americas was only the most startling result of voyages of exploration and trade, which brought closer China and India, civilizations claiming for themselves antiquity much greater than the Bible allowed the earth itself. Orientals, in spite of religious and moral beliefs often the reverse of those in Europe, not only managed to survive, but achieved high culture. The sacred book of the Persians, the *Avesta*, had enunciated the doctrine of the immortality of the soul before the Old Testament. Was this a borrowing of the Jews while captives in Babylon? The Jesuit Joseph Lafitau, returning from five years as a missionary among the Iroquois in Canada, published in 1724 a book claiming for the aborigines of the New World religious ideas and ceremonies enough like those of classical paganism and of Catholic Christianity to support the hypothesis of a religion of nature-rites once universal among mankind. If the moralist La Bruyère observed with raised eyebrows "those bold spirits who corrupt themselves

VOLTAIRE SHATTERS TRADITION

completely by long travels and lose the little religion they had left," who "see from day to day a new religion, divers manners, diverse ceremonies," the *philosophe*, in the curious and detached spirit of science, tried to compare the world's richly various systems of government, ethics, and religion without prejudice in favor of those of his own nation.

Jean Chardin, who while selling jewelry among the Persians observed their manners keenly, laid down the principle: "Doubt is the beginning of knowledge; he who doubts nothing examines nothing; he who examines nothing is, and remains, blind." His Journal furnished local color for the fictitious *Persian Letters* (1721) of Montesquieu, in which a Persian visiting Paris describes for his friends at home the manners of the French, their bizarre principles of morals, government, and religion: a device Swift five years later reversed by sending Gulliver on his travels. Montesquieu's gay youthful satire led toward the serious masterpiece of his maturity, *The Spirit of the Laws* (1748), an explanation of limited monarchy, despotism, and democracy as outgrowths of diverse national characters, themselves largely the result of geography and climate. Voltaire's three years of exile in England, where he met Swift, Pope, and most of the leaders of the nation, introduced him to a society whose large measure of religious toleration and political constitutionalism contrasted with the intolerance and despotism of France.

The *philosophe*, it appeared, could examine historical writings nowhere without breaking into unplumbed depths. The confused chronology of ancient peoples disturbed neat mathematical minds. Not only was it hard to find definite meeting points for the annals of ancient Egypt, Persia, Palestine, Greece, and Rome; it was not easy to fix important dates in the history of a single people. Great mathematicians like Newton and Leibnitz failed to agree in such apparently simple matters. Slowly investigators realized that the ancients had only the vaguest notion of time; little means, or care, for its exact measurement.[1] Again, the conception of invariable laws of nature demanded revision of the history not only of the Christian Middle Ages, but also of the pagan nations, which likewise teemed with wonders and miracles. Yet when Levesque de Pouilly in 1722 presented before the Academy of Inscriptions his doubts of the historicity of the first four centuries of Rome, the Abbé Sallier denounced him as an atheist. Why so grave a charge against a Christian on the basis of his questioning pagan tradition? Fear of what his criteria of certainty might do to early Hebrew history; once disturb its Hebrew keystone, and the wide arch of the world would fall into fragments.

Voltaire dared take the risk. Unlike Descartes, he was unwilling to dismiss as useless any acquaintance with the past prior to the reawakening of science in the sixteenth century. If historians hitherto had accepted with too little scrutiny the accounts of credulous witnesses, severe tests might still sift from them a residue of fact, or at least clear the way for credible recording in the future.

To this high enterprise of revaluing the entire past, he brought impressive qualifications. The most celebrated man of letters in a cosmopolitan age, he had touched European affairs at many points during his adventurous life. As friend and confidant of monarchs and statesmen he had watched how nations were governed; as prisoner, fugitive, exile, he had felt the stern hand of power and learned sympathy with victims of tyranny and intolerance. A shrewd businessman, he followed developments in commerce, finance, and manufacture at a time when a rising middle class was drawing attention to economic forces. He was also a meditative and versatile intellectual, keenly interested in science, psychology, literature, and the fine arts. The *Essay on the Manners and Character of the Nations* (1754-1769) was composed for the most part in the maturity of his sixties, after he had won the independence of Church and State essential to the impartiality of the historian, rare in any era. Only since the fifteenth century in Italy had history been written wholly from a secular point of view; Voltaire dated "well made" history from Machiavelli and Guiccardini. Only now in the eighteenth was it becoming possible for the historian to emancipate himself from flattery of monarchs and nobles and to write as a citizen of the world. Unfortunately, the struggle to be free from French censorship had so embittered Voltaire that he could not write objectively of despotic rule and organized Christianity.

He designed the *Essay* as a refutation of the general history best known in France, the *Universal History* (1681) which Bossuet, Bishop of Meaux, had prepared for the instruction of the heir of Louis the Fourteenth. Bossuet told the story of mankind from the Creation to Charlemagne after the manner commonly accepted in Europe since Saint Augustine. Believing that "religion and political government are the two points about which human affairs revolve," [2] he represented history as guided by the hand of God to the triumph of the Church and of kings who governed in His name. Dividing human affairs into sacred and profane, Bossuet always accepted, in case of conflict, the version given in the Hebrew Scriptures, since in their historical books "God had always maintained the admirable practice of having things written down at the time when they occurred, or while their memory was recent. . . . It has not been thought possible to alter a single word without impiety." Although the story of the Chosen People is the most clear and awe-inspiring evidence of the "particular Providence with which God governs human affairs," the fate of the pagan empires was also the work of His hand. There could be no cause to doubt the miracles involved, for "God gives laws to nature and overthrows them when he pleases." Dismissing Greek philosophy in a paragraph and Latin literature in a single laudatory sentence, Bossuet devoted much space to Rome as the arch-type of political glory and wisdom and brought his history to a climactic close with the revival of the Roman Empire by Charlemagne, whose mantle had descended upon the France of Louis the Fourteenth. The style of this *Universal History*, adequate to its august theme, clothed in the majesty and grace of the Latin classics sublime imaginings inspired by Holy Writ.

Voltaire reproached the Bishop with writing "solely to insinuate that everything in the world was done for the Jewish nation," while omitting China and India, and speaking of the Arabs, "who founded so powerful an empire and so flourishing a religion, only as a deluge of barbarians." [3] Striking at the center of the rival world view, he denied categorically the possibility of a miracle, Christian or pagan: "One wheel in the great machine cannot stop without throwing nature as a whole out of gear." The historian need only "follow the march of the human mind abandoned to itself" in a world of inevitable law.

The distinction between sacred and profane history would not hold, "were it permissible to examine the historical part of the Jewish books by the same rules which guide us in the criticism of other histories." A nomadic people, with little means of preserving records, the Jews had exaggerated the longevity of their patriarchs, the numbers and political importance of their race. What ability to foretell the future their Prophets may have possessed was purely human. Between the Hebrews and other ancient peoples Voltaire found only one genuine difference: their deadly seriousness about tales of their origin. "Roman historians tell us, it is true, that

VOLTAIRE SHATTERS TRADITION

a Vestal Virgin bore two children to the god Mars when there were no Vestals in Italy, and that a she-wolf nourished these children instead of devouring them, . . . that Castor and Pollux fought on the side of the Romans, that Curtius threw himself into an abyss that closed after him. But the Roman Senate never condemned to death those who doubted all these prodigies. It was permissible to laugh at them in the Capitol." Obliged to be circumspect in regard to Christian origins, Voltaire managed to insinuate that they, too, were in no way superhuman.

In regard to alleged happenings not excluded from history by their miraculous quality, he advised: "Let us believe the events attested by public registers, by the agreement of contemporary authors living in a capital, enlightened by one another and writing under the eyes of the principal figures of the nation." Strictly taken, this advice would have confined his own version of the past to a few favored spots and eras; but Voltaire's mind was too adventurous to resist temptation to speculate concerning the most obscure problems of history, including the origin of the world and of the human race. The earth and man, he suspected, were far older than the year 4004 B.C. which Bossuet, following the calculation of the seventeenth century British Archbishop Usher, had assigned to their simultaneous creation; and the earth was much older than man. But his knowledge of geology, chemistry and biology (sciences then in their infancy, which besides he had not followed so closely as physics) permitted him only to hint this drastic revision of chronology. Classical and medieval historians (and even Bossuet) had taken the nature of man for granted, as known; but Voltaire realized that since the discovery of the Americas the various races, the stages and quality of their cultures, must be described. He sketched a slow and painful rise of mankind from a state close to the animals.

Like Aristotle considering man a social animal, he traced the development of government from family and tribe to nation, and except in China found the earliest governments theocracies. This rule by priests he excoriated as the worst of tyrannies because instituted by conscious fraud, by men speaking in the name of gods for their personal profit.

Nevertheless, he acknowledged religion as a natural growth. Dreams of the dead returning had suggested an idea of ghosts and of the human soul. Fear of the forces of nature and effort to appease them produce polytheism. Tribal gods, such as those favoring the Trojans or the Greeks, were created by the desire of groups for protection and for success in war. But each tribe acknowledged the existence of the gods of its rivals, confessing that its own ruled over limited territory. The first chapter of Judges relates that the God of Judea, though master of the mountains, could not conquer the valleys; and the Third Book of Kings records that at a later date the Syrians thought the god of the Jews a god of the mountains only. In paralleling Homer with the Old Testament, Jewish with Egyptian and Persian rites and religious ideas, Voltaire was among the pioneers in comparative religion.

Concerning the most ancient civilizations, the Chaldean, Indian, Chinese, Egyptian, he confessed great ignorance. The early centuries of Rome lay in obscurity. After a brief interval of light in the Greek and Roman historians, darkness descends when the Roman Empire is overthrown by "two scourges, ... barbarians and disputes about religion." Concerning the Northern barbarians, the classical writers were no longer safe guides. "Tacitus, Quintus Curtius, Horace, resemble those pedagogues who, to provoke their pupils to emulation, utter in their presence profuse praise of foreign children, however gross they may be." Pious chroniclers abused the ignorance and credulity of these conquerors by exaggerating the

VOLTAIRE SHATTERS TRADITION

earthly pomp of the Church and concealing its beginnings among humble folk with democratic manners. The so-called Donation of Constantine, a document in which that Emperor, out of gratitude for his cure from leprosy by Sylvester, Bishop of Rome, confesses symbolically the subordination of his secular power to the spiritual power and confers upon the Church temporal authority over Italy and the Western Provinces, drew from Voltaire a withering comment: "Since the entire text was in the incorrect style of the eighth century and full of historical and geographical errors, the artifice was gross; but it was gross men who were deceived." And long they remained so, for the forgery was not exposed until the fifteenth century.

Fortunately, Voltaire thought, Christendom was not the entire human race. While ignorance reigned in Europe, China and India maintained high civilization, and among the Arabs sprang up a religion tolerant of science throughout an empire from Baghdad to Granada. Against this brilliant Eastern background, the West stands out darkly as "a heap of crimes, follies, and misfortunes, sometimes in one country, sometimes in another, for five hundred years." Fanatical Crusades "drained Europe of men and money without civilizing her." Scholasticism, "a bastard child of Aristotle's philosophy," did "more harm to reason and good scholarship than the Huns and Vandals." Reason was likewise flouted in secular affairs. Wittily Voltaire describes trial by combat as an institution whereby "a man accused of one murder was given the right to commit another." If chivalry arose to soften the relations between feudal lords, it did not make them less harsh to inferiors. The perversion of justice by Church and State in the condemnation and burning of Joan of Arc points a lesson to his Parisian readers: "Let the citizens of an immense city, where today the arts, pleasure, and peace reign, where even reason is beginning to be introduced, compare the eras, and complain if they dare. That is a reflection which must be made on almost every page of this history."

Voltaire sees light breaking once more upon Europe in Italy of the thirteenth and fourteenth centuries, where "artisans and merchants, whom obscurity screens from the ambitious fury of the great, are ants which dig dwellings in silence, while eagles and vultures are tearing each other to pieces." In pausing here to describe family life and the useful arts, Voltaire once more widened the bounds of history. On the economic foundation of commercial cities he saw culture rise, until by the sixteenth century the Italians have rivaled the ancient Greeks in sculpture and surpassed them in painting, music, architecture, and some forms of literature. In the epic, progress was clear. After Dante's "bizarre poem," Petrarch had wisely revived imitation of classical models. Soon Homer had been outdone. Ariosto's *Orlando Furioso* surpassed the *Odyssey*, although sharing its defects of "intemperate imagination and the romantic incredible." Tasso's *Jerusalem Delivered* was more decidedly superior to the *Iliad*, "with better management, greater interest, variety, accuracy and grace, and more of that softness which sets off the sublime." By the sixteenth century, too, culture and refinement have spread to France and are moving farther north. Deplorable wars of religion have the undesigned result of teaching some men the wisdom of tolerance, so that they see God as the Father of all mankind, not merely the "benefactor of a few persons in a few small regions."

But as the West advances, the East declines. China follows India into intellectual and artistic decadence, and the Arabs lose their hold on Spain. Since the sixteenth century, Europe has been leading the world. It is not yet at its zenith, for only toward the end of that century did "true philosophy begin to shine on mankind" with Copernicus and with Galileo, who was "not only the first good physicist, but also wrote as elegantly as Plato, with the incomparable advantage over the Greek philosopher of saying nothing that is not certain and intelligible."

At the threshold of the era of Enlightenment the *Essay* comes to an end, for Voltaire had already published in 1751 *The Age of Louis the Fourteenth*, which brought the story of mankind down to 1715. *The Age of Louis the Fourteenth* had been the first attempt to describe the life of an era in all its aspects, intellectual, artistic, and economic as well as political, religious, and military. It opens with Voltaire's celebrated dictum that only four eras are worthy of the attention of men of mind and taste: Greece from Pericles to Alexander, the Rome of Caesar and Augustus, the revival of the arts in Italy, and the present age, symbolized by the France of Louis the Fourteenth, which, enriched by the discoveries of the three others, is incontestably their superior "as regards the human reason in general," since in it "men have acquired more enlightenment, from one end of Europe to the other, than in all preceding ages." When completing the *Essay on the Character and Manners of the Nations* in 1769, Voltaire saw enlightenment still spreading. Yet nothing in his survey of the past gave him confidence that the barbarism and superstition which separated previous great ages might not return. "Any one who would have predicted to Augustus that one day the Capitol would be occupied by the priest of a religion derived from the religion of the Jews would have astonished Augustus greatly. . . . Every event brings in another which is unexpected." [4]

Voltaire's historical writing stirred his contemporaries most by its sweeping denials, by its reversal of the Jewish-Christian version of the past. History, exposed to his clear and malicious gaze, was never quite the same again. But the twentieth-century reader, inured to doubt and to changes of standard, is more impressed by its constructive character. Voltaire broadened history in time, in space, and in themes. He obliged historians to consider not only all peoples of the globe but also every aspect of their cultures. He inaugurated the history of ideas, drew into general history the arts and literature, and made gestures in the direction of economic and social history. By obliterating the distinction between sacred and profane annals, by admitting only human and natural causes of events, he brought a new kind of unity into the portrait of the past. Yet these innovations involved, for him, sacrifice of the other sort of unity and universality which made Bossuet impressive, sacrifice of the uninterrupted unfolding of God's plan, in which the end was foreseen in the beginning. Voltaire's style is swift and sprightly, sparkling with wit, salted with irony; but his narrative has not the steady, majestic pace of the Christian epic. The analytic intellect has shattered history.

Voltaire was the most original and versatile mind among many historians whom pride in the eighteenth century disposed to look backward in self-congratulation. Contempt for the Middle Ages, praise for modern thought and invention run through d'Alembert's "Preliminary Discourse" to the celebrated *Encyclopaedia*, through national histories like the philosopher Hume's *England* and the Presbyterian clergyman Robertson's *Scotland*.

Probably most representative of the educated public, because the views of a lesser man, were *Philosophical Speculations on the History of Humanity* by the Swiss Isaac Iselin, published in 1764. Iselin's immediate audience was the Philanthropic Society of Basel, which sought to learn from history principles that would direct humanity toward more perfect welfare. His thesis was that man's true guide is the intellect,

VOLTAIRE SHATTERS TRADITION

which resists or restrains the seductions of the senses, the emotions, and the imagination. The Greeks became the first enlightened people largely because Lycurgus and Solon, looking centuries ahead, were their wise lawgivers. Had not Alexander died early, world enlightenment might have proceeded without the setbacks of rude Roman imperialism and its ruder destroyers. Rome fell because her ruling class failed to diffuse among the masses the culture borrowed from Greece, and darkness ensued for over a thousand years. The clergy fostered this darkness.

Instead of spreading light, morality and humaneness among European peoples and making them prevail, corrupt Christianity augmented ignorance, anarchy and grossness. It made the wildest passions and the preposterous inclination to marvels, that tyrannized over great and small, into tools of priestly advantage and authority. . . . It is a recognized principle that in the history of the Middle Ages the judgments of the historians, who were all priests, since no one else could read or write, must not be trusted.[5]

Accident lifted the darkness. From the Mohammedan enemy in the Crusades, Christendom learned of Aristotle and Greek medicine. The Turkish capture of Constantinople drove still more Greek learning to Italy, where textual criticism of manuscripts opened a way to free thought. Science revived in unexampled splendor, and from classical literature Boileau derived critical laws that permitted Racine and Dryden to produce works of "purified taste." The seventeenth century "contributed more to the enlightenment of Europe than all preceding centuries," and the eighteenth has continued auspiciously by spreading freedom of thought and refinement into Germany. The economic foundations of culture, no longer the booty of robbery as in Greco-Roman times, appear solid. The weapons of modern science have removed the menace of barbarian invasions. The prospect for civilization would be brilliant, were it not that European sovereigns make war upon one another, were it not that culture is so thinly spread that the common people in most countries of Europe remain "almost as barbarous, as superstitious, as unjust as they ever could have been in the Middle Ages."

II

HERDER AND GOETHE: THE LIVING PAST

AFTER the incisive, malicious glance of the sage Voltaire, a young German groped toward great truths, often felt rather than seen. The lumbering title of his anonymously published book, *Still Another Philosophy of History for the Culture of Humanity*, mocked the widespread habit of using history for didactic purposes. He poured scorn upon "the mole's eye of this most enlightened century," that perceived mere fragments of history "according to exceedingly hasty reasoning about it *à la Voltaire*," that failed to comprehend the Biblical story of human origins out of distaste for "the wonderful and the hidden."[1] The vaunted intellect was only part of the resources of man, who before the waking of reason had invented language and other devices at which reason must still wonder. Like the development of the seed, the embryo and all other productions of nature, history took place in ways the spectacled philosopher would not have approved in advance. Even the freedom of thought he prized so highly was a sorry substitute for what he needed more: "heart, warmth, humanity, life."

Why be puzzled because Leonidas or Caesar might have been a clever man of the eighteenth-century sort, but wasn't? Character is molded by time and place, and "every nation has its center of happiness within itself, just as every ball its center of gravity." Vain therefore the classicist's dream of reviving the culture of some brilliant moment of antiquity. Cultures are inimitable. "The Greek learning the Romans absorbed became Roman; Aristotle, an Arab and a Scholastic." Even within a single people, "culture has never been able to go back a second time to what once it was—the way of Fate is iron." Humanity, like a stream, must flow. The direction of its flow cannot be reversed.

Descartes and Newton, the anonymous author pursued, had misled historians into a wrong analogy. Man is not a machine of dead matter, but alive, and growing in time as well as spreading in space. His history resembles that of other living products of the earth; the Norse *Edda* had the right instinct in imagining it a tree. Decay, which baffled Voltaire, is consequently as appropriate to human affairs as growth. "Everything, every art and knowledge, and what in the world not? has had its period of growth, bloom and decline."

Nevertheless, man need not resign a forward look. Decay of one great society leaves the ground richer for the growth of another. Humanity is advancing, although the nature of the advance, dependent upon a thousand concurrent causes, is beyond the power of the keenest mind to foresee. If, according to Newton, "Man's dwelling house, even to its smallest detail, shows 'God's image'—why not the history of its inhabitants?" God guides humanity, though not by personal whim, as in Bossuet's pages. "The analogy of Nature, the speaking symbol of God," is our assurance of orderly and intelligible progress. History and natural history alike are the "show place of a directing plan on earth, even if we are not to see its ultimate intention; the manifestation of Divinity, if only by indications and by fragments of single scenes." With characteristic enthusiasm the author continued:

If I were to succeed in binding together the disparate scenes without confusion, in showing how they are related, grow out of one another, lose themselves in one another, each singly but a moment, through their continuity only means to an end—what a view!

What encouragement to hope, to believe, even where one discerns nothing, or next to nothing!

He appealed to the reader to suspend judgment by any standard of his century. "First sympathize with the nation," he urged, "go into the era, into the geography, into the entire history, *feel* [2] yourself into it." By imagining himself in the childhood of humanity, he will discover religion, "the element in which all lived and moved," to be no imposture of priests or kings, but honest groping for knowledge; for man wonders at everything before he sees it clearly. Even fear, used for discipline by early priests and kings, was not so harsh and degrading as Voltaire, from the analogy of modern Oriental despotism, had supposed. It was indispensable cement for the foundation of custom laid by instinct, until men were ready to be led by reason. Patriarchal authority was an excellent guide for the nomadic childhood of our race, depicted in Genesis, before agriculture drew men to fixed abodes and severer discipline, represented by Egypt. Egyptian rigidity had been undervalued by judging it after Greek standards and not after its own nature and style, as in the characteristic Egyptian art. Indeed, some cultural values were probably lost in the passage to Greece, for "the human vessel is not capable of any perfect cargo at one time, but must always leave something behind in pressing onward."

The relentless push of nature compelled advance from Greece, the glorious youth of humanity, to Roman manhood which forced unity upon the ancient world. And the Northern barbarians who overthrew Rome were no mere interruptors of Western culture. The Englishman Hurd, in his recent *Letters on Chivalry*, had likened them to the heroes of Homeric Greece. Of course the Middle Ages had their dark side; but, in stressing it, Voltaire, Hume, Robertson, and Iselin had failed to observe their creative power. Medieval Christianity strengthened the union of Northern and Southern Europe; and the unworthy, even repulsive, ideas that mingled with it—an inevitable consequence of the pagan mentality of early converts—were gradually sloughed off. Medieval architecture, the despised Gothic, had merits which the author described with understatement half-tactful, half-imperceptive: "Monstrous Gothic building! overadorned, oppressive, sinister, tasteless—yet how great, rich, roofed, mighty!" Feudalism, tempered with Christianity, produced the admirable code of chivalry: action had its virtues as well as thought.

After so long, so varied a journey, was it probable that humanity should have found its goal, its resting place, in eighteenth-century science and cosmopolitanism? Science was visibly in its infancy, for with Buffon natural history (zoology and geology) had barely made a start. Cosmopolitanism was a mixed blessing, since it threatened to wipe out diversity in customs, national character and artistic taste. How blind, then, a century's despising ages which do not resemble it! History reveals the great principle that nothing is means alone, that "everything is at the same time means and end."

The author of this arresting challenge to both the *philosophe* and the traditionalist was Johann Gottfried Herder, Chief Pastor to the ruler of the small German state of Schaumberg-Lippe. It was his first historical work. His earlier writing had been chiefly literary criticism, in which at thirty he was already a leader in a revolt against French domination of European taste. Although *Still Another Philosophy of History*, appearing in 1774, followed Voltaire's completed *Essay on the Manners and Character of the Nations* by only five years, it was the voice of a new era, for Herder was fifty years Voltaire's junior. Plebeian birth in an aristocratic society and remoteness from the center of culture in Paris had allowed an original young thinker a fresh valuation of history.

Herder was the son of a Lutheran sexton and schoolmaster in an East Prussian village. Individualistic and temperamental, he resembled less his German kinsfolk than the Slavs bordering his native province, whom he met early as fellow students at Königsberg and during his first pastorate in Riga. But his education was Prussian at its worst and its best: worst in the harsh discipline of the village school; best in the University of Königsberg, which in 1770 instituted what today is called an orientation course in the principal fields of knowledge, designed to stimulate "ability to think and to investigate the nature of things without prejudice and without sectarianism." [3]

Although Herder had left the University five years earlier, the encouragement to a wide survey was already there in his student days, represented preeminently by a private tutor, Immanuel Kant, who in the spirit of Bacon and Leibnitz had taken all knowledge as his province. Still unknown to fame in his late thirties, for his great philosophic works had not appeared, Kant was almost equally at home in the abstractions of mathematics and metaphysics and in the concrete data of politics, anthropology, and literature. He followed with lively curiosity every branch of science, from the well-established physics and astronomy, to which he had contributed a Nebular Hypothesis, to "natural history," within which biology, geology, and chemistry were beginning to differentiate themselves. An inspired teacher, who in the phrase of one of Herder's student friends "poured himself over time and space with his bold hypotheses," Kant would illustrate his conviction of the oneness of knowledge by quoting Pope's *Essay on Man* as Newton and Locke in poetic guise. He insisted that the brilliant and impecunious Herder attend his lectures without payment. From him, Herder derived faith in immutable laws of nature, learned of Linnaeus and Buffon, pioneers in the sciences of living things, and of books of travel which were source material for anthropology. Kant's publisher generously permitted the eager student to browse among the newest publications displayed in his bookstore, where he met the daring speculations of Voltaire, Rousseau, Diderot, and d'Alembert.

That Herder was studying for the ministry in no wise interfered with such reading, for his theological professors gave liberal interpretation to the Protestant principle of free examination of matters of faith. They encouraged also his learning Hebrew and Greek as bases for study of the Scriptural text and acquainted him with the work of recent scholars, including J. D. Michaelis of Göttingen, who were interpreting the Bible in the light of Oriental customs and geography. In the preface of his greatest work, Herder recalled with emotion these "early years, when the meadows of learning still lay before me in all their morning splendor." [4]

The Enlightenment might gradually have effaced the most vivid impressions of his village childhood—the *Märchen* or folk tales of the supernatural, the reading aloud in family devotions from Genesis, where the supernatural touched with radiance the simple lives of the Patriarchs, the delight in nature as a refuge from the hated schoolroom—had he not met also at Königsberg a man of letters, Johann Hamann. A rolling stone and untrained thinker, the antithesis of Kant, Hamann had been laboring to express in his disorderly and inarticulate writings opinions brought back from Russia and England. At Riga he had listened with unprejudiced curiosity to Latvian folk songs and found genuine poetry in their words, the anonymous, unwritten compositions of a people still without a prose literature. Comparing this experience with accounts of other primitive peoples, ancient and modern, he concluded that poetry, not prose, must have been the mother tongue of the human race, a spontaneous rhythmical outburst of emotion and imagination before the awakening of reason.

This reversed literary history as most Germans understood it. Following the French, they conceived of poetry, anything deserving the name, as a late appearance, when intellect could guide taste in forms and metres approved by the long line of authoritative critics from Aristotle to Boileau. In England, however, Hamann had found considerable support for his doubt of this absolute standard of poetic merit. For the English had begun to venerate Shakespeare, who with little Latin and less Greek learning composed dramas in a form sprung from the popular theater of the Middle Ages. Hamann read the protest of the poet Edward Young against Pope's apology for Shakespeare's lack of learning:

Though Pope's noble Muse may boast her illustrious descent from Homer, Virgil, Horace, yet is an original author more nobly born. . . . A star of the first magnitude among the moderns was Shakespeare; among the ancients, Pindar, who . . . boasted of his no-learning, calling himself the eagle, for his flight above it. . . . Genius is a master-workman, learning is but an instrument. . . . There is something in poetry beyond prose-reason; there are mysteries in it not to be explained, but admired.[5]

Hamann believed he knew the source of those mysteries. It was the inspiration of God. In a period of deep depression from poverty and loneliness in London he had sought consolation in the Bible, and through its pages had a mystic experience of the relation of God to man and the world. God had not retired, as Voltaire thought, to His Heaven to watch the running of the clockwork mechanism of His Creation. He had remained constantly within nature and within human nature. Hamann discovered himself not alone in this conception of a universal indwelling Spirit. The Neo-Platonists, the sixteenth-century Italian Giordano Bruno, intoxicated with the immensity of the new Copernican universe, and quite recently the English Lord Shaftesbury, in an ecstatic hymn to Nature, each in turn had attained it. Some mortals were favored with an extraordinary influx of this universal Spirit. For Shaftesbury and for Hamann, these were the geniuses. In Socrates' account of the daimon that guided him in momentous decisions, Hamann saw an attempt to describe this inner experience. Did not Plato record Socrates as also saying that all good poets "compose their beautiful poems not by art, but because they are inspired and possessed?" The Spirit blew where it listed, and might stir to poetic utterance rude, unlettered men like the unknown authors of those Latvian songs.

Love of the Bible as inspired poetry brought Hamann and Herder together. Herder, steeped from childhood in folk tales, needed no convincing as to the quality of the oral literature of untutored peoples. But he was unprepared for the heights attainable without the aid of classical literary forms, that were revealed when Hamann, to teach him English, plunged him into *Hamlet*. The Bible and Shakespeare inspired. This enlarged one's ideas of inspiration.

That Herder might see for himself the artistic possibilities of an untutored people, Hamann recommended his friend for a pastorate in Riga on the conclusion of his Königsberg studies. Herder was in Riga barely four years, from 1765 to 1769. When he left for Paris at the age of twenty-five, he had read as much and as variously as the young Coleridge, and, what is even more remarkable, his reflections had a boldness and a clarity Coleridge was never to attain. With the rare gift of perceiving similar tendencies in diverse fields of thought and action, that unconscious convergence which gives to an age its "style" or "spirit," he dared speculate by analogy, a dangerous tool in less skillful hands. In his chief interests, literature, languages, theology, philosophy, and science, he discovered common principles for that highest synthesis of thought and action which was his conception of history.

Several of these principles radiated from a single fact: the fact that poetry, so superlative a human manifestation as often to be accounted Divine, could be produced by no mere effort of will guided by reason and taste, and appeared among unschooled peoples and individuals from the earliest times. Evidence of this fact, embarrassing to Enlightenment historians, had been accumulating of late, not only from travelers among barbaric peoples but also, more impressively, by resurrections from the neglected past of Northern Europe. The *Poetic Edda* had been partially translated into French by Mallet in his *Monuments of the Mythology and Poetry of the Ancient Scandinavians* (1756). In 1762 James Macpherson had published *Fragments of Ancient Poetry Collected in the Highlands of Scotland*, which he attributed to the Celtic bard Ossian. Bishop Percy's *Reliques of Ancient English Poetry* (1765) contained English and Scottish popular ballads of tragic dignity. The barbaric conquerors of Rome were revealed as creators of impressive poetry and of a mythology of Valhalla which had served, like that of Olympus, to support epic strains. Nor did this exhaust the achievement of primitive peoples; for it was being discovered that Homer was a primitive.

That the eighteenth century was misunderstanding Homer from ignorance of the principle that "every kind of writing, but especially the poetic, depends upon the manners of the age when it was produced," [6] had been the thesis of *An Enquiry into the Life and Writings of Homer* (1735) by James Blackwell. This ignorance explained, Blackwell asserted, the baffling failure of the best modern pens, including Voltaire's, to produce even a passable epic. Among the Greeks of Homer's time, who lived insecure lives of piracy and brigandage and who thought in prescientific terms, it was natural to find the marvelous and the wonderful as the nerve of the epic strain; but how false and ridiculous to imitate it in an age of science and well-policed states! The simple, unaffected manners of times when "the folds and windings of the human breast lay open to the eye," embarrassed sophisticated moderns. Living within doors, they considered similes taken from nature as "low." Such was their attitude as readers; yet as writers in the epic tradition they obeyed Boileau's instruction "to strip the common accidents of life of their plain dress, and in order to keep up their dignity, ascribe them to some superior power; and for inanimate things, to give them life, clothe them with a person and proper attributes." [7] The insincere imitation deceived no one, for "the manners not only of the age in which we live, but of our city and family stick closely to us, and betray us at every turn." [8] The natural voice of Homer confirmed the Greek tradition that he had been a strolling, indigent bard like those Highlanders whom Blackwell, an Aberdeen Scot, had heard recite from memory. Homer probably composed orally in troublous times which stirred men to passionate and metaphorical language.

In 1765, the year of Herder's arrival in Riga, Robert Wood had joined this effort to aid the eighteenth-century reader to imagine the conditions under which the Homeric poems had been produced. His *Essay on the Original Genius and Writings of Homer* described the effect of reading them on the legendary site of Troy, an experiment apparently without precedent since the Greek orator Aeschines in the fourth century B.C. Looking with Homer's eyes westward across the length of the Mediterranean, Wood pictured to himself the peril of voyages in those far-off times. He understood how much was romantic to Homer which already ceased to be so when "the author of the *Aeneid* found Circe's island in his neighborhood, and the country of the Laestrygones among the gardens of the Roman nobility." [9] Reminding his contemporaries that even they were not far removed from a time when great statesmen did not know their alphabet, he found no difficulty in supposing Homer to have lived in an age that did not possess the art of writing. Those offended by pictures of primitive simplicity, to whom "the courage of Achilles must appear brutal ferocity and the wisdom of Ulysses low cunning," [10] should reflect upon an analogy between the manners of Asiatic Greeks of the heroic age and those of the Bedouins who have lived in the same region since time immemorial. This analogy was less exact than that which the untraveled Richard Hurd, in his *Letters on Chivalry and Romance* (1762), had made with the "Gothic manners" of the early Middle Ages; but it attracted Herder because it ran parallel to Michaelis' theory that the Book of Job had been written among Arab nomads. Job, Homer, the Eddas weighed heavily in favor of primitive peoples.

The superiority for poetic purposes of the language of such peoples, rich in synonyms and idioms, highly flexible in construction, was a notable exception to the doctrine that all things could be improved by reason and refined taste. So, too, the French language, over which refinement and reason had been tightening their grip for more than a hundred years. The French aristocracy had set up its own current speech and interests as the standard of "good usage," to the exclusion of popular, provincial, and even slightly outmoded words and expressions. Scientific minds, regarding language as a vehicle for the communication of ideas only, had been endeavoring to attach to each word a single, invariable meaning and to formulate grammatical rules admitting of no exceptions; they frowned upon synonyms as superfluous, upon idiomatic expressions as confusing irregularities. Pure reason and aristocratic taste, respecting each other and working together, had thus contrived to reduce by almost two thirds the rich vocabulary of the sixteenth century; and the impoverishment of the language was continuing. This meant disaster for poetry,[11] disaster the greater because the French, unaware, thought they had improved their language for every purpose. The "Preliminary Discourse" of the *Encyclopaedia*, where the *philosophes* proudly displayed the recent advances in knowledge and in the arts, counted among them the fact that Voltaire, "sure to obtain in the very small number of great poets a distinguished place, and a place peculiarly his own, possesses at the same time in the highest degree a talent which hitherto no poet has possessed even in a moderate degree: the talent for writing prose."[12] Today, Voltaire remains only among the prose masters.

The triumphs of French prose had been impressive. French had become the international language of diplomacy and of polite society, and was replacing Latin in international scholarship and science. The desire to reform other tongues after the French model was contagious. No less a writer than Jonathan Swift proposed a plan to improve and to "fix" English, so that future generations need not struggle with obsolete expressions.[13] In Germany, so ravaged by feudal anarchy and wars of religion that little good poetry had been written since the extinction of the Hohenstaufen dynasty in the early thirteenth century and almost no good prose since Luther, French was irresistible. Leibnitz entrusted to it his greatest works; Frederick the Great invited Voltaire to Potsdam to correct the French verse he composed. Among those few Germans, mostly of the middle class, who had hope for their native tongue, Professor Gottsched of Leipzig, a literary dictator with greater sway than his contemporary Dr. Samuel Johnson, tried to save it for literary purposes by throwing out compound words (rare in French) and German idioms.

While in his native land the menace to poetry was great, Herder found encouragement in England, where that menace, though considerable,[14] was least. Although the British Royal Society antedated the French academies for scientific purposes, individualism and national pride had thwarted attempts to found in England an Academy on the French model for the control of language and literature. Even Dryden, who by judicious imitation of French virtues had become the father of modern English prose, observed that for poetry

> Their tongue, enfeebled, is refined too much
> And like pure gold, it yields at every touch.

Blackwell, a generation later, saw a political cause for this enfeeblement:

An *absolute* Court must have a pernicious influence both on the variety of characters in a nation, and the extent of their dialects. . . . All must conform to the Court-model. . . . We may view in our native isle the happy instance of the connexion between liberty and learning. We find our language masculine and noble: of vast extent, and capable of greater variety of style and character than any modern tongue.[15]

None the less, it required considerable hardihood for him to defend Homer's Greek during the high popularity of Pope's translations. "Does it not sound something like treason in Apollo's court, to say that a *polished language* is not fit for a great poet? . . . What we call polish diminishes a language; it makes many words obsolete; it coops a man up in a corner, allows him but one set of phrases, and deprives him of many significant terms and strong and beautiful expressions."[16] Thirty years later, Robert Wood put the question in its historical setting: "If we examine the rise and progress of language, with a view to its application and use, we shall find that the several stages of its advancement are not equally favorable to every display of genius; and that the useful Artist and the Philosopher will find their account in several improvements, which rather impede than forward the Poet's views." [17]

The study of languages, into which professional need of Greek and Hebrew for interpreting the Bible, as well as interest in primitives, drew Herder, began to open windows upon history. Italian Humanists, led by love of stylistic beauty to contrast classical with medieval Latin, had been the first to observe that languages went through historical change. In 1440 Lorenzo Valla proved the usefulness of language as a test for the authenticity and the dating of documents by showing that the so-called Donation of Constantine contained words and constructions which were not introduced into Latin until several centuries after Constantine's time: a discovery Voltaire used for anticlerical purposes. Two centuries after Valla, the significance of language as a depository of what is now called prehistory, history before the invention of writing and mathematics, became apparent. Herder was fascinated by glimpses into forgotten origins which languages had given Leibnitz, Blackwell, Wood, and Michaelis.

Blackwell had observed that

the primitive parts of the languages reputed original, are many of them rough, undeclined, impersonal monosyllables, expressive commonly of the highest passions and most striking objects that present themselves in solitary, savage life. . . . The two usual words in Hebrew for meat and food, *Lechem* and *Tereph*, signify . . . the one fighting, the other rapine and plunder. *Gur* signifies to go abroad, to travel; and the adjunct to it, to *dread*, to be *in fear;* and *Ger* or *Gur*, a stranger and a young lion. The old word for wealth in Greek, λεία, means nothing originally but spoil, the product of war or piracy . . . and the great variety of words they have to signify *good* or *better*, take their origin from strength or violence. . . . It gives us an idea of a dismal way of living, to find the [Hebrew] word *karab*, that signifies to *draw near one*, to approach, signifying at the same time, to *fight*, to *make war;* and thence the word *kerab*, a battle.[18]

Leibnitz, in his posthumous *New Essays* (1765), discovered similar survivals of primitive psychology in modern German, and advised the use of the Teutonic languages as tools of research into the origins of Northern Europe: "The names of rivers, ordinarily descended from the greatest known antiquity, best mark the old language and the old inhabitants. . . . Languages, generally being the most ancient monuments of peoples, before writing and the arts, best mark their racial relationship and migrations." [19]

Even for later times, the value of language as a clue to the psychology of peoples remained great. "We have no better guide to the rise and progress of Greek knowledge," Wood remarked, "than Greek etymology; which is in this respect Greek history." [20] The strikingly "botanical" poetry of the Jews revealed to Michaelis its authors as herdsmen and tillers of the soil. The Babylonian Captivity, by wrenching Jewish literature from its native soil, sowed seeds of decline. Comparing Ezekiel, who wrote after it, with Latin poets who followed the Augustan Age, Michaelis found "some resemblance in the style, something that indicates the old age of poetry." [21] In Greek, Blackwell and Wood observed similar stages of childhood, maturity and senility. Blackwell maintained: "When the Greek language was brought to express all the best and bravest of human feelings, and retained a sufficient quantity of its original amazing metaphorical tincture; at that point did Homer write." [22] The golden moment for Greek art had come later, in the time of Pericles, according to Johann Winckelmann's *History of Art in Antiquity* (1764).

Since in the Periclean age, chosen by Voltaire as one of the high points in cultural history, the Greek language had already lost something of the "noble simplicity" Wood praised in its Homeric stage, Herder inferred that no era was likely to have a monopoly of the virtues, and that each, therefore, merited attention for those it possessed. In the *Sacra poesia Hebraorum* (1753) of Robert Lowth, he met an admirable statement of the duty of the historian to give each era a sympathetic hearing on its own terms: "We must act as the Astronomers with regard to that branch of their science which is called comparative, who, in order to form a more perfect idea of the general system and its different parts, conceive themselves as passing through and surveying the whole universe, migrating from one planet to another, and becoming for a short time inhabitants of each." [23]

That the illustration should be from astronomy was highly significant. The science which was the model for the thinking of the *philosophes*, the comparative method Voltaire had been using against the claims of Christianity to uniqueness in creed and ritual, prescribed an attitude of imaginative sympathy impossible to Voltaire's mind but consonant with the principles of relativity and pluralism which the study of literature, language, and the arts had been impressing upon Herder.

In the foremost rank of the rationalists, in Leibnitz and Hume, Herder met acknowledgment of the limitations of pure reason. Leibnitz, codiscoverer with Newton of the infinitesimal calculus, which permitted the calculation of the orbits of heavenly bodies, was, unlike Newton, more interested in pure than in applied mathematics. In 1765, almost fifty years after his death, *New Essays on the Human Understanding* had been published from his manuscript. A reply to Locke's work with a similar title, these essays contained surprising deductions from the idea of a series of infinitesimals. Taking exception to Locke's famous image of the human mind at birth as a "blank tablet" whose contents would be written in entirely by sensations from the outer world, Leibnitz maintained that a tablet absolutely blank, without some vein or irregularity distinguishing it from all others, did not exist. The perfectly blank tablet was one of those "abstractions of the intellect" [24] which did no harm so long as they were recognized as such. But taken literally, this abstraction obscured the fact that no human brain was exactly like another, and that therefore individual difference must be reckoned with from babyhood. Locke had also erred in considering as contents of the mind only those sensations of which the mind is aware; for reflection upon infinitesimals revealed that our brains record much of which we are unconscious. We hear each wave of the sea, though we are aware only of its general roar; habit deafens us to a waterfall or a windmill close at hand. Incessant influx of "tiny perceptions," "unconscious perceptions," [25] stores the brain with unconscious memories. That these memories appear in dreams, proves waking never absolute. Close continuity is still another characteristic of infinitesimals; and here again a construction of pure mathematics proves relevant to the real world.

The law of continuity imports that Nature leaves no void in the order she follows. . . . Beginning with ourselves and going to the lowest things, there is a descent made by very slight *degrees*, and by a continued series of things which in each removal differ little from one another. There are fishes with wings, to which the air is not a stranger, and birds living in water whose blood is the cold blood of fish. . . . There are animals approaching so closely to birds that they hold a middle place between them and the beasts. Amphibians hold a similar position between the creatures of the sea and those of the air. . . . There are beasts which seem to have as much knowledge and reason as some animals that are called men; and there is so great a proximity between animals and vegetables, that if you take the most imperfect of one and the most perfect of the other, you will scarcely notice any considerable difference. And so on until we arrive at the lowest and least organized parts of matter, we find everywhere that species are linked together by almost imperceptible degrees.[26]

Herder saw at once how emphasis on individual difference lent support to historical relativity, and how unconscious memory explained unplanned creativeness. The principle of continuity, too, helped to fuse the fragments in which Voltaire had left the past without need to abandon Voltaire's conviction that man and his affairs were completely within the laws of nature. But according to Voltaire, the laws of nature were the mechanical laws of physics. Leibnitz, by revealing continuity in the whole scale of living things, suggested to Herder that human society might be better understood from the analogy of an organism. It was true that Leibnitz had stopped short of making his picture of nature a picture of growth. Although the success of gardeners in artificially varying flowers and fruit had raised in him doubt of the fixity of species, suggesting that the lion, the tiger and the lynx were offshoots of an extinct species of cat, he did not pursue the idea of development. His conception of the Creator as "an inactive God ... outside the world," [27] stood in the way of his envisaging creation as a continuous and continuing process. This barrier Hamann's conception of an immanent God permitted Herder to leap. His mind took fire from Leibnitz's statement: "I approve very much the search for analogies; plants, insects and the comparative anatomy of animals will furnish more and more of them, especially when the microscope comes better into use." [28] Since Leibnitz's death, Linnaeus had advanced botany and Buffon biology, to the extent of giving Herder confidence that man could be incorporated within the scheme of nature without thereby being made into a machine.

Leibnitz had warned mathematical minds against the pitfalls of abstractions. Hume, in the English tradition of inductive thinking, found other limits to pure reason while examining candidly into historical facts. Nowhere did he find greater disparity in the answers to the philosophical question of foundation in reason and the historical question of foundation in human nature as a whole than in religion, which he investigated in *The Natural History of Religion* (1757). While as a rationalist he could readily concede that "according to the natural progress of human thought, the ignorant multitude must first entertain some grovelling and familiar notion of supernatural powers, before they can stretch their conception to that perfect Being, who bestowed order on the whole frame of nature," [29] historical research led Hume to other conclusions that were disconcertingly paradoxical. There seemed "no theological absurdities so glaring, that they have not, sometimes, been embraced by men of the greatest and most cultivated understanding. No religious precepts so rigorous that they have not been adopted by the most voluptuous and abandoned of men. . . . It is justly regarded as unsafe to draw any certain inference in favor of a man's morals, from the strictness of his religious exercises, although he himself believes them sincere." [30] In human nature, "nothing is pure and entirely of a piece. . . . The most sprightly wit borders on madness; the highest effusions of joy produce the deepest melancholy; the most ravishing pleasures are attended with the most cruel lassitude and disgust." [31] From this vision, which anticipates late Romanticists like Keats, the placid and rational Hume shrank. "The whole is a riddle, an enigma, an inexplicable mystery. We happily make our escape into the calm, though obscure regions of philosophy." [32] In spite of his effort to be objective, rationalistic prepossession held him back on the brink of a discovery. In surveying relics of primitive religious practices he had come upon a curious fact recorded by Strabo and Suetonius: "In the temple of Aricia near Rome, whoever murdered the present priest, was legally entitled to be installed as his successor. A very singular institution, for, however barbarous and bloody the common superstitions are to the laity, they usually turn to the advantage of the holy order."[33] What Hume dismissed with an anticlerical sneer was to be the point of departure for Sir James Fraser's *Golden Bough*.

Herder, however, could build upon such puzzling data; for as a clergyman he knew that priests could act against their advantage and from the experience of his own temperament he was willing to accept the contradictions of human nature. To his already lively interest in origins, Hume contributed the suggestion that religions, in retaining ritual whose meaning had often passed out of memory, might, like languages, be miraculously preserved archives of prehistory, revealing ways of thinking peculiar to the peoples who produced or adopted them. It was natural that each primitive folk, in attempting to understand the world, should devise a cosmology in the form of myths, inchoate philosophy, or science with "theological coloring,"[34] and that those myths should reflect the climate of their origin. The Hindus imagined the earth carried on the back of an elephant; the Scandinavians, its destruction by frost giants. In an unpublished essay "On the Various Religions," written after he had read Hume in 1766, Herder declared: "The Edda, the cosmogonies, theogonies and heroic songs of the most ancient Greeks, and the common reports concerning Indians, Spaniards, Gauls, Germans and every sort of barbarian: all is a combined voice, a single sound of poetic records of times past."[35] What Christian theologians dismissed as error thus might be of great historical value: "If I have noted the error and coolly refuted it, the most important thing remains to be done: to explain how it arose. . . . No proposition is so foolish, as not to have been maintained by a philosopher, no religion so silly, that no nation has believed it. The circle of errors has already been run through and has returned upon itself; and yet our philosophy still lacks this history of wisdom and our natural theology, a history of religions."[36] Herder was but twenty-two, when he arrived at this insight.

Since the intellect had led so many wild goose chases, Herder mused, would not it be well to call to its aid imagination, feeling, the urge to action, in order to bring into play the whole man, whose resources the Enlightenment had whittled down to a single faculty? Not only does poetic and artistic creation come from "the dark regions of the soul";[37] most human inventions are likewise born of mere accident, not conscious research.

I intend to invent this, means really: I intend to invent what, since I can name it, is already invented. . . . Had we a history of inventions, it would show that we have the god of Chance to thank for most of them, and those the most precious. The inventor went for a walk, let us say, with no object in view, or else with some different purpose. He fell to dreaming, stumbled upon something, picked it up. At first it was not recognized for what it was; but later it became known as a gem and was worked over. . . . Causes operated together, simultaneously and in sequence, so secretly that the inventor often could not give an account of them: not even immediately afterwards, if his fire of creation had died within him, and judgment had begun to mingle with feeling.[38]

Nevertheless, the mystery of origins did not oblige Herder to accept the pre-Enlightenment theory of Divine gifts coming to man fully formed. Holding with Hamann that God works immanently, he insisted that "the whole course of nature, the history of the human mind and of all the arts, sciences and accomplishments," runs counter to the assumption that such precious things as speech and poetry were "quite perfect in their origin, but thereafter deteriorated, instead of improving, like everything else in nature and art, by constant use and adaptation."[39] Nothing need be despised for its low beginning. If, as Hume maintained, religion arose out of fear and sore need, anguished prayer produced poetry.

No investigator into the earliest days of humanity, those days Herder thought most in need of investigation, could avoid declaring himself about Genesis, reputed the earliest of historical documents and that offering certain knowledge of the first events. In Riga, Herder composed an essay interpreting the opening chapters of the Bible as a prescientific attempt to account for the origin of things, comparable to cosmogonies of primitive peoples the world over. For he perceived that the *philosophes*, although right in thinking parts of the Old Testament childish, had not risen to the higher sophistication of enjoying the fresh imaginativeness of childhood and honoring the first efforts of man to account for the workings of nature. He left the essay unpublished, probably from fear of uniting against him the skeptics and the orthodox. In youthful impatience with literal-mindedness and mistaken loyalty, he broke out:

O quantum est in rebus inane!—Poetry, a very ancient sensuous Oriental song, becomes, several centuries after the birth of Christ, a text chopped up for dogma. . . . That every letter, every word has been taken as if it were actually written for quite dry scholastic purposes as a chapter of physics and metaphysics, has shackled the human mind and cast it into unworthy dust. In former times, indeed at the beginning of this century, a few of the ablest critics scarcely dared call the first chapters of the Bible poetry, and stopped short with merely naming it so. In our day the name has been repeated, but again merely as a name. The interpretation that would put this work in all its national light—that is still to come.[40]

That interpretation, in which history and literature joined hands, was to be one of Herder's signal achievements. But it had to wait until his position as a clergyman was secure.

Meanwhile, a literary problem gave an opening for his novel views of history. The problem was: What is the proper model for German literature? Critics had been commanding authors to follow the Greco-Roman tradition, which had inspired Corneille, Racine, and Molière and had aided the scientific temper in creating a modern European prose. Behind them was a great line of interpreters of this tradition, from Aristotle and Horace through the Italians Vida and Castelvetro to Boileau and Pope. Pope's "Essay on Criticism" paraphrased the Frenchman Rapin's statement that Aristotle's *Poetics* was "nature put into method and good sense reduced to principles" in the familiar couplet:

> These rules of old, discover'd, not devised,
> Are Nature still, but Nature methodized.

While Herder was at Riga, this position was being assailed by the brilliant German writer Lessing, who proposed Shakespeare as a better model for his countrymen. He pointed out that the dramatic principles actually stated by Aristotle, as distinct from interpretations and amplifications by his successors, had been merely generalizations concerning the plays most successful in the Greek theater. Shakespeare, faced with new theatrical conditions, had attained as great literary effects by another dramatic form. In 1767, the year of Lessing's best statement of this argument in his *Hamburg Dramaturgy*, Herder, fifteen years his junior, came to his support with fuller historical reasoning in his first published book, *Fragments on Recent German Literature*.

Herder admitted the superiority of modern French, and of Latin of the Augustan age, in finish and sophistication, in the communication of ideas, but claimed for the German language compensating advantages. By combining the observations of Wood, Blackwell, and Michaelis concerning the history of Greek and Hebrew with an analogy drawn from the revolutionary educational theory of Rousseau's *Émile* (1762), he showed the impossibility of the demand that "a language should possess at the same time the virtues of all ages." [41] Just as a child's mind, according to Rousseau, cannot be forced, but must slowly recapitulate the mental history of the race, so German literature could not leap at once beyond the cultural immaturity of the German people and the undeveloped state of their language. Instead of bewailing this backwardness and seeking to overcome it by imitation of the French and the Augustan Romans, German authors should exploit the youthful virtues of German. A language like French, at ease with abstractions, crystal clear, was "bad for the poet, who . . . must live from superfluity; who does not define conceptions clearly, but seeks to express conceptions and creations movingly and richly." [42] For the youth of a literature, the Romans and French were not proper guides, since from despising their own literary youth they had largely forgotten or lost its records; the Romans out of deference to the more mature literature of the Greeks, the French out of admiration for the Romans. Hebrew literature, indeed, had preserved its youth and even its childhood records; but the mental processes of Orientals were difficult for Germans to follow. Fortunately, one great Western literature remained extant in every stage from childhood to old age—the Greek.

But before Germans could imitate wisely, they must see it as it really was. A historical critic should do for Greek letters what Winckelmann had done for Greek art. As Winckelmann had refused to look at Greek sculpture, according to the practice of centuries, through Roman eyes, so this critic must efface the image of the Greeks as they appeared in the dramas of Racine, where their manners were those of the French aristocracy, their motives sometimes Christian. He must trace the Greek drama backward from its maturity in Sophocles toward its origin in lost dithyrambs in praise of Dionysus the wine god, of which traces lingered in the wildly impetuous odes of Pindar.

In the barbaric side of Homer, so disturbing to fastidious readers, he should see a remnant of the primitive heroic songs of the rhapsodists, who resembled the bards and the skalds of the North. Homer and Pindar, then, were proper stimulants for a youthful literature like the German, provided that their spirit be imitated, not their form. Still more helpful would be the indigenous popular literature of Northern Europe, especially Shakespeare, and of Germany's own medieval past.

This first book of Herder's involved him in controversy with a Professor Klotz, who maintained doggedly that Homer could be imitated without allowance for time and place. Seeing where Herder's historical theories would lead if applied consistently to the Bible, he also questioned his orthodoxy. The question struck home, throwing the young clergyman into an alarm exaggerated by fatigue from overwork. By nervous reaction he fell into disgust with writing and even with his highly successful pastoral labors.

Seeking refreshment from change of scene, he boarded a cargo sailing ship, which took six weeks to land him in France. In Paris, where he met d'Alembert and other *philosophes*, he found what he expected, an aging culture producing encyclopedias, dictionaries, and grammars instead of creative writing. But on the voyage he had stumbled upon more useful discoveries.

The first days aboard ship, he had suffered acutely from want of books and from lack of stimulating conversation, for he was the only passenger. Nothing but the misty Baltic and its flat coasts. Out of boredom he observed the crew. The sharp commands, the unquestioning obedience roused his unspoken protest, for he had always chafed against authority. But when the cordage creaked and waves dashed high, he saw this discipline bring prompt, efficient action. Reluctantly he came to admit that here, and in all primitive societies at the mercy of nature, despotism was necessary. The skilled hands and sharp eyes of the sailors, their instinct for coming storms, disgusted the pale young man in clerical dress with his own uselessness as a mere "inkwell of learned writing . . . a dictionary of the arts and sciences." [43] With his quick turn to generalization, he admitted he had undervalued men of action and their role in history. The sailors' superstitions and tales of wild adventure recalled the poetry of the Greeks, the great seafarers of antiquity; now he knew why they created myths of the sea, and the Egyptians myths of the solid earth. The sunny Mediterranean must inevitably have shaped poetry otherwise than this dim Baltic. On the way through the narrow Skagerrak to the broad North Sea, glimpses of the bleak, mist-shrouded mountains of Norway, their green bases bathed in deep fjords, told him why the Eddas and Ossian exhaled wildness of a different quality from that of the *Odyssey*. In vivid retrospect, Herder wrote of this voyage:

Suddenly out of business, tumult and the foolish rivalries of the *bourgeois* world, out of the easy chair of the scholar and the soft sofa of society, thrown abruptly, without amusements, libraries, learned or popular periodicals, upon a deck on the open boundless sea among a little state of men who have severer laws than the republic of Lycurgus; in the midst of a wholly different, living and moving Nature, surrounded daily by the same endless elements and only now and then observing some new coast, new people, ideal region—here past the cliffs of Olaf, famed in so many wondrous stories, . . . past the lands where of yore skalds and Vikings with sword and song wandered through the sea on their horses of the earth-girdle [ships], now afar past the coasts where Fingal's deeds took place and Ossian sang melancholy songs, under the same changing sky . . . believe me, there skalds and bards get read far differently than from a professor's desk! [44]

The stuff of history, Herder now believed, was action, instinct, atmosphere, the spirit of a people in its geographical

THE LIVING PAST

setting. History should be displayed as "pictures," not analyzed into abstract generalizations. Its charm was "absence," remoteness. In remoteness Herder discovered the impelling force of his own temperament and activity:

Thence my taste for speculation and for the somber in philosophy, in poetry, in tales, in thought! my inclination toward the shadows of antiquity and the remoteness of centuries that have flowed past! My inclination toward the Hebrews, the Greeks, Egyptians, Celts, Scots, etc. . . . From it my first scenes of activity, my youthful dreams of a water-world, my trembling before psychological discoveries, new thoughts emerging from the human soul, my style, half-comprehensible, half-obscure, my perspective of fragments, groves, torsos, of archives of the human race—everything! My life is a procession through Gothic arches.[45]

An unpublished fragment of his *Journal of My Voyage in 1769* contains Herder's vision of his life work: "History of the progress and energies of the human spirit, in the flowing together of whole eras and nations! . . . A spirit, a good *daimon* has encouraged me to it, in the guise of night!—May that be the career of my life, my history, my work! . . . and that alone can keep me ever alert, since I shall always be wandering in the gallery of great men!"[46]

This ambitious work was slow in maturing. Five years were to pass before he should publish its preliminary sketch, *Still Another Philosophy of History*. Years beginning with widening horizons in France, Holland and the Rhineland, but soon passing into the isolation of Bückeburg, the village capital of Schaumberg-Lippe with its stuffy Court. Those years, spent in awakening a German literature of Northern inspiration, developed his historical ideas and witnessed the beginning of his friendship with a writer whose genius, even more universal than his own, would aid in the planning of his masterpiece: *Thoughts on History*.

The meeting with Goethe was in Strasbourg, where Herder was undergoing an eye operation. Goethe, a law student of twenty-one, made the advances, for Herder, five years his senior, had considerable German reputation as a literary critic. Herder remained for some time the dominating personality. Goethe tells us: "Herder's books taught me that the poet's art was a world gift, a gift to the nations, not a private inheritance of a few polished and cultivated men." [47] At Herder's instigation he hunted out folk songs among the Alsatian peasants and reported the discovery of twelve, "out of the throats of the oldest grandmothers . . . with the old melodies, as God made them." [48] Herder's faith in the early Greeks, especially Pindar, as inspiration for German lyric poetry quickly bore fruit in Goethe's odes and songs of untrammeled energy. His urging that themes from the German Middle Ages be treated in the manner of Shakespeare's chronicle histories resulted in Goethe's *Götz von Berlichingen*, which a generation later pointed Scott toward the historical novel, still the most popular union of history and literature.

The manifesto of the new literary school, *German Character and Art* (1773), a joint work by Herder and Goethe, led directly to Herder's writing history. Goethe's essay on *Germanic Architecture* was an enthusiastic tribute to the architect of Strasbourg cathedral. Although he erred in thinking the international medieval style we call Gothic to be of German origin (the English were also to claim it before architectural history got on a firm footing), his felicitous comparison of the structure to a "highly noble, wide-spreading tree of God, which with a thousand branches and twigs, and leaves like the sands of the sea . . . proclaims abroad the splendor of God its master," [49] contributed to the understanding of the medieval spirit. Herder's two essays, by stressing the relativity of taste, laid the foundation for a comparative study of national literatures. His "Correspondence about Ossian and the Songs of Ancient Peoples" was, in effect, a miniature form of his later work, *Folksongs* (1778–1779), where he was to reveal himself as an inspired translator of primitive poetry among many nations, ancient and modern. His hint of the loss of German popular verse through neglect led to the discovery of ballads and songs almost rivaling those of Scotland and England (*Des Knaben Wunderhorn*, 1805, by Brentano and Arnim, was to be the German equivalent of Percy's *Reliques*); and his surmise of a similar, and apparently irremediable, loss of ancient Roman folk poetry invited the historian Niebuhr's attempt to restore the true origins of Rome.[50] Herder's essay on "Shakespeare" proclaimed his plays as natural an outgrowth of time, place, and race as those of Sophocles. "As everything in the world changes, so must the nature that produced the Greek drama";[51] and the efforts of the French to maintain it as an absolute norm were as mistaken as their persuasion that it had been reproduced in modern plays. Herder's conceptions of the plurality of cultures, of their mortality and irrecoverability, had become ripe for inclusion in *Still Another Philosophy of History* the following year.

In tracing the main ideas of that book back to their origin, we have come to understand how Herder could mediate between Voltaire and Bossuet. He was as loyal to science as Voltaire, to religious values as Bossuet: his broader and more flexible understanding of both made them reconcilable. He followed Voltaire in breaking down the compartments between sacred and profane history, between man and nature, but without belittling the Jews or making man a mechanism. He accepted enlightenment from science without letting its brilliance cast too dark shadows on the Middle Ages or on the childhood of our race. Against the tyranny of the analytic intellect, he maintained the value of the senses, of imagination, of feeling. By a more catholic taste in literature, he enlarged Voltaire's innovation of cultural history. Where Voltaire reported chaos in human affairs, Herder discerned plan. But that plan, unlike Bossuet's, was not imposed upon man arbitrarily or capriciously: it unfolded according to the laws of the growth of living things. The principles of imaginative sympathy and of relativity of taste taught by literature have revealed in history the continuity of a seamless, though many colored, fabric. Continuity implies movement in time; and time is irreversible. Tradition therefore could not fetter the future. Humanity was ever marching upon an invisible goal. The route had the fascination of the unexplored, but not the bewilderment of the capricious; for a backward look revealed that all had come to pass according to law. Science, in expanding the universe and in showing the complex workings of human nature, had increased man's reason to wonder and admire.

This first historical work of Herder's was a manifesto, like *German Character and Art* of the previous year, and had the characteristic fault of manifestoes, overstatement of a case. In exposing the blind spots of Enlightenment historians, it failed to do justice to their boldness and acuteness in using the methods and results of science, even if narrowly conceived. Such injustice was a passing phase with Herder. In the intellectual isolation of Bückeburg he had felt the influence of correspondence with the mystic Hamann and with a strange religious enthusiast, Lavater. His pulpit mannerisms in style and his disorderly presentation are in sorry contrast to Voltaire's limpid neatness. Soon a more stimulating environment restored the equilibrium his mind had enjoyed in Riga and in Strasbourg.

Good fortune once more joined Herder to Goethe. In 1776 he was called to head the official church of the Duchy of Weimar. Goethe had persuaded the Duke, who wanted "absolutely no clerical squabbles about orthodoxy," that Herder was his man. The Weimar clergy, suspicious from rumors of Herder's worldly ideas, manner, and dress (he had arrived in Bückeburg wearing a blue coat with gilt trimmings, a white vest and hat), were unanimously opposed. The Duke forced his will on them. Although knowing of this opposition, Herder accepted, and held the uncomfortable post for the rest of his life.

In Weimar, Herder was introduced to a cultivated and enlightened Court inclined to the usual frivolity and moral laxity, and a clergy morally upright but intellectually narrow. He endeavored to bring mutual understanding by an interpretation of the Bible that would open the eyes of the aristocracy to the moral grandeur and the poetic beauty of "the despised book" and would win the pastors away from their exclusively dogmatic conception. His hopes went even further. Such an interpretation might save historical writing from becoming involved in theological dispute, as threatened since Voltaire had laid violent hands upon the records of Jewish civilization; and it would scarcely fail to contribute richness and unity to the world history which was to crown his life's work. In Weimar, he had the extraordinary advantage of ready consultation with Goethe, the greatest poet of the time, and with its greatest Biblical scholar, Johann Eichhorn, teaching at Jena, only a few miles away. Eichhorn, who had studied with Michaelis, had the expert knowledge of Semitic languages and customs that would further Herder's Riga plan to put the Old Testament in its national setting. More useful still, he was disclosing well-preserved examples of primitive ways of recording history, for centuries unnoticed, in the best-known and most diligently studied book in Europe.

Over a hundred years of serious and scientific research into the history of the Bible—beside which Voltaire's suppositions were amateurish trifling—had gradually prepared the way for this disclosure. The chief problems had been raised by the Jewish philosopher Spinoza in his *Tractatus theologico-politicus* (1670) and by the French Catholic priest Richard Simon in his *Critical History of the Old Testament* (1678).

Spinoza could not reconcile what he had been taught in Rabbinical schools—that God dictated the Pentateuch to Moses word for word—with the arrangement of its materials.

> If one pays attention to the way in which all the histories and precepts in these five books are set down promiscuously and without order, with no regard for dates; and further, how the same story is often repeated, sometimes in a different version, one will easily discern that all the materials were promiscuously collected and heaped together, in order that they might at some subsequent time be more readily examined and reduced to order. Not only these five books, but also the narratives contained in the remaining seven, going down to the destruction of the city [Jerusalem], are compiled in the same way. For who does not see that in Judges ii 6 a new historian is being quoted, who had also written of the deeds of Joshua, and that his words are simply copied? [52]

Besides, Moses could hardly be the author of passages narrating events subsequent to his death, including a circumstantial account of his burial. Nevertheless, the historical books, from their interconnection and from the unity of their point of view, seemed clearly the work of one man. Spinoza suggested he might be Ezra, who could have gathered the precious memorials of his nation's past when the Jews returned from captivity in Babylon. "Ezra did not put finishing touches to the narratives, but merely collected the histories from various writers." [53] Portions of lost sources could be discerned in repetitions, such as the identity of the last four verses of Second Kings with the last four of Jeremiah, and the reappearance in the first chapter of First Chronicles of the genealogy of the kings of Edom set down in Genesis. Ezra could not, however, have been the author of the book bearing his name, nor Nehemiah of "Nehemiah," since the contents of both books show they must have been composed after Judas Maccabeus restored worship in the Temple. Spinoza came to the general conclusion that "the sacred books were not written by one man, nor the people of a single period, but by many authors of different temperaments, at times extending from first to last over two thousand years, or perhaps much longer." [54]

To avoid alarming the general public, Spinoza had written in Latin, and anonymously. But in 1678 not only did a French translation of his *Tractatus* appear in Holland, but a priest, Richard Simon, published in his native French a book refining its theories. Inquiring into the origin and transmission of the Old Testament, Simon discovered that Fathers of the Church had been in doubt as to the authorship of certain books. Saint Jerome did not think it possible that Moses could have set down all the Pentateuch. Theoderet denied to Joshua the book bearing his name and considered Kings the work of more than one author. Certain Fathers, including the scholarly Origen, had anticipated Spinoza's theory that Ezra, as official scribe for the Jewish nation, had put together historical books out of "ancient memoirs," often as abridgments. As to the accuracy of the events recorded, Simon declared: "It is not absolutely necessary that all statements should have been written down by contemporary authors who were witnesses of the things they relate; otherwise one will not have faith in everything contained in Genesis." [55] Conspicuously, this was the case in matters of chronology, where the ancient Hebrews, not finding in their histories enough genealogies to fill up the full space of time, made a single person live several centuries. The diversity of style in the books attributed to Moses argued against a single author. "Sometimes the style is very abrupt, sometimes very much expanded, although the difference of subject matter does not require it" [56]—an observation that was to have far-reaching consequences. To admit that some of the historical parts of the Pentateuch were composed after the death of Moses should do no hurt to Christian faith, Simon explained, for it was not the history of his nation, but the Divine Law which God revealed to Moses.

This distinction between the historical and the religious content of the Old Testament, between the letter and the spirit, a distinction also made by Spinoza, satisfied Simon's superiors in the Oratorian Order. His *Critical History of the Old Testament* was approved for publication by the Royal Censor, and was sponsored by an influential priest who intended to ask Louis the Fourteenth to accept its dedication. But a glance at the table of contents had been enough to scandalize Bossuet, who rushed to the Chancellor and got its publication forbidden. In vain, for the offending book, still in French, appeared in Holland under a pseudonym. Simon had the courage to defend it, insisting that he must be proved wrong on the basis of Hebrew manuscripts. For his obstinacy he was punished by expulsion from the Paris Oratory and banishment to a country parish for the rest of his days. But vindication came forty years after his death by means of a former private physician to Louis the Fourteenth.

Dr. Jean Astruc, pondering over the evidence against the single authorship of Genesis presented not only by Simon and Spinoza but also by the English philosopher Hobbes and the Huguenot Leclerc, had the happy thought of relating to the odd fact, noted by Saint Augustine and Tertullian among others, that the Hebrew text had two names for God, Jahweh and Elohim. Separating the passages containing each name into parallel columns, he found they had fallen into two straightforward narratives, without the transpositions of chronolog-

and the repetitions, which had seemed greater than should be expected even from a primitive and unpracticed writer. Apparently, Moses had combined two originally independent accounts of the origin of his people. There remained a residue of passages not mentioning God, chiefly explanation of etymologies and other editorial comment, but including fragments of still a third account of the Flood. The discovery was so brilliant as to justify the exultant motto from Lucretius:

> Avia Pieridum peragro loca, nullius anté
> Trita solo
>
> I roam through the pathless haunts of the Muses,
> Trod by no foot before

which Astruc prefixed instead of his name to his *Conjectures on the Original Memoirs Apparently Used by Moses in Compiling Genesis* (1753).

One of Herder's first acts on arriving in France in 1769 had been the purchase of Astruc's book. Already he had learned of Spinoza and Simon from Michaelis, Eichhorn's teacher. So he was admirably prepared by knowledge of its antecedents to understand Eichhorn's epoch-making *Introduction to the Old Testament* (1780–1783).

Eichhorn claimed for the Old Testament a new sort of uniqueness: historical. In it, "the history of the culture and enlightenment of an ancient people is more fully described than in the extant account of any other people." [57] He asked readers to imagine with him how primitive history, such as Genesis, got recorded. Before written documents, such as those Astruc supposed Moses to have had before him, there must have been a long period of oral tradition. Racial discoveries, such as the use of metals and the institution of property, were attributed to individuals who were revealed as convenient fictions by the etymology of their names: Tubal (smith), Cain (possessor).

As in Greek myth, later discoveries were hung upon old names by an extension of the meanings. In a conscious effort to record events, piles of stone or altars were erected upon the spots; and after memory of the event became blurred, the pile or altar remained, to be related to some subsequent happening. Likewise, illustrious names attracted to themselves deeds performed much later, and the sagas gathered about them were embroidered by imagination. "Is it not very pardonable," Eichhorn asked, "if late posterity has taken mere pictures and poetic ideas in a historical sense?" [58]

As human intelligence grew, it became curious as to origins and causes. Thinking only in human likeness, it imagined causes as indwelling spirits. Curiosity about the origin and relationship of peoples produces among almost all nations "a dark saga" that the human race is descended from a single pair. So long as there is no writing, ideas of time are exceedingly vague. "The play of the imagination with figures, as it still goes on among peoples in their childhood," produces fantastic genealogies.

The earliest writers of history had no choice but to record these orally preserved accounts, for only as to contemporary events had they any measure of exactitude. Even for these, they continued to employ metaphorical expressions from lack of abstract terms: "Great thoughts and weighty decisions become inspirations and commands of the Divinity, and according to the phraseology man seemed in continual intercourse with Him." [59] Thus it was clear why the editor or editors who put Genesis together should have collected accounts often exaggerated or contradictory and set them down side by side without comment. A faint echo of their state of mind could be heard in a later and more sophisticated age, when Herodotus declared: "My duty is to repeat all that is said; but I am not obliged to believe it all alike; a remark which may be understood to apply to my whole History." Fortunate it was for posterity, commented Eichhorn, that no attempt to reconcile contradictions was made by the editor or editors of Genesis; for the art of comparing sources so as to get at the truth was of course unknown, and any move in that direction would have destroyed invaluable data concerning the primeval mind. That its sources have been preserved in their original state is proof of the authenticity of Genesis. No forger would have worked thus.

Guided by these conceptions of primitive recording and by differences in vocabulary and style, Eichhorn assigned the residue of text in Astruc's third and fourth columns to one or the other of the two narratives distinguished by the names for God.[60] He confessed the difficulty of the operation: "It demands the greatest acuteness, to distinguish manners of writing down to imperceptible shadings, and also hours when the mind is watchful enough not to miss the slightest similarities or dissimilarities."[61] But the rewards of this new way of approaching Genesis were great, he told his readers.

Read it as two historical works of high antiquity, and thus breathe the air of its age and land. Forget the century you are living in and the knowledge it offers you; if you cannot, do not dream that you are reading the book in the spirit of its origin. The youth of the world, which it describes, requires that one sink into its depths. The first beams of dawning intelligence will not bear the bright light of the intellect. The herdsman speaks only to the herdsman, and the Oriental of gray antiquity only to the Oriental. Without intimate acquaintance with the customs of pastoral life, without acquaintance with the manner of thinking and imagining among uncultivated peoples gained through the study of the ancient world, especially Greece of the earliest times, and of untutored nations of modern times, one easily becomes the betrayer of the Book, when one tries to be its rescuer and interpreter.[62]

In promoting understanding of the later Scriptural books, Eichhorn met the problems of explaining the function of the prophets and the inclusion of works with pronounced secular or worldly tone, like Ecclesiastes and the Song of Solomon. The vast majority of Christians of his time thought of the prophets as Divinely inspired predicters of the future; the *philosophes*, on the contrary, classed them with pagan soothsayers and oracles. Fontenelle's *History of Oracles* (1686), aimed obliquely at Judaism and Christianity, had given ammunition to Voltaire. But Eichhorn saw nothing derogatory to the prophets in an original association with oracles. "Oracles and prophets presuppose some growth of the human understanding. Man's awakened intelligence learns in course of time that many a thing returns in fixed order and that certain occurrences continually have their regular sequence," [63] in the moral as well as the physical realm. The gift of foreboding comes to individuals of exceptional intelligence and much experience. "Those instructors concerning the future—what important persons! As images and earthly representatives of the Godhead they direct everything. They are the common voice of nations. They are not merely advisers; they are lawgivers and all-powerful rulers of kings and peoples." [64] No wonder that they spoke as though inspired, were carried away into pictures, similes and fictions, gesticulated as they improvised oracular sayings. The great service of the Hebrew prophets was in spiritualizing the ceremonial Law of Moses.

Embarrassment regarding the Song of Solomon and Ecclesiastes would disappear, were the Old Testament understood as "the Hebrew national library." [65] Solomon's renown accounted for their inclusion, although their vocabulary and grammar now reveal their composition after his time. They were ascribed to him for the same reason that ascribed certain Psalms to his father: "Poets of later times knew no greater adornment to give their songs than to dedicate them to the name of David." [66] Such conclusions of "higher criticism"—

as distinguished from "lower criticism" (*niedere Kritik*), which concerns itself merely with establishing a correct text—Eichhorn explained as the result of methods well established in the study of other documents. "For a long time there have been attempts not only to determine the age of anonymous Greek and Roman writings from their contents, or often, when this is not sufficient, from their language; but also to separate out of ancient works pieces of later origin which by chance have been mixed with the older." [67]

Biblical scholars in this critical tradition had generally been so much occupied with such problems as to pay little attention to the literary quality of the Scriptures. Herder regretted that Spinoza "had only a metaphysical sense of the poetry of the Prophets." Richard Simon's rigid conception of poetic form obliged him to reject the suggestion of Saint Jerome and of the Jewish historian Josephus that Job and the Psalms were in verse: they showed, he said, no arrangement of long and short syllables after the manner of Greek and Latin poetry. In artistic matters clergymen who rejected critical scholarship, notably Bossuet with his exquisite sensibility, were frequently better judges. The first book on the Old Testament as literature came from the pen of an Anglican bishop, Robert Lowth, in the form of Latin lectures to Oxford students collected under the title of *Sacra poesia Hebraorum* (1753). Lowth found it strange that "the writings of Homer, of Pindar, of Horace should engross our attention and monopolize our praise, while those of Moses, David and Isaiah pass totally unregarded," even though "in the sacred writings the only specimens of the primeval and genuine poetry" [68] are to be found. The chief reason for this neglect was the loss of the principle of Hebrew versification, so long ago that the rabbis of the seventh century A.D. responsible for the Massorete text made no distinction between verse and prose. This ignorance might still be remedied, were it granted that "each language possesses a peculiar genius and character, on which depend the principles of versification and in great measure the style or color of the poetic diction." [69] Books and passages obviously poetical in spirit were distinguishable from the rest of the text by "an accurate recurrence of the clauses": this must be the base of a peculiarly Hebrew versification. Such "parallelism," accompanied by a special vocabulary or "poetic dialect," not only characterized entire books like Job, but also permitted Lowth to find short poems, like the song of Lamech, embedded in historical narrative. He defended parallelism against the charge of tiresome repetition and tried to overcome the prejudice of his student hearers against "poetic imagery from common life," although he forgot his own objection to criticizing "according to foreign and improper rules" to the extent of trying to fit Hebrew verse into the Greek genres of elegy, ode, idyll, and drama. In doing justice to the Hebrew union of sublimity with simplicity in style, diction and manners, Lowth represented the growing liberality of British taste that influenced Herder in his formative years.

Michaelis corrected Lowth's overstatement of the uniqueness of Hebrew poetry in notes affixed to the German edition of the *Sacra poesia* in 1770.

There is need [he wrote] of uncommon force of argument to convince me that the sacred writings are to be interpreted by rules in every respect different from those by which other languages and writings are interpreted. . . . It is indeed very improbable that in so long a poem [the Song of Songs], no intimation should be found to direct us to apply it to the Divine love; nothing which does not most clearly relate to the human passion. . . . It is much to be lamented that no commentator has arisen, sufficiently qualified to explain this beautiful poem. Those who have attempted it have been scholastic divines, rather indeed mystics, and have entirely overlooked the obvious and elegant meaning. Indeed the task is by no means easy. Besides a very accurate and idiomatic acquaintance with Oriental languages, an intimate acquaintance with the manners of antiquity and no small information concerning natural history will be requisite. To these must be added a good deal of reading in Arabic poetry, particularly of the amorous kind, and last of all a fine taste for poetry. Very few of these qualities have existed separately, and never all of them together in those who have undertaken to illustrate this poem.[70]

Before meeting Eichhorn in 1780, Herder acted upon Michaelis's suggestion by publishing anonymously, as a sort of trial balloon, a translation of the Song of Songs under the secular title, *Songs of Love: the Oldest and Most Beautiful from the Orient* (1778). He printed the German text as lines of verse in the Hebrew parallel manner, and arranged the songs as an anthology of popular love poems. But he called Solomon their collector; for among the highly various qualifications of the ideal commentator listed by Michaelis, knowledge of the history of the Hebrew language was not Herder's strongest.

Here, and in other matters of technical scholarship, it was exceedingly fortunate that Herder could lean upon Eichhorn in preparing a larger work, *The Spirit of Hebrew Poetry*, similarly addressed to the nonscholarly public. This was to prepare the way for a still more ambitious undertaking, a translation of the entire Bible in which, Herder planned, "every book and part of each book would be restored to its original state, without division into chapters and verses, and poetry and history carefully separated," so that the whole might appear "not as the Bible but as a collection of ancient writings."[71] It is intriguing to speculate upon what history and poetry might each have gained from the clarification of the public mind if Herder had carried out this project, which was not to be executed in any language for over a hundred years.

The arrangement of the Song of Songs apparently was well received, for Herder signed his name to *The Spirit of Hebrew Poetry* (1782–1783). In plan, this book resembles the ideal history of Greek literature on the analogy of Winckelmann sketched in his *Fragments:* Hebrew poetry is presented as the natural outgrowth of a people; of its language, its mentality, its history. The word "spirit" in the title indicates consciousness of a further parallel to Montesquieu's *Spirit of the Laws*.

"Before one says much about the beauty or ugliness of anything, one must first learn to understand it," said Herder's Preface: "Correct understanding of words, images, and things gives to those who have feeling, without much talk and eulogy, the conception of beauty." [72] Understanding of Hebrew poetry must begin with the language, whose very handicap in the expression of abstract ideas was its advantage for poetry. The sensuous tongue of a sensuous people living close to nature, it is rich in synonyms for concrete objects, in verbs representing action. Sincerity, lack of sophistication are the charm of its antique style: "the artistic poetry of the Greeks is variegated ornament beside this pure childlike simplicity." Poetic form, responding to stages in the national culture, developed from the bare rudeness of Lamech's sword song, through the song of deliverance from the Red Sea, a chorus with a leader, to considerable complexity in the Psalms. The war song of Deborah, the lament of David for Saul and Jonathan, the Psalms, stand comparison with the best of their kind in other literatures. Characteristically, Herder lamented the disappearance of the poetry of common life, songs of harvest and of the wine press, the song of the grinder at his work. Of the great tree of Hebrew poetry there remained "only two branches, poetry of religion and poetry of kings." [73]

Vindication of the right of the Hebrews to a distinct place in world poetry was preliminary to Herder's chief purpose:

definition of the "spirit" of their verse. Regretting that dictionaries of the Semitic languages gave little help here, he looked forward to a time when they "through taste, sound intelligence and comparison of various dialects will come to distinguish essential meanings from incidental, and also, in the derivation of words, the application of metaphors, become a true art of the discovery of the human spirit and enter into the logic of early times." [74] Assuming that among all peoples history grew out of sagas, he compared the stories of Eden, of the Deluge, of the Tower of Babel with Greek stories of origins, like those of Prometheus and Pandora. He found local color in Hebrew theology: its Heaven is that of tent dwellers who look up at a cloudless sky. The conception of the land of the dead went through changes that record "the pulse-beat of the nation." The plural name for God, Elohim, reveals an original polytheism which located a spirit in every natural object: the singular verb sometimes accompanying it indicates that a later editor has become a monotheist. Herder thought it unhistorical to deny that other ancient peoples had taken this step away from polytheism: "Why be jealous and not grant to the Persians, Hindus, Celts, the strides which each in his measure took in maintaining and developing the primitive religion of the earth?"

He did not employ the comparative method, like Voltaire, to disparage the Jews, but indicated essential difference within similarity, stressing the spiritual and ethical genius of the Hebrew people, their priority in discovering some plan and order in history, and the peculiar vividness of their manner of recording it. With them, "history itself is really poetry, the handing down of a tale pictured as if it were really present," [75] so that it brings the earliest state of the human heart before our eyes. "What with other peoples were wonderful tales of heroes and adventures are with this people tales of God and the Patriarchs, documented by genealogies and monuments. . . . With the Hebrews, up to their kings, history almost always preserved the saga style." [76] Herder aided the imagination of the eighteenth-century reader by portraits of great figures: of Moses steeped in Egyptian ideas and customs, of Abraham the nomad, of Job the emir on the border of the Arabian desert. He praised the prophets as leaders of civilization:

Look upon the savage or backward peoples. Note to what frightfulness humanity sinks, if it is not driven upward by force and awakened out of its sullen sloth. Then you will acknowledge the merit of those early guardian angels of our race, who lighted the way forward with their spirit, embraced nations with their heart, and against their will elevated them with a giant's strength.[77]

Herder could not restrain an expression of pride in the collective achievement of which *The Spirit of Hebrew Poetry* was a part. "If our time and nation has any desert, it is in this cool effort, unintoxicated by glosses and esoteric interpretation, to get at the simple original meaning of these poets, and to hear their god-like utterances in the historical atmosphere of the earliest times." [78]

The inclusion of Hebrew history and literature on honorable terms left Herder with only a final step toward an allembracing synthesis of history. But that step was the most difficult by far. For he must unite man with the earth and with all living things, his fellow travelers through time. Herder's belief that man is molded by the kind of world he lives in, his poetic sense that nature is alive, his religious intuition of God within nature, urged him to put an end to the separation of matter and spirit. Since writing *Still Another Philosophy of History*, he had been encouraged by discovering the progress made in that direction by Spinoza, whose *Ethics* (1677) had treated human emotions and actions as "natural phenomena following nature's law." Spinoza had been handicapped by the science of his day, which offered only mathematical and mechanical illustrations of natural law. Herder hoped to do better with the aid of the sciences of living and growing things.

The seventy years since Leibnitz had thought of an unbroken continuity from "the lowest and least organized parts of matter" to man himself had seen that brilliant speculation buttressed by great collections of facts. So long as matter had been defined, according to a phrase from Newton's *Optics* (1707), as "solid, massy, hard, impenetrable, moveable particles," theories smacking of materialism had been the just abhorrence of those who knew the higher human values. But recent discoveries of electrical phenomena had been giving to matter a more vital and spiritual character. Buffon, the foremost scientific speculator of Herder's day, had written in 1749: "The true mainspring of our existence lies not in those muscles, veins, arteries and nerves which have been described with so much minuteness; it is to be found in the more hidden forces which are not bound by the gross mechanical laws which we would fain set over them." In 1757, five years after Franklin had established the identity of electricity with lightning, the Swiss physiologist Haller described the stimulation of dead animal tissue by the newly invented "Leyden jar" into muscular activity which counterfeited life. Electricity, intangible, mysterious, was apparently at the same time a physical force and something very like the nervous and vital force in men and animals. So Herder conceived of the basis of the universe as "force" (something very like "energy" in modern scientific terminology),[79] manifesting itself in various degrees as chemical affinity and electricity in matter, as sensitivity and irritability in plants, and as nervous activity and thought in man—all forms of the omnipresent spiritual essence of God. Eloquently he described the position of man in this universe of energy.

In the human body, nothing is without life. From the tips of the hair to the end of the nails everything is pervaded by one sustaining and nourishing force, and as soon as this leaves the smallest or largest member, that member separates itself from the body. Then it is no longer in the realm of the living forces of our humanity, but it never escapes from the realm of natural forces. The dead hair, the cast-off nail, now enters another region in which it again acts or is acted upon only in accordance with its present nature. Now examine the wonders which the physiology of the human being or of any animal unfolds for us. You see nothing but a realm of living forces, each fixed in its place, producing by its activities the connection, structure, and life of the whole, and each the consequence of its essential nature. So the body forms and sustains itself. So it spends itself duly, and finally expends itself entirely. All that we call matter is thus more or less imbued with life.[80]

To place animals and plants in the universal scheme, Herder drew upon full and precise data collected by two great pioneers, the Swede Linnaeus and the Frenchman Buffon. Linnaeus had studied the effect of natural environment on the flora of such different parts of the world as Lapland, which he visited in early life, and the Americas, Japan, and the Near East, whence his pupils brought specimens and reports. He observed a struggle preserving equilibrium in the vegetable kingdom: "Every vegetable seems to have been given her special insect for the purpose of keeping her under and preventing her from spreading too much and ousting her neighbors." With vast patience he classified all known plants according to apparent resemblance, inventing for the purpose in 1748 the present binomial system of identification.

Count Buffon, who as Keeper of the Royal Garden in Paris (the present Jardin des Plantes) commanded exceptional means for organizing research, was the first scientist who attempted to put nature, animate and inanimate, under law as a single whole. His encyclopedic *Natural History*, begun in

1749 with *A Theory of the Earth and General Views on Generation and on Man,* had passed through volumes on quadrupeds and birds to concern itself with minerals while Herder was writing. Buffon found great difficulty in distinguishing sharply between animals and plants, and between species of both. Among the mammals, where he had the aid of the comparative anatomist Daubenton, he noted the physical resemblance of the higher apes to man. He entertained, before rejecting with possible irony, the hypothesis that resemblance of organisms might imply genetic relationship at odds with the orthodox theory of special creation.

Not only the ass and horse, but even man himself, the apes, the quadrupeds and all animals might be regarded as forming members of one and the same family. . . . If the point were gained that among animals and vegetables there had been, I do not say several species, but even a single one, which had been produced in the course of direct descent from another species, . . . then no limit could be set to the power of nature, and we should not be wrong in supposing that with sufficient time she could have evolved all organic forms from one primordial type.

And there had been sufficient time. In *Epochs of Nature* (1778) Buffon estimated that forty thousand years had passed since the appearance of life on our planet. Fossils were remains of living things and their absence from granite showed the earth still older than any form of life. De Saussure, in his *Travels in the Alps* (1779) added the information that fossils were determinants of the relative ages of rock strata and indications of great fluctuations of climate, indications supported by the discovery, a few years previously, of remains of elephants in Siberia by a Russian expedition headed by the German Simon Pallas. By studying the effect of climate and geography on the physique and habits of man, Buffon inspired a new sort of anthropological investigation, for which Herder also found rich materials in reports of recent exploration: the voyages of Bougainville and Cook in the South Pacific, Cook's subsequent voyages into the forbidding Aleutians and Antarctic, the travels of Pallas among the Siberians, and of Carver among North American Indians.

Before the anthropological sections of his *Thoughts on History* were ready for publication, Herder learned that his friend Goethe had proved erroneous a supposed physical distinction of man from the higher animals—the lack of an intermaxillary bone. The announcement came in an enthusiastic note of March 27, 1784: "I have found, neither gold nor silver, but what gives me inexpressible pleasure, the intermaxillary bone in man! I was comparing with Loder [Professor of Anatomy at Jena], came upon the clue, and see, there it is. . . . It will make you, also, rejoice heartily, for it is like the keystone to humanity. . . . I have thought of it in connection with your whole [*Thoughts on History*], how fine it will be there." [81]

Embryology, though condemned to slow progress until the invention of the compound microscope in the nineteenth century, also supported Herder's surmise of the relationship of all living things. The Dutchman Swammerdam had compared the metamorphosis of insects to the change of the tadpole into the frog and to stages in the development of the human embryo, which begins as an egg and passes through a form resembling a worm. In 1759 Caspar Wolff, brother of a distinguished disciple of Leibnitz, had described in his *Theoria generationis* how the organs of the chick in the egg appear one after another in rudimentary form, and develop gradually. From these hints, strengthened by the analogy of Rousseau's theory that the intellectual development of children retraces the steps of civilization, Herder adumbrated one of the most intriguing of biological speculations, the hypothesis that an embryo recapitulates, in abbreviated form, the stages of the evolutionary descent of its species. From comparative literature and religion to comparative anatomy, anthropology, and embryology Herder's thought coursed.

Copious notes to the text, referring to a multitude of books now forgotten except by historians of science, show how thorough and discerning was his effort to base his History on the best scientific knowledge. It was his misfortune to write just before the foundation of modern biology by Cuvier, Lamarck, St. Hilaire, Bichat, and Blumenbach, of modern chemistry by Lavoisier, of modern geology by Hutton, whose *Theory of the Earth* appeared just a year after the geological portions of Herder's book. But he had the aid of Goethe, at once the poet with an intuitive understanding of life and growth and the patient, objective, sharp-sighted observer, in foreseeing paths science was to enter. "Herder's work makes it probable that we were formerly plants and animals: what nature is now going to stamp out of us, must remain unknown to us," [82] was the impression of one of his earliest readers, his Weimar friend Frau von Stein. He was obliged to bridge by theological speculation gaps in knowledge not filled until Darwin, some indeed still to be filled as the modern physicist revises our conception of matter; but the admixture of speculation with fact did not seriously distort his view of man's place in nature as a determinant of history.

Thoughts on History, Herder's most ambitious work, appeared in four installments between 1784 and 1791. The Preface announces it as a development of his thesis of 1774 that history has a plan, discernible through scrutiny of nature. To find the plan there, will be an arduous task; but no other way will suffice: "Whoever wants mere metaphysical speculations, has them by a shorter route: but I think that speculations, apart from experiments and analogies with nature, are only a pleasure jaunt, which rarely leads to the goal." [83] The heartening analogy is with what has been accomplished in the sciences of space. "Is Time not ordered, then, as Space is? Both are indeed twins of one Fate. Space is full of wisdom, Time full of apparent disorder; and yet man is obviously so created as to seek order, to survey a spot of time in order that the future may build upon the past. For that purpose he has recollection and memory." [84] This faith Herder reaffirms in Part III: "The God I seek in history must be the God who is in nature; for man is only a small part of the whole, and his history, like that of the worm, is interwoven with the fabric he inhabits." [85] The Preface closes with offering the book to God in all humility: "And so I lay at thy feet, Great Being, Thou unseen higher Genius of our race, the most imperfect book which a mortal wrote and in which he dared think after Thee, follow after Thee." [86]

The note of humility is sustained as the curtain of the human drama rises to reveal the earth, its stage, as a "star among stars," in the immensity of space. But Herder bids man not to be overwhelmed by his insignificance; for it was the human intellect which attained astronomical knowledge, and every individual is "a force in the system of all forces." [87] Earth is not only man's dwelling, but his mother, who existed long before any form of life. Life was brought forth by the action upon primeval rock of air, water, and fire: exactly how, we do not know, for Buffon is only the Descartes of the new knowledge; but the phenomena of electricity hint that matter is itself alive, and "we know no spirit which works without, and outside of, all matter." [88]

Among living things man was a late comer.

Nature everywhere still today brings forth everything out of the minutest elements and . . . does not reckon according to our measure of time. . . . Many combinations of water, air, and light must have taken place before the seed of the first plant organism, perhaps moss, could come forth. Many plants must have appeared and died, before there was any animal organism; and among the animals, insects, birds and aquatic and nocturnal creatures preceded those of the land and the daylight, until at last after them all appeared the crown of the organisms of our earth, man the *microcosm*.[89]

The development of the human embryo through similar stages is a marvelously preserved record of man's relationship to the life that went before. Herder repeatedly returns to wonder at it. Signs of this relationship do not cease after man's birth. "It is manifest that human life, so far as it is vegetation, shares the fate of the plants. . . . Our ages are the ages of plants; we sprout, grow, bloom, fade, and die. . . . Our organism takes part in the life of a tree, as long as it is growing, and there are men who cannot physically bear its fall, or mutilation in its green youthful form. Its withered top gives us pain. We bewail a beloved flower that fades."[90] Man's sexual behavior, which he dignifies by the name of love, "serves the laws of nature almost as blindly as the plants. Even the thistle, we say, is beautiful when it blooms. . . . As soon as nature has assured the continuation of the race, she lets the individual existence gradually sink."[91]

Animals are "man's elder brothers. . . . There is no virtue, no instinct in the human heart, which does not find analogy in the world of animals."[92] Where the handsomest men live, Buffon has observed, are also the largest and handsomest dogs: both respond to environment. Like animals and plants, man has survived through struggle. "The whole Creation is in war. . . . Nature lets Earth bear what she is able to bear. . . . Always and everywhere we see that Nature must destroy while she builds up again, that she must separate while she unites anew. From simple laws as well as from rude forms she steps forward to something more compact, artful and fine."[93] Nature maintains an equilibrium with which it is perilous for man to interfere. "Seldom has a plant or animal species been made extinct in this or that region without the habitability of the whole soon experiencing the most obvious damage."

Man is nature's best product; and even in his species is "a ladder visible, from the man close to the animals to the purest genius in human form." [94] Comparative anatomy shows him most closely akin to the apes, but not their descendant. His advantage over the animals seems to have arisen from his adaptability to every climate without need of bodily change, his unique upright carriage, the refinement of his instincts into intelligence through speech, and his capacity to cooperate for mutual aid, which has freed him from the worst effects of the struggle for existence. As a social animal with capacity for reason, humaneness, and religion, he has moved into a position midway between the brutes and God, a position which is his glory and his torture.

Between man in the state of nature and man in his present stage lay long ages in which he was the creature of his imaginings and irrational customs. He has been slow to acknowledge his natural origin and to distinguish and classify the varieties of his species because he has found it hard to face unflattering facts and thus make himself the subject of scientific study. "The historian must observe dispassionately, like the Creator of our race or the Earth-Spirit, and judge dispassionately. To the investigator of nature who desires to arrive at the knowledge and ordering of all classes of his realm, the rose and the thistle are alike dear, the stinking, slothful beast and the elephant. He investigates most where he learns most." [95] The anthropological map of the world was still incomplete, but all evidence pointed to the unity of mankind. The various races are not genetically separate, though diversified by geography, climate, and ways of living. Herder's anthropology is

THE LIVING PAST

remarkable for its wide survey of source materials and even more for their interpretation. He observed how quickly and easily cultures got set in prerational patterns that were propagated by the tribal training of children.

The Greenlander and the Siberian now really sees what he only heard tell of in his childhood, and thus believes it a true happening. Wherever there is movement in nature, wherever a thing seems to move and change without the eye being aware of the cause of the change, there the ear hears voices and speech which explain to him the riddle of the seen by means of the unseen. The power of the imagination is excited and then satisfied after its own manner, that is, through imaginings. The ear is the most apprehensive, the most timorous of the senses. It apprehends vividly but only darkly. It cannot hold things together, cannot compare clearly, for its stimulations go past in a bewildering stream. . . . Dreams are wondrous mighty among all peoples rich in imagination; indeed dreams were probably the first Muses, the mother of fiction and poetic art. They brought men upon forms and things which the eye had not seen, but for which desire lay in the human soul.[96]

The Eskimo thinks of his soul as wandering out of the body at night, but staying at home while he is on a journey. Magicians are not always conscious deceivers. They are "themselves people, and were also deceived by older myths." [97] Only after the meaning of a religious symbol has become dim or is lost, does priestcraft arise out of the mechanical repetition of a superstition that serves to the advantage of the priest.

Myth, legend, and poetry are the chief sources of history until the Greeks set themselves seriously to its writing. "The Greeks alone have true history. The Oriental has genealogical lists or legendary tales, the Northerner has sagas, other nations have songs. The Greek, in course of time, built out of traditions, songs, legends and genealogical tables the sound body of a narrative which is alive in all its limbs." [98] Such importance did Herder attach to prehistory, that he devoted almost as many pages to it as to history proper up to the Crusades. For man's place in nature explained much in civilization which otherwise must be an enigma. It accounted for the persistence of animal instincts, the struggle for existence counterbalanced by gregariousness, geographic and climatic influences with their counterbalance of genetic characters, the stages of growth and decay in individuals and in civilizations, and the tendency of each culture toward an equilibrium. Prerational societies, in which imagination and trial-and-error fashioned customs and beliefs handed down uncritically, prepared the mind of the eighteenth-century reader to allow for the stubborn persistence into his own time of beliefs and customs of a similar sort. An immense and shadowy past remained at work through the eras of man's self-consciousness, and speculations as to his future must still reckon with it.

Of peoples with written history, the most ancient appeared in the great land masses of Asia and Africa, where geography encouraged uniformity of behavior and belief. Herder could say little else about them, for Egyptian writing was still undeciphered, and information concerning India, China, and Mesopotamia was fragmentary and uncertain. He saw the contribution of these peoples to European civilization passing chiefly by way of the Jews, who along with exalted religious and moral ideas brought the retarding influence of a priestly class which frowned upon the plastic arts, showed no scientific curiosity, and enforced the mental habit of rigid adherence to the letter of social and political precepts pertinent to certain stages of culture, after those stages had passed.

Europe, on the contrary, with its highly indented coasts and irregularly set mountains, encouraged variety in thought and action. The first civilization characteristically European appeared in Greece, which had these geographical characteristics in a high degree. The *Iliad* and the *Odyssey* reveal the

Greeks at the dawn of their history as seafarers and adventurers, who look with curiosity on the strange customs of other peoples. In Athens, a sea power, political freedom aided in a brief flowering of the arts, philosophy, and historical writing, which set a goal for European culture. Even after freedom was lost, Greeks of the colonial port of Alexandria gave scientific form and order to all the knowledge of the ancient world.

Natural causes accounted for the decline of Greece. "Let no one say that an unfavorable god guides the fate of man and in envy tries to throw him down from his height: men are their own unpropitious spirits." [99] History as a whole is "a purely natural history of human forces, actions and instincts, according to time and place. . . . The soundness and endurance of a state does not rest upon the point of its highest culture but upon a wise or fortunate *equilibrium* of its living and working forces." [100] Habits of luxury, and overweening pride in their own type of culture contracted from the vanquished Persians, set the victorious Greeks upon the downward path. Herder expressed regret that his contemporaries had not devoted to Greek history the attention they had given to Roman, for it was especially instructive. "As the scientist can only fully observe a plant when he knows it from its seed and germ to its blossoming and fading, so the history of Greece should be such a plant for us." [101]

Rome, which swallowed up Greece and most of the ancient world, was a parasite state, feeble in invention except in law and government, and even there unable to expand the constitution of a city to the needs of an empire. Like Athens, it broke down from within: from the uneconomic practices of a robber state accustomed to live from plunder, from class struggle, from "tyranny over the noblest men," [102] and, most of all, from militarism, the defect of its strength, for when the empire ceased to expand, unemployed legions devoured its vitals. Rome presented to Herder the problem of destructive forces in nature. Strong passions, he thought, were indispensable, since "an apathetic human race would never have built up its intelligence; it would still be lying in some troglodyte cave." [103] Astronomy shows that the harmony of the solar system represents an equilibrium of violent forces, and man himself has learned to control and use to his advantage many forces of nature. These analogies led Herder to hope that a larger perspective upon time would make evident what "our short history" faintly indicated: that passions are becoming less anarchic. Although the Roman world state was not, as some believed, providentially designed to disseminate Christianity, still Rome, and the barbarian invasions, did undesignedly promote the brotherhood of man by bringing together diverse peoples, mingling their blood and customs. The piling up in the European mentality of many traditions, "the monstrous snowball the ages have rolled up for us," insured against the permanent lowering of culture by the invasions. "The stream never returns to its source, as if it had never run from it." [104]

The Christian church preserved learning among barbarians, giving it a home in universities, institutions unknown in the world hitherto. It softened the manners of knights whose ancestors had deified incessant warfare in Valhalla, and protected against them the industrious guilds of the towns. None the less, the introduction of the fraternal gospel of Jesus into the melting pot of peoples meant its being covered with the accretions of "a new Christian mythology," [105] which the union of temporal and spiritual power in Rome and Constantinople forced upon Europe as a uniform system of belief. There was real danger of spiritual and mental slavery, but the danger was averted by the excess of fanaticism itself; for the Crusades permitted the seeping in from the East of Greek science and philosophy under the strange guises of alchemy and scholasticism. In describing how alchemy led to science, how scholasticism wakened the dormant intelligence of Christendom by encouraging debate and discussion, by developing language capable of fine shades of meaning, Herder's sympathetic comprehension of primitive stages in culture was again fruitfully at work. He was equally happy in explaining why this period of half-awakened intelligence should have brought forth the greatest revival of the plastic arts since Greece and should have refined into chivalric romances the sagas of the heroic age of barbarian migrations and the Celtic legends of Arthur. The superlative achievement of the age, Gothic architecture, was the work of the towns and their craft guilds. "Cloisters and knights' castles could never have been models for the boldest and most original art of the Gothic builders; it is the splendid possession of the community. . . . According as men think and live, so do they build" [a principle developed from Winckelmann, which was to illuminate the history of art]. Towns and guilds were in their turn products of a revival of commerce, stimulated by the Crusades but soon expanding into the Hanseatic ports with their global possibilities: "All that Genoa, Pisa, Amalfi did, remained within the Mediterranean; to the Northern seafarers belonged the ocean, and with the ocean the world." [106] Commerce provided the economic basis for culture, spread knowledge of printing, paper, glass, Arabic numerals, gunpowder, painting in oils and the useful arts. The universities, although the invention of the Church, responded to this lay development by training civil servants. Thus was added to knights and priests "a third estate . . . of learning, practical activity and artistic emulation on a world scale."

In breaking off here, at the threshold of modern times,

Herder was not blind to the dangerous use of the inventions which were to be their glory. But his survey of the ages had taught him to trust mankind to arrive at wisdom ultimately. "A sharp knife in the hands of a child hurts the child. However, the art which discovered the knife is one of the indispensable arts. Not all who use such tools are children, and even the child will learn from pain its better use." [107] A reassuring thought, as we ponder over atomic energy.

Herder's purpose with *Thoughts on History* had been to cut paths that would let light into the tangled wilderness of historical facts. He was aware that the light of science still was dim and that much which was accessible in the guise of fact might not be dependable. But already in his Preface he had been content to incite futurity to do the rest: "A well-disposed man will rejoice much more over what he awakened than over what he said." [108]

III

GIBBON, VICO, AND THE MASSES

TO a passage in the Seventeenth Book of *Thoughts on History* describing the servility of spirit into which his favorite Greeks had fallen under Byzantine Christianity, Herder appended a footnote of thanks for solid factual support: "With appreciative pleasure we can here name the third classical English historian, who rivals Hume and Robertson, and perhaps surpasses the latter: Gibbon's History of *The Decline and Fall of the Roman Empire*, a highly finished masterpiece." [1] Gibbon's six volumes (1776–1788), the perfect Enlightenment history, had been appearing simultaneously with Herder's work. Their theme was the worst disaster in human annals as the *philosophe* saw them. The style was of a fitting Augustan stateliness, varied by the grave irony of Pascal and the mockery of Voltaire. The author was a bilingual cosmopolitan who in youth had seen Voltaire and in maturity had been welcome in Parisian salons. A visit to Rome had determined the choice of his life's work. "My temper is not very susceptible of enthusiasm, and the enthusiasm which I do not feel I have ever scorned to affect," he wrote in his *Autobiography*, "But at the distance of twenty-five years I can neither forget nor express the strong emotions which agitated my mind as I first approached and entered the *eternal City*. After a sleepless night, I trod with lofty step the ruins of the Forum: each memorable spot where Romulus *stood*, or Tully spoke, or Caesar fell, were at once presented to my eye: and several days of intoxication were lost or enjoyed, before I could descend to a cool and minute investigation." [2]

For Gibbon, the chief agents of Rome's downfall were those singled out by Voltaire. "I have described the triumph of Barbarism and Religion," was the phrase summarizing his long narrative of the fate of the Western Empire. Ashamed to recall his conversion to Catholicism from reading Bossuet in his susceptible youth, he tried to sap the solemn creed of Christianity by solemn sneers at asceticism and credulity. He examined the manners of the Northern barbarians with scientific curiosity but without sympathy. "I have read the *Introduction to the History of Denmark* by Mallet, with the translation of the Edda, the sacred book of the Celts," he noted in his Journal: "We have at present half a dozen of these bibles (including our own). It would be a pretty work to make a philosophic picture of the religions, their spirit, their reasoning and their influence on the manners, government, philosophy and poetry of each people."[3] He went on to reflect that it must not have been difficult for the superior religion of Southern Europe to detach the Northern invaders "from a cult founded only on barbarity and ignorance." His dismissal of the Crusades, "I shall abridge the tedious and uniform narrative of their blind achievements, which were performed by strength and are described by ignorance," was a neat condensation of his youthful rejection of the future theme of *The Talisman*:

The history of Richard First of England and his Crusade against the Saracens would please on the side of the marvellous. . . . Richard was a worthy hero to the monks. The ferocity of a gladiator and the cruelty of a tyrant employed without success in a cause in which superstition imposed silence upon religion, justice and policy; and against one of the most accomplished princes in history! How little Richard would interest us! Besides, this event is too far off, too much buried in the darkness of the Middle Ages, to attract much attention today.[4]

Thus Gibbon was completely at home in what he was pleased to call his "philosophic age." He sifted critically the immense accumulation of facts bearing upon his great theme by the patient labor of scholars, notably the French Benedictine Jean Mabillon, the Jansenist Louis de Tillemont and the Italian librarian Ludovico Muratori, and marshaled the infinity of detail that passed through this ordeal into a coherent narrative, giving body to what Voltaire and Herder had left in outline interspersed with comment. "To say that he applied the mind of the eighteenth century to the learning of the seventeenth would fix Gibbon's position exactly in the movement of European letters," is the comment of his latest biographer, Mr. G. M. Young. In the admirable proportions of its immense structure, *The Decline and Fall* is a great work of art in the neoclassical manner, a St. Peter's as compared to the Greek temple of Bossuet and the uncompleted Gothic cathedral of Herder. Observing with regret that France had not "formed and fixed the idiom to the proper tone, the peculiar mode of historical eloquence," [5] Gibbon had made many experiments before he could "hit the middle tone between a dull Chronicle and a Rhetorical declamation." [6] Yet with his belief that "history is the most popular species of writing, since it can adapt itself to the highest or lowest capacity," he was not wholly surprised that his book was to be found "on every table, and almost on every toilette: the historian was crowned by the taste or fashion of the day." [7]

He designed his narrative to "connect the ancient and the modern history of the world." Beginning with the Roman Empire in the age of the Antonines, "the period . . . during which the condition of the human race was most happy and prosperous," he traced its decline to the extinction of its last remnant in Constantinople in the fifteenth century, when Italy was ready to put the world once more on the path of enlightenment. Convinced that "wars, and the administration of public affairs, are the principal subjects of history," Gibbon paid much less attention than Herder and Voltaire to social and economic conditions, to literature and the arts, resembling in this the historians of antiquity. Yet he keeps the reader constantly aware of their importance by brief asides, such as that concerning gunpowder: "If we contrast the rapid progress of this mischievous discovery with the slow and laborious advances of reason, science and the arts of peace, a philosopher, according to his temper, will laugh or weep at the folly of mankind." While, like Voltaire, he considers periods of high culture precarious accidents, he does not share Voltaire's and Iselin's fears for the future of civilization in Europe. Political organization has become too firm, superiority in the arts and machines of war too great, for an irruption of barbarians, "since, before they can conquer, they must cease to be barbarous."

These confident words, published in Gibbon's third volume in 1781, were not qualified in the completed History in 1788. As if to pay the great ironist in his own coin, the French Revolution broke out the following year.[8] In 1792 Gibbon was writing to English friends from retirement in Switzerland: "What a strange world do we live in: you will allow me to be a tolerable historian, yet, on a fair view of ancient and modern times, I can find none that bear any affinity to the present. . . . Where indeed will this tremendous inundation, this conspiracy of numbers against rank and property, be finally stopped? Europe seems universally tainted, and wherever the French can light a match, they may blow up a mine."[9]

GIBBON, VICO, AND THE MASSES

The Revolution swung historical writing out of the orbit of the Enlightenment. Thereafter, every historian was obliged to take popular movements into account and to entertain, at least, doubt as to the finality of any social system. The moment had come for the wide influence of Herder, the Fourth Part of whose *Thoughts on History*, written three years after the outbreak of the Revolution, faced the future calmly. It had also come for the resurrection of an almost forgotten Italian work, the *Scienza nuova* of Giambattista Vico, which had appeared in its final form in 1744, the year of Herder's birth.

Vico was the most independent historical thinker of the century and the most isolated. Chronologically, this study of history should have begun with him; but his isolation made an approach through Herder more convenient. His discoveries, which anticipated many of Herder's,[10] were made from scantier and less tractable evidence: from Homer and not from the popular poetry of Northern Europe, from Roman institutions rather than medieval, from the religious symbolism of the Greeks and Romans without comparison with that of backward peoples of the modern world. He aspired to make of history a "new science" (*scienza nuova*), but the genetic method of the nonmathematical sciences was not ready when he published in 1725–1744; indeed it was scarcely ready for Herder's use a generation later.

Writing under the eyes of the Inquisition, Vico was debarred from drawing out of the Hebrew Scriptures examples of primitive religious notions and practices, and was obliged to leave Hebrew history outside of his historical science. Although the speech and the mentality of the Italian peasant gave him glimpses into prehistory, he did not seek them also among reports of travelers among savages and barbarians. In the classical literatures of Greece and Rome, by sheer divination, he penetrated to records of forgotten social conditions, rivaling Herder's anthropological flair with observations like the following:

> Ears of grain were called apples of gold, which must have been the first gold in the word while metallic gold was still in ore and the art of refining it in bulk and, even more, of giving it luster and splendor, was unknown. . . . Later, in expressing further the idea of so great price and rarity, fine wools must have been called golden; for in Homer Atreus laments that Thyestes has stolen his golden flocks, and the Argonauts stole the golden fleece of the Pontus. Μῆλον meant both apple and sheep to the Greeks . . . so the golden apple, which Hercules first brought back or gathered from Hesperia, must have been grain; and the Gallic Hercules with links of this gold, that issue from his mouth, chains men by the ears: something which later will be discovered as a myth concerning the fields. Hence Hercules remained the deity to propitiate in order to find treasures, whose god was Dis (identical with Pluto), who carries off Proserpine (another name for Ceres or grain) to the underworld described by the poets, according to whom its first realm was Styx, its second the land of the dead, its third the depth of furrows. . . . It was of this golden apple that Virgil, most learned in heroic antiquities, made the golden bough Aeneas carries into the Inferno, or Underworld.[11]

Roman history, in which Gibbon saw no parallel to the French Revolution, led Vico to discover the great role of the anonymous populace. By giving careful attention to the Empire only, Gibbon missed the full purport of Rome's story, which Vico had come upon by pushing backward through the Republic to vestiges of social states unrecorded in history. These vestiges he first met with while examining, as Professor of Jurisprudence in the University of Naples, fragments of the Laws of the Twelve Tables, supposedly the work of the Decemvirs at the opening of the fourth century after the founding of Rome. Gibbon, who without knowing Vico's work examined those fragments while studying the background of Justinian's *Institutes,* very properly doubted the tradition that the Decemvirs owed the substance of those laws to Hermodorus, a wise and widely traveled Greek. But he did not pursue his skepticism so far as to note that some laws were related to social conditions posterior to the Decemvirs. This observation Vico had made, and it led him to examine other matters of early Roman chronology, until he became uncertain of all dates before the Punic Wars. Previous events dissolved, in his phrase, into "an obscure memory, a confused fantasy." Nevertheless, he was unwilling to resign the origins of the Roman people as lost. If records failed, much might lie concealed in language, in myth, in poetry. "A language of an ancient nation which has remained in use until it has come to maturity ought to be a great witness to the customs of the first eras of the world," [12] Vico reasoned, and accordingly found in Latin testimony to the savage and peasant beginnings of the Romans. The word for law, *lex,* originally meant a collection of acorns, then came to mean a gathering of any sort of vegetable, by further extension signified a gathering of citizens and, finally, the law which such a gathering made. From similar etymologies he was able to surmise concerning early institutions and to conclude that the Latins and the Greeks were descended from a common stock.

"Confused fantasy" in the form of myth, legend and poetry introduced him to the way of thinking of an entire people not yet capable of abstract thought. A statement by the late Greek philosopher Iamblicus, that the Egyptians ascribed to the god Hermes Trismegistus all inventions useful in human life, illuminated for Vico the sacred books of ancient peoples and the attribution of early laws and institutions to some far-sighted lawgiver, a Hermodorus or the Decemvirs. Glimpses of a mentality still more primitive he caught from

Homer, who was obviously not an individual but "the ideal or heroic character of the Greek people."[13] The Odysseus who seeks herbs for poisoning his arrows is a relic of a savage era. The Homeric trials by combat, the anarchic temper of Achilles, had their parallel in the feudal Middle Ages, "barbaric times come back again."[14]

By this route Vico arrived at the conclusion that the earliest institutions embody the wisdom of the human race, "judgment without any reflection *felt* in common by a whole order, a whole people, a whole nation or the entire human race."[15] Arranged roughly in chronological order, they could yield history: history entirely anonymous, without gods, without heroes or legislators, history revealing Divine Providence in its course of guiding man by means of his instincts until he attained to self-consciousness. To this, the true knowledge of his past, man had come by three stages.

An initial Age of Gods, in which advances in civilization were attributed to direct Divine gift or counsel, gradually passed into an Age of Heroes, when they were attributed to great individuals, lawgivers, rulers, philosophers, and this was now at last yielding to an Age of Men, who saw those advances truly as the collaborative, largely anonymous work of entire peoples. To those stages corresponded appropriate forms of government: theocracy, or the rule of priests; aristocracy, or the rule of privileged individuals; and a republic or limited monarchy, in which a people governs itself. Each stage of culture, each form of government, rests upon a phase in the development of human nature. "The nature of people is at first crude, then severe, then benignant, afterwards favorable to intellectual curiosity, and finally dissolute."[16]

The adjective "dissolute" represents a further stage of society than those mentioned: one in which the people, ruling themselves, fall into selfish individualism and no longer co operate for the common good. For a civilization thus disintegrating, history shows two possible fates. It may fall prey to barbarians, men in the age of gods or of heroes, who by rejuvenating it will in time bring back the Age of Men, which Vico also calls the Age of Reason. But if such barbarians are not at hand, it will destroy itself by anarchy, which he describes with prophetic appositeness to the Europe between the two World Wars of the twentieth century:

If they become rotten in that ultimate civic disease, . . . then Providence, in their extremity of ill, uses the following drastic remedy. Since such peoples, like beasts, have become accustomed to think of nothing but individual advantage . . . and have been living in solitude of spirit and desires, not even two of them able to agree, with the result that by obstinate factions and desperate civil wars they make forests of cities, and of forests holes for men to hide in, . . . the sinister subtleties of malicious minds, more frightful than beasts because of the barbarity of reflection, which is worse than the primal barbarity of sense, begin to defeat themselves.[17]

For they reduce everyone to want of the bare necessities of life. This extremity forces a few men to unite for production of material goods. Observation of the advantage they thus gain induces others gradually to imitate them and to return to the simple virtues of the primeval world—to loyalty, truthfulness, religion. So Providence, working through men against their conscious will, preserves mankind and renews civilization eternally.

By penetrating into prehistory, Vico gained perspective on the course of humanity. He found faith in its unconscious wisdom, which could be trusted to save peoples when their rulers failed to govern and their thinkers failed to guide.

Recognition of Vico was delayed not only by his unpropitious place and time, but also by his concessions to that time and that place. His effort to accommodate his thought to the geometrical framework congenial to the early eighteenth century put an obstacle between him and his readers, for instead of clarifying his ideas it rendered them more opaque. His impetuous imagination kept breaking away from the frame and having to be drawn back into it by force of will, producing digressions and repetitions that added to the difficulty of a style stiff with Latinisms and often obscure, especially where tendencies of his thought needed concealment from the Inquisition or from the foreign despots, Austrian or Spanish, who were Kings of Naples. Herder, though clearer and more orderly, lacked, except in brief passages, the charm of style which gave Bossuet, Voltaire, and Gibbon so wide an appeal. Headlong and restless in the pursuit of ideas, he polished none of his books and left his histories incomplete. Nevertheless, the ideas of Herder and Vico were incitements to historical writing in which the senses, evocative imagination, and sympathetic emotion would have full scope, writing that would make the past as vivid, as colored, as pulsating with life as the present, and more beautiful by reason of the wonder, the pathos, of distance.

Before the French Revolution, prose thus appropriate to the poetry of history had appeared in the fiction and the autobiography of Jean Jacques Rousseau. Goethe's *Götz von Berlichingen* had brought it to the halfway mark of historical drama. The Revolution drew together firmly the converging lines of Romantic literature and of historical works of similar inspiration. By writing large the fact that no society is exempt from change, it forced men to contemplate the past, whether with regret of something lost whose charm was only fully perceived in the losing, or for aid and example in building toward a better future. "The time was when we were witnessing many unheard of and incredible events: when our attention was attracted to many forgotten and decayed institutions by the sound of their downfall," [18] Niebuhr recalled vividly. The present generation, from its similar fate, can measure the impact of the revolutionary convulsion which shook Western civilization for twenty-five years. Out of this vast stir of emotion, out of the widespread consciousness that the events of the day were as large and as laden with fate as any the world had known, out of the stimulus to the imagination of the recent discovery that their stage was an infinite universe, that an immense backward and abysm of time was their background, and that their influence might extend to an apparently limitless future, came historical writing unexampled in poetical quality and power.

PART TWO
THE FULFILLMENT

IV

THE FASCINATION OF ORIGINS: NIEBUHR, OTFRIED MÜLLER

THE French Revolution thrust the mass of mankind into the foreground of historical writing. When the raw volunteers of the Republic withstood at Valmy the best-drilled soldiers of Europe, Goethe, who had watched the battle from the Prussian lines, said prophetically: "Here today begins a new epoch in world history." The advent of the common man brought threats to civilization: the Reign of Terror and Napoleon's diversion of the energies of the French people into wars of conquest. But French nationalism soon created its counterpoise by awakening nationalism in other peoples. The Spanish showed genius as guerrillas; the Prussians rallied quickly from defeat at Jena; the stubborn resistance of the Russians turned the tide against Napoleon. These events set historians to scanning popular revolutions in the past, especially in the great republics of Rome and Athens, for analogies interpretive of the present, and to reading popular literature for the psychology of the masses in all times and places. At the juncture of the political with the literary interest in antiquity stands Barthold Niebuhr's *History of Rome*.

Niebuhr was to the highest degree sensitive and imaginative. To a friend who found him greatly agitated, he confessed that he "often could not endure reading more than a few pages of the ancient tragedians, so vividly the characters lived, spoke, acted and suffered before his eyes. He saw Antigone leading her blind father; he saw the grove and old Oedipus entering it; he heard the melody of their speech, and was certain it was the genuine Greek intonation, though he could not reproduce it with his barbarian tongue."[1] From childhood, his reading of Greek and Latin had been guided by Johann Voss, the German translator of Homer, who taught him to draw out of the classical authors what they took for granted and mentioned only casually: their conception of the earth and of the gods, their household habits and way of life. Thus he came to know Homer and Virgil as if they were his contemporaries, separated only by an interval of space. His phenomenal memory not only permitted him before thirty to acquire nineteen languages, including Slavic and Oriental, but made him aspire to know dead languages as perfectly as living tongues. Born in 1776, he read close upon their appearance the masterpieces of Goethe, Herder, and Schiller, and Friedrich August Wolf's epochmaking *Prolegomena to Homer*. Equally familiar were the foreign works that had inspired the revival of German literature: Shakespeare, Ossian, the Eddas, English and Scottish popular ballads.

Uncertain health, which forbade regular schooling, and isolation in a Danish village encouraged his inclination to dwell in a dream world of the past. But the plans of his father, sole survivor of a celebrated Danish expedition into the interior of Asia Minor, pushed Niebuhr into practical life. His frail body ruled out his father's career as an explorer. A confiding loquacity and naïve enthusiasm stood in the way of his becoming a diplomat. But there remained the possibility of civil service. For this he was prepared by formidable training in Roman law, constitutional history, economics, mathematics, and science. At nineteen he became private secretary to the Danish Minister of Finance. Three years later, in 1798–1799, his education was completed by travel in England, whose constitution his father admired because it had resisted the infiltration of French democratic ideas, and by study in Edinburgh, where Playfair explained to him Hutton's uniformitarian theories, the basis of modern geology.

Leaving the Danish civil service for the Prussian at the unlucky moment of the battle of Jena, Niebuhr had to flee from Berlin to Memel, where he managed the service of supplies for the Prussian army until stricken with typhus. On recovery, he aided the Baron vom Stein in reforms, including the abolition of serfdom, which solidified the Prussian nation against Napoleon. In 1810, after twelve years of public life, he was given the more congenial occupation of lecturing on Roman history at the University of Berlin. From this quiet haven, he reviewed his recent past with a triumphant sense of having gone through the severest tests as a man of action: "Our first entrance into this city was simultaneous with the dissolution of the State to which I had gone over, and now, amid distress and grief, I went through scenes far more remarkable than any in my whole former life. My position was perpetually fluctuating; I was forced to act with foresight, to be cool and resolute. It was a great tragedy, and no longer the tedious drama of my former middle class life. I learned to stake my all at every step on a pin's head, and fortune was on my side. The wreck on which I had pumped so long was cast ashore, and behold! on this shore I found the home of my useful aspirations, leisure that I could devote to research and letters, surrounded by highly favorable and agreeable circumstances." [2]

Among his University colleagues were Savigny, who was reinterpreting Roman law, and Buttmann and Heindorf, pupils of the celebrated F. A. Wolf, who had broadened classical scholarship from textual and aesthetic considerations into a study of every manifestation of human nature in the antique world. The Preface of the first volume of Niebuhr's *History of Rome* acknowledges their aid: "There is an inspiration which emanates from the presence and association of persons beloved, an immediate influence through which the Muses appear to us, waken our desire and strength and clear our vision; to which I have owed a grateful debt for what has been best in my life." To their learning and his own, he was conscious of adding insights gained in practical affairs: "The return to studies I had long been deprived of, with the fullness of other experiences, was a blessedness one enjoys only once in a lifetime." [3]

Niebuhr set himself the arduous task of restoring knowledge of the political life and institutions of the Roman people, largely misunderstood by the Romans themselves after the extinction of their Republic. Livy, writing under the patronage of Augustus, already had no clear notion of the causes of conflict between the plebians and the patricians, and did not distinguish, in the story of the early days of Rome, between homespun tradition and imitation of Greek heroic legends.

Born the year of the American Revolution and of the first version of *Faust*, Niebuhr had been freed by the political and literary innovations of his time from Gibbon's reverence for the Augustans. His interest lay in the early centuries which Gibbon does not touch, centuries in which the Roman people freely evolved institutions that still are the admiration of the world. Concerning these, the Roman historians of the Empire were as incapable of answering the questions Niebuhr's generation was most eager to ask, as the rationalist and neoclassical minds of the seventeenth and eighteenth centuries had been of understanding the Middle Ages. Save for Vico, whom neither they nor he had read, Niebuhr's predecessors subjected the account of Roman origins to almost purely negative criticism. Voltaire laughed at the mythical adventures of Romulus and Remus, which Livy had set down while declining "either to affirm or to refute." Louis de Beaufort's *Dissertation on the Uncertainty of the First Five Centuries of Roman History* (1738) maintained that few records had survived the sack of Rome by the Gauls in 390 B.C., and that the earliest Roman to write history, Fabius Pictor, coming so late as the Second Punic War, had depended largely upon the funeral orations and memoirs of noble families, whose tendency to self-glorification was illustrated by the claim of Caesar's Julian clan to descent from Venus by way of Aeneas. "In no history is it later before we reach what is absolutely certain," [4] Niebuhr admitted.

Nevertheless, Europe of the past half-century had provided him with means to recover, in spite of the imperfection of the record and the unreliability of factual detail, the large outline of the development of Roman institutions. The equipment upon which Niebuhr relied was the analogy of early Rome to the heroic age of medieval Europe, the understanding of collective authorship and political creativeness, the establishment of exact etymologies, the utilization of inscriptions and scattered fragments of Roman authors to supplement the connected narratives of the historians, and the willingness to accept without prejudice what was strange and alien in a past civilization.

How historical characters and incidents could be embedded in legend and myth he knew from the *Nibelungenlied*, which had been rediscovered in a castle in the Tyrol in 1755. Its most recent editor, Von der Hagen, had sent Niebuhr a presentation copy in 1810. The poem reflects historical fact: Burgundians under their king Gundahar (Gunther) had been massacred by Huns in the fifth century A.D. The Etzel (Attila) and Dietrich (Theodoric) of the poem are historical characters, although neither was present at the massacre, as the poem relates. But this historic kernel is wrapped in the heroic husk of the Siegfried legend and the prophecy of Danube mermaids. And about seven centuries after the historical events, the anonymous poem, which had slowly developed by word of mouth, was given a surface coloring of Christianity and courtly love in the final written version Niebuhr saw. The historian, Niebuhr thought, could recover the original shape of events so transformed by passage through many minds, if he reversed the process, guided by familiarity with the propensity to create legends.

That collective authorship had operated similarly in classical antiquity, he had learned from Wolf's *Prolegomena to Homer* (1795). Wide variations in the text of the *Iliad* and the *Odyssey* noted by the ancient *scholia* (marginal commentaries) to a manuscript in Venice published by the French scholar Villoisin in 1788, and the quotation by classical writers, including Plato, Aristotle and Virgil, of Homeric lines not in our manuscripts, had convinced Wolf that Robert Wood was right in thinking the art of writing unknown to the Greeks of Homer's time. Homer, Wolf believed, had composed orally the greater part of the two epics out of national legends. But his work had been added to and altered for about four centuries by rhapsodists, who transmitted it by recitation until it was set down in writing at Athens in the middle of the sixth century B.C. Even thereafter, the text had been modified by grammarians and editors. So Wolf came substantially to the conclusion of Vico, whom he had not read, that in a very real sense the Greek people had been Homer. What in Vico had been largely inspired conjecture, Wolf supported by impressive classical learning, classifying and criticizing the sources of our knowledge of Homer. Not only had writers of antiquity, including the historian Josephus, asserted that the Homeric epics had been composed and transmitted by word of mouth, but the extraordinary powers of memory among unlettered modern peoples (old men in the Hebrides were said to recite Gaelic verse to greater length than the *Iliad*) showed its possibility and probability. Although scholars still fail to agree about a single author or many, since Wolf it has been clear that the poems ascribed to Homer resemble much more closely folk epics than self-conscious creations of a single author, like the *Aeneid*.

Of the wars of Aeneas, Niebuhr wrote: "We feel only too uncomfortably how little the poet succeeded in raising those shadows, characterless dummies of commonplace barbarians, into living creatures like the heroes of Homer.... Perhaps it is a problem that defies solution, to form an epic poem on an argument which has not lived for centuries in popular songs and tales, as the common property of a nation."[5] He adopted and expanded Herder's theory (in the Second Part of his *Folksongs*, 1779) that the Romans had possessed native heroic verse comparable to Homer, which had been lost when the Roman poets were overwhelmed by the sophisticated culture of the Greeks. Fortunately, he thought, some of its contents had been preserved, especially by Livy, in what purported to be historical annals. "That which began as poetry, became popular belief,"[6] and lived on in the guise of history. How similar the accounts of early Rome to old Germanic heroic poems such as the lay of Hildebrand recently published as *Hildebrand and Hathubrand*, by Jakob Grimm. "In them I find," wrote Niebuhr in 1812, "the other end of the fallen-in gallery, whose corresponding end I have discovered in antiquity, and from which I shall begin to clear out the rubbish."[7]

The masterpiece of the Roman popular mind was the story of the kings.

The Lay of the Tarquins, even in its prose shape, is still inexpressively poetical; nor is it less unlike real history.... The whole story of the lost Tarquinius; the warning presages of his fall; Lucretia; the assumed idiocy of Brutus; his death; the war with Porsenna; finally the truly Homeric battle of Lake Regillus; all this forms an epic poem, which in power and brilliance leaves everything produced by the Romans in later times far behind it.[8]

Horatius' defense of the bridge [9] Niebuhr likened to modern Greek and Turkish ballads. From the founding of Rome to the expulsion of the Tarquins nothing was historical. Nevertheless the coloring of the whole gave historical information.

This poetry is pervaded by a plebeian spirit, by hatred of the oppressors, and by evident marks that at the time it was sung some plebeian houses were already great and powerful. . . . All the favorite kings are friends of freedom. The best of them next to the holy Numa is the plebeian Servius. The patricians appear in a despicable light as accomplices in his murder. [Among them] the only noble characters are the Valerii and the Horatii, houses friendly to the plebeians.[10]

Onward from the first threat of the common people to secede from Rome, Fabius Pictor had been in possession of "real history, though in many parts tinged with fable," which unfortunately has reached us in a very defective state. Much of its original sense could be restored if one allowed for "the old practice of dressing up a legal right in the shape of an incident." [11] Stories told the truth about the Roman constitution, though not about individuals. The Senate was not an invention of Romulus, but an institution widespread in the antique world. Plutarch failed to observe how the symbolic number thirty runs through the legends as well as the institutions of Rome. The Volscian wars should be viewed "in masses as they combine in the distance." Although "the spirit of absurdity . . . always came over even the most sagacious of the Greeks and Romans the moment they meddled with etymology," [12] modern linguistics revealed that "consul" originally meant "colleague," and that Mucius Scaevola was represented as holding his *left* hand steadfastly over the flame, for the reason that "left" was the root meaning of his cognomen.

The fundamental error of modern students of the Roman constitution, even experienced magistrates like Montesquieu, had been in thinking the Romans very like themselves.[13] The historian must concede their *otherness*, and try to understand it.

The state of the law concerning landed property and the public domains of ancient Rome differed in such a degree in its peculiarities from the rights and institutions we are used to, that the confounding of our ordinary notions of property with those of the ancients . . . gives rise to the most grossly erroneous opinions on the most important questions of Roman legislation; opinions under which the voice of justice must pronounce condemnation against actions and measures perfectly blameless; or an indistinct feeling of enthusiasm for great and noble characters must plead on behalf of the most dangerous projects and enterprises.[14]

The chance that his boyhood home, South Ditmarsh, was an exception to the almost universal European system of aristocratic landlordism, and retained under Danish rule its communal constitution of peasant proprietors, helped Niebuhr to know what had been at stake in the economic struggles of the Roman Republic. Like his contemporary Wordsworth in northern England, he had observed how ownership of land developed character and citizenship. When he read, at the time of the French Revolution, the Latin scholar Heyne's explanation of the agrarian laws of Tiberius and Gaius Gracchus as designed to distribute the public domain conquered by the armies of the Republic more widely among the Roman people, the Gracchi became his heroes. On the appearance of Savigny's book on *The Right of Possession* (1803), a pioneer interpretation of Roman property law, Niebuhr began an essay on the history of agrarian laws. "No nobleman and landed proprietor will like it," he wrote his friend Von Moltke in 1804, "but I shall write, as I think and speak, in the strength of my unalterable convictions, as the old Romans would approve and praise, were they still among us." [15] In the second volume of his *History of Rome* he likened the public domain of the Romans to communal landholding in India and Ireland before British conquest. "Through one of the most calamitous mistakes that ever brought ruin on a country, notwithstanding the most benevolent intentions on the part of the government, the Zemindars of Bengal succeeded under Lord Cornwallis in getting themselves recognized as independent princes and absolute proprietors of the soil." [16] Likewise in Ireland, "after Tyrone's rebellion, ignorance of the native law occasioned the confiscation of all lands belonging to the subjects of the insurgent chiefs." [17]

The assassination of the Gracchi by members of their own social class marked the decline of the political genius of the Roman Republic, which had flourished through the willingness of the patricians to concede rights under pressure and of the plebs and other underprivileged groups to accept partial concessions rather than risk revolution in order to attain absolute equality. In regard to the perversion of the term "agrarian law" by his contemporaries, Niebuhr wrote bitterly:

The regulation of Cleomenes, the equal partition of land demanded by the frantic levellers in the French Revolution, are termed agrarian laws; while in cases where the word might suitably be applied, where a strict right of property has been unfeelingly applied against tenants at will, cultivating a piece of ground transmitted to them from their forefathers, the word is never thought of: and the rapacious landlord, who turns a village into a solitude, regarding its fields as a property he may dispose of in whatever way he can make the most of it, if he has ever heard of the name of the Gracchi, will condemn their agrarian law as an atrocity.[18]

THE FASCINATION OF ORIGINS

His task of piecing together, out of a multitude of fragmentary, dry, often misleading references, a clear notion of the functions of consuls, tribunes, praetors, censors, dictators, and of public bodies like the Senate and the Curia, so as to exhibit the Constitution of the Republic as a functioning organism, Niebuhr compared wryly to the fabled Chronos digesting stones. But in his triumphs he felt akin to the artist and scientist: "Our labor is . . . to be likened to that of a student of nature who frees a skeleton of fossil bones carelessly put together, from the additions that have been made to it; and if favored by fortune creates what is now wanting, and from the notion he has conceived of its structure represents the outline of the once living figure. . . . My restoration [of a partly obliterated inscription revealing factional quarrels among the patricians] is like that of a statue by the hand of a sculptor who has seized its idea. Such a thing can no more be established by arguments than any intuition; its certainty results from its completeness." [19] At times his tone is ecstatic: "When an enquirer, after gazing for years with ever renewed undeviating steadfastness, sees the history of mistaken, misrepresented and forgotten events rise out of mist and darkness and assume substance and shape, as the scarcely visible aerial form of the nymph of the Scandinavian tale takes the body of an earthly maiden beneath the yearning gaze of love." . . .[20]

The original version of the first two volumes (1811, 1812) was composed in "a time full of hope, when the University of Berlin opened; and the enthusiasm and delight in which months rolled away, while the contents of the first volumes of this history were digested for lectures and worked up for publication; to have enjoyed this, and to have lived in 1813, this of itself is enough to make a man's life, notwithstanding much sad experience, a happy one." [21] But the continuation of the

History in the decade 1820–1830 by a third volume was undertaken to distract his mind from gloomy apprehensions about public affairs. For although the overthrow of Napoleon, only foreshadowed in 1813, had become a reality, and Niebuhr's post as Prussian representative with the Vatican from 1816 to 1823 gave him the opportunity to enrich his pages by examining the monuments of Roman antiquity at first hand, he saw, as in his History he approached the disturbance of the balance of power among the social classes that had been the strength of the Roman Republic, a similar fate in store for his contemporaries: "Under the terror of wild revolutions, all Europe is congealing into an iron despotism." [22] Even in England, which seemed to have inherited some of the Roman genius for compromise, there was "a fearful and ever-widening gulf between the wealthy and indigent classes; they are two hostile nations." [23] The lesson of his third volume, that "a state has this advantage over an individual, that by constantly raising in an ever-increasing circle more persons to its highest freedom, it can carry back its life more than once to youth, and live through it again with fresh energy," [24] seemed lost upon modern Europe when the French people were provoked by reactionary royal decrees to a second Revolution in 1830. He recorded the bankruptcy of his hopes. "We say that there must be an aristocracy, indeed an aristocracy of many grades; but we add, that at this moment there is no tolerable aristocracy existing, and that that which calls itself such, is a phantom from which all vital energy has fled." [25] His death a few months later left the History, which was to have reached the point at which Gibbon began, with the First Punic War.

Yet this third volume had given Niebuhr moments of his former exaltation. On demonstrating that Quintus Fabius had been called the Great for his wise domestic policy rather than for his military victories, he confessed: "There is one thing which gives happiness,—to restore forgotten and overlooked greatness to a position where it can be recognized. He to whom fortune grants this enters into a relation of the heart with spirits long departed, and he feels himself blessed, when similarity of deeds and sentiments unites with the feeling for them, that feeling with which he loves a great man as a friend." [26] On completing revision of the first two volumes, he told a member of his family:

The most important points are the result of sudden flashes of light and divinations, with regard to which it seriously crossed my mind, whether I had not been inspired by the spirits of the ancients, as a reward for my faithful efforts in behalf of their memory. . . . I have separated the principal legends from the annals which had become suspicious through their intermixture with these, have restored them to their proper shape, and recovered the pure line of the annals themselves. It is incredible how rich and uncorrupted they are.[27]

The French historian Michelet, who followed immediately upon Niebuhr's footsteps to complete his design of joining hands with Gibbon, has described the character of his achievement: "His book is like the *Forum Boarium*, so imposing with its monuments well or badly restored. A Gothic hand is often evident; but it is always a marvel to see with what power the Barbarian lifts the enormous débris. . . . He knew antiquity as antiquity did not always know itself. Compared with him, what are Plutarch and so many other Greeks, for the understanding of the rude genius of the first ages? He understands ancient barbaric Rome because he bears something of it in himself. He is one of the long-haired authors of the Salic Law, Wisogast or Windogast, who might have acquired civic rights and sat with the wise Coruncanius, the subtle Scaevola and Cato the Elder. Do not dare to attack this colleague of the Decemvirs, or speak of him lightly." [28]

The practical, politically minded Romans created impressive heroic legends, like that of Coriolanus, but little in the form of myth. The imaginative Greeks, the superlative mythmakers of the world, bathed their early history in supernatural light. Therein lay the peculiar difficulty of Otfried Müller's attempt to do for Greece what Niebuhr had done for Rome. But he had Niebuhr's work before him, and began to write just as linguistics had made a great advance.

Born in 1798, an almost exact contemporary of Keats, he shared Keats' enthusiasm for Greek art, literature, and nature myths. Except for political affairs—he taught at Göttingen from the age of twenty-two to his early death at forty-two—he was almost as many sided as Niebuhr, a geographer, anthropologist, archeologist, linguist, philosopher, critic of literature and of the arts. Studying at the University of Berlin shortly after Niebuhr had left it, he was encouraged by Niebuhr's friend Buttmann and by August Boeckh, both disciples of Wolf, to make firsthand acquaintance with every sort of classical knowledge the basis of his equipment as an historian. "It is obvious," he remarked in his first mature work, "that a hundred special studies in the hands of a compiler would never become a history of Greece." [29]

Mythology was a lively topic of discussion in Germany during Müller's student years. The philosopher Schelling found in the Mysteries of Samothrace traces of a Hellenic religion older than Homer's Olympians. Like Dr. Casaubon in George Eliot's novel, Görres and Creuzer traced all myths to a single source: they were deformations of an original revelation by God to the peoples of the earth. Kanne supported this theory of a single revelation by maintaining that etymology reveals in all tongues the same names and symbols for fundamental religious ideas. Müller's teacher Buttmann declared, on the contrary, that myths had no genuine religious significance, but were mere play of fancy, inventions of poets. Müller took a middle course with a method of comparative mythology which owed much of its success to the recent creation of a science of comparative linguistics.

While keen minds from Leibnitz onward had been right in suspecting that etymologies reveal very early stages of human intelligence, no precise use of them was possible so long as Greek and Latin, or even Hebrew, were compared directly with the languages of Northern Europe. Similarity of spelling was highly misleading. Through it Jakob Grimm, though more cautious than Kanne, had attached to the same root the proper names Uta, Berther, Berta, Berka, Erka, Hildeberta, Hildur, Hulda, Holle, Hutte, Hodur, Hother, Hütchen, Hödeken, Robin Hood, Otnit, Rother, Ruther, Rucker, Rücker, Rucher, Holger, Olger, Ogier, Ulysses, Odysseus, and so on. There was need of some clue to the kinship of languages, some way to determine whether Hebrew, Greek, and Latin had a common ancestry, and what were the relationships of modern tongues. As early as 1786 Sir William Jones had suggested Sanskrit, the ancient language of India, as the link among Greek, Latin, Gothic, and Celtic. This idea, which occurred to others, including Friedrich von Schlegel, remained speculation until Franz Bopp tested it by comparing grammatical structure, beginning with the verb in his *Conjugation System of the Sanskrit Language Compared to Greek, Latin, Persian and Germanic* (1816). He maintained that there was an Indo-European family of languages, which had no affinity with Hebrew and the other Semitic tongues.

Seeing at once the superiority of Bopp's method, Jakob Grimm applied it to the Germanic languages in his *German Grammar* (1819). For the second edition of this book in 1822, he took the scarcely traveled road of phonetics, setting himself the laborious work of studying the role of every letter of the alphabet in chronologically arranged documents of the Germanic languages. The result was the triumph of the historical method in the formulation known as Grimm's Law. To a previous regular consonantal shift of certain labial, dental, and guttural consonant sounds between Greek or Latin and the Germanic languages observed by Kanne, the Dane Rask, and others, Grimm added a later shift between General Germanic and Old High German: "The relations of Gothic to Latin are exactly those of Old High German to Gothic." [30] Grimm foresaw great consequences "for the rigor of etymology." [31] For he had established the paradoxical and revolutionary principle that where spellings agree there need be, except for borrowed words, no relationship. Where two or more consonants in a word have followed the regular shift between languages, relationship is certain. "Thus identity rests in constant fashion on exterior diversity," [32] Grimm stated succinctly.

The new linguistic science permitted Müller to rule out so-called etymological proofs of the derivation of Greek myths from the Egyptians and the Hebrews, and to show that the mythologies of the Greek and Germanic peoples had developed independently after they had been separated from their Aryan kin of India.

If myths could not be reduced to a single source, neither could they be explained as lawless fancy, nor as the fabrication of priests, according to a view lingering from the eighteenth century. Müller's conception of myths was substantially Herder's. Myth was the form taken by each people's earliest observation and reflection: thus it revealed each people's characteristic ways of life and thought. Myth mingles the ideal and the real without distinguishing them; it "makes all beings into people, all relations into actions," [33] Müller explained in *Prolegomena to a Scientific Mythology* (1825). While the phallus appears as a symbol only "where belief lets a continual fertilization, a continual production proceed from the gods," as in the cults of Demeter, Hermes, and Dionysus, in heroic myth

> countries, mountains, rivers beget peoples and heroes. . . . That Homer calls Hector the son of Zeus, and Stesichorus calls him the son of Apollo, is only a deduction from the interest these gods take in him. Preceding circumstances are often the parents of succeeding. . . . Wholly distinct races living together in the same land are put into genealogical relation. That the gods of a nation or race beget its progenitors or ancestors is a simple expression of naïf piety.[34]

Even hostile brothers may turn out to have been neighboring cities of different origin, whose only bond is their enmity.

"Mythical expression," Müller concluded from such examples, "must be regarded as a peculiar sort of simple childish speech, whose dictionary and grammar have to be searched for."[35] Its strangeness should be its fascination for us.

What do we usually want from history? he asked; To see men act and think as we do, and to observe with self-satisfaction our own stage of culture? If so, let us turn to contemporary life and watch activity in cabinets and drawing rooms. But it is just out of this narrowness that history should lift us. It should cause us to value man as a whole above men of a single epoch. We should learn to understand different ways of living. It is my belief that knowledge of antiquity exalts and humanizes us in no way more than by putting before our eyes an alien humanity in its full, robust, self-sufficient existence. And of all parts of our knowledge does not mythology lead us farthest out of the circle of the present into workshops of ideas and forms whose whole construction and arrangement is still a problem for our minds?[36]

What distance between the Enlightenment and this attitude of Müller's in 1825!

The nearest surviving European analogy to the myth was the *Märchen* or fairy tale, of which the Grimm brothers had published three collections between 1812 and 1822. The *Märchen*, Müller explained, "is related to myth somewhat as belief in ghosts is to paganism. It carries over obscure notions of an earlier time into an alien epoch of spiritual culture, for experts in our German tales find in them traces of a pre-Christian time."[37] But how thin and pale these tales taken from the lips of German peasants beside the rich complexity of antique myths, which ignore the nice compartmentation of the modern mind. The interpreter of Greek myth must rid himself of scientific and ethical preconceptions, must accept indecency and even jests about holy things, in order to build up a feeling for myth-making from an acquaintance with thousands of isolated passages in Hellenic literature. This recovery of a lost state of mind was not, Müller warned, within everyone's reach. It required "a special talent, a special frame of mind; yes, even a special inspiration."[38] As to the degree of his own success in *Orchomenos and the Minyae*, the first volume of his *History of Hellenic Races and Cities* (1820–1824), he would accept the verdict of only those "in whom beside deep and thorough learning there lives a mellowness and warmth of feeling, such as literary life tends to awaken and nourish."[39] To create in himself the mood to understand the *Eumenides* of Aeschylus, Müller composed a poetic tragedy, *Manoah*, on blood revenge.

The geography of Greece, which separated cities and peoples by mountains while uniting them by sea, gave myths a historical basis attractive to the literary taste and curiosity of Müller's time. It was a time of enthusiasm for nature; a time when nationalism was awakening localism; a time when Wordsworth wrote a series of poems *On the Naming of Places*, when Walter Scott was making the place names of his native land so familiar to the world that historians in centuries to come may be puzzled to decide whether Scott was named after Scotland or Scotland after Scott. While a student, Müller called the local mythology of Greece "a closed Paradise," which he was eager to be the first to enter. Volcanic action on rocks and mountains, meandering streams, peculiar effects of light must have left, he thought, traces of definitely recognizable geography upon the myths of the various Greek tribes. It seemed no accident that Boeotia should have been "the fatherland of Hellenic theogony," for "like Palestine, it was a land of caverns and grottoes, full of lonely gorges, of isolated marshes, of underground streams . . . ordained to send up oracles out of the mysterious depths of the cleft earth."[40] Great diversity of fruitfulness from region to region and accessibility by sea encouraged migration, colonization, and commerce, which confused and amalgamated myths originally local. The Greek language, in its growth toward uniformity out of dialectical diversity, told a parallel story. By reversing the process of amalgamation of myths, Müller endeavored to resolve them into their original elements and thus recover the history of the migrations, commercial relations, and religious outlook of the branches of the Greek race, and even the history of the religion and customs of races submerged by Greek conquest. The Northern migrations and conquests of the early Middle Ages offered helpful analogies.

Orchomenos and the Minyae (1820) was characteristically Romantic in exploring historic dawns and strange, half-forgotten rites and peoples. Through the Minyae and their city Orchomenos, whose glory the *Iliad* puts back in the remote heroic age of the Trojan war, Müller set out to recover pre-Homeric Greece and its pre-Olympian religion. The site of Orchomenos, compared by Homer in riches and splendor to Egyptian Thebes, was known through the ruins of its treasure house, whose antique design Pausanias in Roman times had likened to the "Cyclopian" walls of Tiryns in the Peloponnesus, and which Lord Elgin had recently linked with another ruined treasure house, so-called of Atreus, in Mycenae. The Minyae had constructed still another wonder of Hellenic antiquity, underground canals to reduce the level of Lake Copias so as to permit Orchomenos and other cities to expand on its banks. Having thus come upon traces of the civilization of the heroic age which modern scholars call Mycenean, Müller studied its character through local Minyan myths.

The fabulous Minyas, whose name the people bore, was called the son of Orchomenos, because that was their chief city; the son of Chryses, because he inherited much gold from his ancestors; the son of Ares, because the Minyae were warlike; the son of Poseidon, because they were seafaring. Behind Minyas lay the tribal gods Trophonios and Agamedes, renowned as builders of treasure houses, and a tribal ancestor Athamas, whose legend reveals a forward step in the religious consciousness of the tribe. Athamas, offering himself as a human sacrifice for guilt, was replaced, through Divine intervention, by a ram with golden fleece; but his descendants the Minyae were doomed by the ancestral curse to continual migration, until Jason, one of the Minyae of Thessaly, reconciled his people with the gods by recovering the Golden Fleece of the sacrificial ram. The placing of the Fleece in the Black Sea region was to Müller a sign that Minyan commerce had gone in that direction. The roundabout legendary return of the Argonauts by way of North Africa was explained by the existence of a colony of Minyae in Cyrene.

While such interpretations traced the growth of colonization, trade, and religion, the myth of Trophonios and Agamedes and the Cadmus myth of neighboring Boeotian

Thebes led farther back to a primitive stage of agriculture and nature religion. The story ran that the brothers Trophonios and Agamedes, builders of the treasure house of Orchomenos, stole from it by entering through a stone block they had cunningly left detachable, until Trophonios, finding his brother caught there in a mantrap, cut off his head and carried it away in order to conceal his identity and preserve their secret. Müller connected this fable with the better-known story of Cadmus by their common agrarian symbolism, belonging to a remote state of human consciousness. From the symbolism peered forth

the deep thought, which conceives of agriculture as a very intimate living with nature, especially as communion with the underworld, Pluto as Plutus, gold and harvests as robbery from its inhabitants. The taking out of the seed from the chambers and vaults of the earth is theft from the treasure of the underworld. The hewing off of the head of grain is clearly identical with the murder of Cadmilos, the tearing to pieces of Dionysus. The god, appearing in the world, is killed both physically and ideally.[41]

Although the sagas of later warrior-peoples represent the priest-kings who ruled these agricultural peoples as evil, destructive-minded enchanters, their religious ideas did not wholly die out. Even in classical times they persisted in the worship of Dionysus and Bacchus, originally distinct local gods whose cults had coalesced at Thebes; in the Theban rites which, after migration to Samothrace, appeared in Athens as the Samothracian Mysteries; and in the Demeter-Proserpine mysteries of Eleusis. The dark and bloody side of Greek religion which disturbed the classicist was a remnant of prehistoric cults.

The brightest side of Greek religion, ethical and philosophical, was the creation of the Dorians, to whom Müller devoted two volumes published in 1824. Doris, their fabled ancestor, was a son of Apollo: an Apollo who was neither a god of fertility nor even originally the sun-god, but was simply the god who protects, the unmarried god of a warrior tribe coming from the North. His statues, stern and stocky in their archaic form, acquire grace and enthusiastic expression as the Doric people matures. Closely associated with him were his sister, the warrior-maid Artemis, and the demigod Hercules, the cleanser, the destroyer of the scourges of mankind. The emphasis of Herodotus upon the migrations of the Dorians as compared with the stability of the Ionians, Müller found confirmed by the wide distribution of the Apollo cult in early times from Delphi to Crete, Delos, and the Peloponnesus. The legend of the return of the descendants of Hercules to reclaim his heritage of Mycenae and Tiryns, a parallel to the return of the Children of Israel to Canaan, indicated a possible double migration of the Dorians before they could establish themselves by the overthrow of Mycenean civilization. Müller contrasts the overadorned richness of Mycenean art with the severe Doric simplicity, and surmises that Doric architecture in stone retains the forms of an original architecture in wood.

The great imaginative tale of the Hyperboreans, which attains its highest beauty in Pindar, a Doric poet, was possibly a vague reminiscence of the coming of the Dorians by way of Thessaly, where the Hercules myth is localized. The idyllic mildness of the Hyperborean climate is accounted for by the primitive reasoning that the bitter north wind fled from that quarter, did not blow toward it. The stories of Hercules are apparently fragments of a national epic saga. His conquest of Hades was the almost unconscious symbol of the struggle of the Dorians, whose minds were set upon the improvement of this world, against the cults of the underworld. His character reflects the confidence of the Doric people in the self-sufficiency of humanity: "a proud consciousness of the strength dwelling within mankind, whereby it could rise, not by the permission of mild and gracious Fate, but through labor, hardship and battle, to equality with the gods themselves. . . . As with Apollo divinity steps into the circle of human life, so with Hercules purely human strength strives upward to the gods." [42] Doric customs, Doric art and poetry, reveal a landed, aristocratic people, virile and self-sufficient, with no longing for the infinite, no desire to mix itself with nature, a people whose "glance is directed, not upon what is becoming, but on what *is*." [43]

Turning from the Dorians to the rival Ionians by way of special studies of Phidias and Aeschylus and a general history of Greek literature, Müller was ready in 1839 to complete his preparations for a history of the entire Hellenic people, by a visit to Greece. Intoxicated by the sight of what he had had to imagine from maps and books of travel, he presumed too much upon his robust constitution in passing a day bareheaded under the sun of Delphi after a night in the swamps of Lake Copias. He paid for the indiscretion with his life.

But he had already built a firm foundation for the history of ancient Greece by discovering the primitive epoch behind its heroic and historical epochs, and by distinguishing the character and the migrations of its peoples. Herder's pioneer investigation of myth had mingled inspired guesses with much that went wide of the mark. Müller's insight grew out of stricter attention to factual detail, more careful use of geographic and linguistic evidence. His delicate balance of learning and art gave to the study of Greece a truly Greek harmony of powers.

V

THE ROMANTIC GARB: CHATEAUBRIAND, SCOTT, THIERRY, CARLYLE

MÜLLER and Niebuhr brought to bear upon classical antiquity the spirit of the new Romantic literature, but not its form. Niebuhr wrote little narrative, for he was constantly engaged in explaining that narration was impossible for want of enough reliable details. His text was clogged with what should have been footnotes or appendices. Müller's effort was likewise analytic, the stripping away of accretions and the correction of distortions to disclose the original form and spirit of myths; only by moments has his account an equable flow. Romantic art came into historical writing by way of two men of letters, René de Chateaubriand and Walter Scott.

Chateaubriand's travels in Greece, Palestine, North Africa and Spain as preparation for his prose epic, *The Martyrs* (1809), whose theme was the conflict in the last years of the Roman Empire between Mediterranean and North European peoples, between paganism and Christianity, brought natural background into history. Events take place beneath the brilliant sky of Greece or against "the dark and flat horizons of Germany, that sky without light which seems to crush you under its depressed vault, that impotent sun which paints objects with no color," [1] in the crowded Roman Circus, or in the grand, sterile vacancy of the Dead Sea valley. Bretons prepare a human sacrifice beneath sacred mistletoe and Druidic stones, while a Christian hermit is mortifying his flesh in the Thebiad desert in protest against the lush sensuality of pagan Egypt. Customs and manners become a second local coloring. Rival peoples, Romans, Gauls, Franks, appear in their dress and habit as they lived. Every sense gives its report. A cultivated Greek shrinks from the grease, smoke, and foul odors of the huts of his Frankish captors. The dazzling gleam of a thousand disciplined Roman swords drawn at once is answered by a savage roar from a host of Franks clad in skins of beasts. The war song, "Pharamond, Pharamond, we have battled with the sword," addressed to the mythical Frankish king, borrowed its authentic Northern flavor from the old Norse song of Ragnar Lodbrog. The Roman province of Gaul offered food for the Romantic taste for the grotesque: "Never did country present such a mixture of manners and religions, of civilization and barbarism." [2] Local color is reinforced with time color, by the precise flavor of an epoch, by distinctive detail preserving the life and soul of the past. "Sometimes in portraying a person of my chosen epoch," Chateaubriand's Preface announced, "I have introduced into my picture a word, a thought, drawn from his writings; not because this word and this thought were worthy of quotation as a model of beauty and taste, but because they fix the time and the characters"; a technique which historians were to find of astonishing efficacy in calling back the spirit of the past to reanimate its forms. Chateaubriand fused this great variety of concrete detail in a rapid, graceful, flowing narrative, tinged with the melancholy of old, unhappy, far-off things, with sympathy for vanquished faiths and peoples.

Scott did not have Chateaubriand's seductive style and narrative art; but he wisely chose, instead of the obsolete trappings and supernatural machinery of the Homeric and Miltonic epic, the popular form of the novel, with its rich inheritance from the historical plays of Shakespeare and Goethe. Nothing stood in the way of his readers' associating themselves as intimately with historical personages as with characters in novels of contemporary life. If less richly woven than Chateaubriand's, his tapestry was larger, broadening from the Scottish scene of the novels immediately following *Waverley* (1814) to England with *Ivanhoe* (1819) and to Continental Europe with *Quentin Durward* (1823). He drew his readers gently backward from the feudal survivals in the eighteenth century to the medieval heyday of the twelfth. In showing feudalism and chivalry in gradual decay, Scott appealed to the loyal fears of a vast body of readers who, like himself, had seen the French Revolution menace their extinction. He brought into historical writing patriotism and the popular touch. What he had heard about the revolutionary mobs of Paris lent force and vividness to the great Edinburgh mob scene in *The Heart of Midlothian*, which offered hints to Carlyle and Michelet. His sympathy embraced peasant and king, lost and triumphant causes, ruling and subject races, the Saxons under the Normans, Celtic Highlanders tenaciously loyal to the Stuarts. His celebrated portraits of James I and Louis XI, by stressing the incongruity of the men with their royal station, gave readers an unwonted intimacy with the mighty. To the static, analytic, abstract manner of the Enlightenment, Scott, like Chateaubriand, opposed movement, atmosphere, color, feeling for nature.

Augustin Thierry, the first historian to don this rich garment of Romantic style, owed an equal debt to Scott and to Chateaubriand. He knew the history of his native France only through a dry military and dynastic textbook prescribed by Napoleon, until *The Martyrs*, just off the press, came into his hands when he was fifteen.

I felt at first a vague charm, a dazzling of the imagination. . . . Nothing had prepared me for those terrible Franks of Chatea briand, clad in the skins of bears, seals, aurochs and wild boars, for their intrenched camp with its leather boats and chariots hitched to big oxen, for that army in triangular array which seemed only lances, skins of wild beasts, and half-naked bodies. As the dramatic contrast of the savage warrior and the civilized soldier gradually unfolded before my eyes, I was more and more spellbound. The impression of the Frankish war song was electric. Jumping from my seat and walking from one end of the room to the other, I repeated aloud, making the pavement resound under my feet, "Pharamond, Pharamond, we have battled with the sword." That moment of enthusiasm was perhaps decisive for my future vocation.[3]

Thierry came to his first historical subject in protest against French praise of the institutions of the English conquerors of Napoleon as a perfect balance of aristocracy with liberty. It seemed obvious to Thierry, of humble origin and a liberal journalist, that aristocracy predominated. He found why, while reading Hume. The English had been more or less a subject people since the Norman Conquest; class inferiority was a relic of race inferiority. He himself had felt the rude hands of a conquering army laid upon the Champagne country, where he was a schoolmaster when Napoleon had been forced to retreat. Still in 1817, he saw about him in the Paris streets English, German, and Russian troops of occupation, who were forcing upon the French people an unwelcome Bourbon King. So with bitter comprehension of the feelings of a subject race he tried to prove his thesis by facts drawn from Sharon Turner's *History of the Anglo-Saxons* and other secondary sources. Soon he realized he must be more concrete, in order to arouse his readers' resentment of injustice, but he did not know how until in 1820 he read *Ivanhoe*.

Walter Scott had cast one of his eagle glances upon the historical period toward which all the effort of my thought had been directed for three years. With characteristic boldness he had placed on English soil Normans and Saxons, victors and vanquished, still quivering with resentment in each other's presence one hundred and twenty years after the Conquest. He had colored poetically one scene of the long drama I was laboring to construct with the patience of a historian.[4]

Thierry resolved to reform the writing of history, to produce "art at the same time as science," to wage "war on writers without learning who have not known how to observe, and on writers without imagination who have not known how to paint." [5] Selection of significant concrete detail from primary sources obliged him to "devour long folio pages, in order to extract a single sentence, or even word, among a thousand." [6] This absorbing labor ruined his eyes within five years, but the result was evocative writing. In an early page of his *History of the Norman Conquest of England* (1825) we encounter the effect of a war horn blown from a Norman Viking boat raiding the Seine valley. "From the moment those dread sounds were heard from afar, the Gallic serf quit the soil of the field to which he was bound, to hide with his few possessions in the neighboring woods, and the Frankish noble, seized by the same terror, lifted the drawbridges of his castle, ran to the donjon to array his armed retainers, and ordered the burying of the tribute money he had levied on the neighborhood." [7] The technique of fiction had won a place in sober history.

Hitherto the history of England had been written from the point of view of the Normans or of the ruling classes. The tale of the subject Saxon masses must be assembled from sources long despised and neglected, from popular verse, from legend and tradition. No historian has been more dependent on literature than Thierry. Not only is his narrative a mosaic of quotations, but also he prints in full, usually in an appendix, poems of considerable length illustrative of the Saxon spirit from *The Battle of Brunanburgh* to Robin Hood ballads. A his sympathies widen from the Saxons to the Celtic peoples they had conquered or driven into mountain fastnesses—Scott had shown him "the eternal hostility of the mountain races and men of the plain" [8]—Welsh bards and Scottish Highland singers take their places beside Anglo-Norman poets like Wace. *Popular Songs of Modern Greece,* edited by Thierry's friend Fauriel in the year of Byron's death for Greek freedom, are used to illustrate the pertinacious hopes of submerged peoples like the Irish, the Welsh, and the Highland Scots, whose fate runs parallel to the major theme of the History—the gradual transformation of the story of the English people from race war to class war. Thierry used the present constantly to illuminate the past, for he was sure that "no one, no matter what his intellectual capacity, can go beyond the horizons of his century, and every new epoch gives to history new points of view and a characteristic form." [9] By holding consistently to narrative, he attempted to "give a sort of historical life to masses of men as well as to individuals," in order that "the political destiny of nations might offer something of the human interest unintentionally inspired by the naïf detail of the changes of fortune, the adventures of a single man." [10] In the final volume, this design had grown into an eloquent profession of faith in the role of the masses:

The essential object of this history is to envisage the destiny of peoples and not of certain famous men, to present the adventures of social life and not those of the individual. Human sympathy can attach itself to entire populations, as to beings endowed with feeling, whose existence, longer than our own, is filled with the same alternations of pain and joy, of hope and dejection. Considered from this point of view, the history of the past gains something of the interest of the present; for the collective beings of whom it tells have not ceased to live and to feel: they are the same beings who still suffer and hope before our eyes.[11]

Although Thierry became totally blind in 1828, at the age of thirty-three, he was able by employing secretaries to complete in 1840 *Accounts of Merovingian Times* as a sequel to Chateaubriand's picture of Roman Gaul. The attraction of this age was in the confusion of races and cultures: "There are Franks remaining purely Germanic in Gaul, Gallo-Romans despairing and disgusted at the rule of barbarians, Franks more or less won over to civilized morals and manners, and Romans more or less barbaric in mentality and conduct." [12] Adopting Chateaubriand's use of local and poetic coloring, Thierry let the age paint its own portrait with the minimum of outside aid. From his chief source, the contemporary chronicler Gregory of Tours, he gleaned "episodic stories, local facts, manners which are there, and there only." [13] Ernest Renan, one of the young admirers who read for him, describes Thierry at work in his later years: "Few historians had greater skill in drawing from a text all it contains concerning the social relations and manners of an epoch. . . . I never watched without astonishment the lively and prompt operation by which he grasped the original document, took it in, sometimes went beyond it, and assimilated it into his narrative. The slightest remnant revealed to him an organic whole which, by a sort of regenerative power, sprang complete before his imagination." [14]

The year after the publication of his history of the *French Revolution* (1837), Thomas Carlyle, a fellow countryman, paid eloquent tribute to Scott: "These Historical Novels have taught all men this truth, which looks like a truism, yet was unknown to writers of history and others, till so taught: that the bygone ages of the world were actually filled by living men, not by protocols, state papers, controversies and abstractions of men. Not abstractions were they, not diagrams or theorems; but men, in buff and other coats and breeches, and the idioms, features and vitalities of very men." [15] Carlyle's emphasis upon biography, his reliance upon memoir writers, his astonishing portraiture, whereby the outer and physical semblance of men is made to betray the very intent of their souls, lie here in germ. The Waverley novels, just off the press in his formative years, dissatisfied him with the standard versions of his national past in Robertson's *Scotland* and Hume's *England*. He turned late to history, after having tried his hand at fiction, poetry, biography, and literary criticism; and his practice of those arts told him what historical writing ought to be.

There are a thousand purposes to which History should serve beyond "teaching by experience"; it is an address (literally out of Heaven, for did not God order it all?) to our *whole* inner man; to every faculty of Head and Heart, from the deepest to the slightest; there is no end to such purposes; none to one's amazement and contemplation over it. Now for *all* such purposes, high, low, ephemeral, eternal, the first indispensable condition of conditions, is that we *see* the things transacted, picture them wholly as if they stood before our eyes.[16]

German literature, which had revealed to him "a new Heaven and a new Earth" soon after he had begun to read Scott, had already introduced this technique into history. "Herder's very description of animals and animated beings are animated, cordial, affectionate," Carlyle jotted down in a youthful notebook, "much more those of men in their varied *Thun und Treiben*." Schiller's *Revolt of the Netherlands* and *Thirty Years' War*, by showing what a born dramatist could do to enliven the record of the past, gave hints for Carlyle's handling of the clash of character among the chief figures of the French Revolution, the ironic juxtaposition of anniversaries of great events.

Carlyle's statement approving Schiller's acceptance of the

chair of history at Jena, "the love of contemplating things as they should be, began to yield to the love of knowing things as they are," unconsciously foreshadowed his own turning away from creative writing. Never able wholly to shake off inherited Calvinistic prejudice against fiction as literally untruth, he found freedom only in historical writing and in pamphleteering. History was true, real; yet it contained the ideal. Actual and living, like the present, it had romantic strangeness from remoteness in time. The wonder of it had come to him in boyhood, when on Burnswark Hill overlooking his native village, he gazed at a newly excavated remnant of the Roman fortified border station of Blatum, a "strange face to face vestige of the vanished eons." [17]

To his mature meditation, time was a greater wonder than the infinite space which had captured the imagination of the century of Galileo. Had he the choice of the wishing hat of Fortunatus that annihilated space, or of a similar hat which would annihilate time, Carlyle declared his preference for the latter.

Simply by wishing that you were *Anywhen*, straightway to be *Then!*, this were indeed the grander; shooting at will from the Fire-Creation of the world to its Fire-Consommation: here historically present in the First Century, conversing with Paul and Seneca; there prophetically in the Thirty-first, conversing also face to face with other Pauls and Senecas, who as yet stand hidden in the depth of that late Time! [18]

His interview in 1824 with the butcher Legendre, who had dared demand that Robespierre hear Danton speak in his own defense, had brought almost miraculously the already remote heroism and horror of the Terror back into Carlyle's everyday world, and he in turn tried to bring it home to readers of his History by reminding them that Marat's sister was still living in Paris. The casual mention in Jocelyn of Brakelond's Chronicle of King John's repaying the hospitality of St. Edmund's Abbey with a shabby sum of money drew from Carlyle the reflection:

How much in Jocelyn, as in all History, is at once inscrutable and certain; so dim, yet so indubitable; exciting us to endless considerations. For King Lackland *was* there, and did leave these *tredecim sterlingii,* if nothing more, and did live and look in one way or another, and a whole world was living and looking along with him! There, we say, is the grand peculiarity; the immeasurable one; distinguishing, to a really infinite degree, the poorest historical Fact from all Fiction whatsoever.[19]

His stylistic innovations, the omnipresent present tense, the breathless narration, the ejaculations and inversions, the punctuation perfectly devised to carry the tone and inflections of the speaking voice of the historian and of those actors in the drama of history whose conversation he abundantly reports, reinforce this impression of the immediacy of the past. In their defense he urged: "The common English mode of writing has to do with what I call the *hearsays* of things; and the great business for me, in which alone I feel any comfort, is in recording the presence, bodily concrete colored *presence* of things."[20] Thence his preference for sources like Jocelyn, naïf, garrulous reporting, and for biographers who, like Boswell, abound in vivid detail.

Constantly he reminds us that amid the greatest and most stirring events the life of most men went on its monotonous round. Louis the Sixteenth is guillotined: "In some half-hour it is done; and the multitude has all departed. Pastry-cooks, coffee sellers, milkmen sing out their trivial quotidian cries; the world wags on, as if this were a common day."[21] At the height of the Terror, twenty-three theaters, some sixty public dance halls flourished in Paris. The twelfth-century scene of Book II of *Past and Present* (1843) is made solid reality by homely touches. Old women of St. Edmundsbury brandish distaffs at tax collectors who have seized their household goods in default of the reaping-penny while "Jerusalem was taken by the Crusaders and again lost by them; and Richard Coeur-de-Lion 'veiled his face' in sight of it." [22] To produce such effects Carlyle shunned the easy course of consulting cold notes of his reading, the materials of the antiquarian whom Scott in *Ivanhoe* had stigmatized as Dryasdust. He tells us how he struggled "to keep the whole matter simmering in the *living mind* and memory rather than laid up in paper bundles or otherwise laid up in an inert way. . . . Only what you *have living* in your own memory and heart is worth putting down to be printed; this alone has much chance to get into the living heart and memory of other men." [23] He described his research in editing *The Letters and Speeches of Cromwell* (1845) as "a mole's work, boring and digging blindly underground; my own inner man sometimes very busy (too busy), but the rest is silence." [24] Like his master Goethe, Carlyle understood the creative role of the unconscious mind.

From Herder he adopted the Norse tree Igdrasil to symbolize the organic relation of the past with the present of humanity. More prosaically, he repeated: "The Centuries . . . are all lineal children of one another; and often, in the portrait of early grandfathers, this and the other enigmatic feature of the newest generation shall disclose itself, to mutual elucidation." [25] The past interested him only in so far as it bore upon the present. "The Art of History," he said in the opening pages of the *Cromwell*, "the grand difference between a Dryasdust and a sacred Poet, is very much even this; To distinguish well what does still reach the surface and is frondent for us; and what reaches no longer to the surface, but moulders safe underground, never to send forth leaves and fruit for mankind any more." [26] That portions of the past should die in no wise belied the continuity of history, for the zoological analogy still held. Decay, as Herder had observed, is essential to growth. Carlyle borrowed Herder's term *Palingenesis* to describe the continual rebirth of institutions and ideals from soil enriched by the death of those that have lost their capacity of adjustment to changing environment. From Goethe, he took the conception of alternating ages of Faith and of Doubt, of construction and of destructive analysis, as another means of representing the phenomenon of decay within a living society.

Finding his own place in the flux of history at a moment of transition from an age of destruction, the Enlightenment, and an emergent age of construction, Carlyle studied the conditions of revolution in France and in Cromwellian England for what light they might throw upon the future. Deeply involved emotionally, he described the *History of the French Revolution* as "hot out of my own soul." His finger is ever pointing over the shoulder of the reader of *Cromwell* or *Past and Present* to some contemporary parallel. *Past and Present* was no plea for return to feudalism, but a demonstration of the functional and therefore always provisional character of institutions, the character emphasized in contemporary France by the Saint-Simonian group of thinkers to whom Augustin Thierry had early attached himself. Carlyle stresses the evidence in Jocelyn of Brakelond that already in the twelfth century feudal ties were loosening: "All manner of Ideals have their fatal limits and lot; their appointed periods, of youth, of maturity or perfection, of decline, degradation, and final death and disappearance." [27] His restoration to English history of the imposing figures of Cromwell and Abbot Samson translated what seemed vital in the decisions of two men of action into the dialect of the present, a translation doubly difficult with Cromwell because of his inarticulateness as a speaker and writer. To Carlyle, the essence of history is dynamism. The world is a Sphinx, forever posing problems of adjustment, on penalty of death for too rigidly organized societies.

VI

RESURRECTION OF THE PAST: MICHELET

"I am large, I contain multitudes," Jules Michelet might have urged, like Whitman, in favor of his self-contradictions. For they permitted him to learn from many masters, and to identify himself with many episodes in the history of humanity. Although he had pushed up "like a blade of grass without sun, between two paving stones of Paris," [1] he had a feeling for nature that made him a delicate interpreter of the intimate relation of peoples to their lands. Struggle to escape bondage to some manual occupation forged him into a man of action, without stripping away his love of solitude, revery and speculation. Shyness born of social inferiority vanished before the eagerness to share his hard-won knowledge which made him an inspired teacher. "Those young generations, lovable and confiding, reconciled me with humanity. . . . If ever a special merit sustained me as a historian, beside my illustrious predecessors, I owe it to teaching, which to me was friendship. Those great historians were brilliant, judicious, profound. But I have loved more. Also I have suffered more." [2] The intellectual passions that devoured his youth, his aspirations to chastity and mystic religion, did not conquer the carnality which gives many of his pages a strong odor of humanity. Self-contradiction is visible in his appearance and in his style. His lips, delicate but firm, hold the balance between the brow and eyes of a dreamy enthusiast and the heavy, square plebeian chin. The surface of his writing is emotional stir, but beneath is solid structure. His abundant imagery is never vague; color and warmth never blur French precision, French clarity. His art, like that of his favorite Michelangelo, unites strength with delicacy. Mathematics, natural science, medicine attracted him almost equally with literature, philosophy, and the arts. A command of narrative and characterization that might have endowed a great novelist, the imagination and divination of a poet, a philosopher's desire to generalize, never made him impatient with the scrupulous attention to detail, the critical analysis of sources which the sciences were pressing upon the conscience of historians.

Michelet's curiosity about the past was first awakened when, in his twelfth year, his mother took him to the Museum of French Monuments, a collection of medieval sculpture saved from the iconoclastic rage of the Revolution. When he returned from such visits to slave away at the family printing press while his father was imprisoned for debt, his imagination

> retained the emotion, always the same and always intense, which made my heart beat when I entered those dark vaults and contemplated those pale faces, when I went searching, ardent, inquisitive, fearful, from hall to hall and from era to era. What was I looking for? I do not know. For the life of those days, perhaps, and the genius of the times. I was not quite sure they were not alive, those marble sleepers on their tombs; and when from the sumptuous monuments of the sixteenth century, dazzling with alabaster, I passed to the hall of the Merovingians and the cross of Dagobert, I was not quite sure Chilpéric and Frédégonde would not sit upright before my eyes.[3]

From his mother's peasant family in the Ardennes came oral legends and old chronicles of the northern border, preparing him for Froissart and Scott.

His training in history came by way of languages and literature, studied just as Romantic taste was entering upon a belated conquest of France, the stronghold of neoclassicism. At the University of Paris, Villemain taught him to see literature as the expression of society and encouraged him to read foreign works for the reflection of national character. The new taste in history lagged behind that in literature. In 1820, the year after his winning the degree of Doctor of Letters by a Latin thesis on Plutarch, he was reading Bossuet's *Universal History*, along with Rousseau, Byron, and Lamartine's *Poetic Meditations*, just off the press; in 1821, Hume's *England* and Voltaire's *Essay on the Manners and Character of the Nations*, along with Chateaubriand's *Atala* and four Scott novels.

The joining of philosophy to languages and history as the subjects Michelet was appointed to teach at the Collège de Ste. Barbe led to a discovery which brought harmony into his thinking. While seeking to relate philosophy to history, he read, in January, 1824, when he was twenty-six, Dugald Stewart's *History of the Metaphysical, Moral and Political Sciences*. In its third volume he observed a note by the French translator criticizing, on the authority of the Italian Salfi, Stewart's failure to mention Vico. The *Scienza nuova* was still little known in France, and unknown in England. Coleridge was to begin to read Vico in 1825, and through him the *Scienza nuova* was to influence the English historian, Thomas Arnold.[4] Wolf had not read it until five years after the publication of his *Prolegomena*, and Niebuhr showed no awareness of its existence, although a German translation had appeared in 1822. Michelet, a man of the people, seized with enthusiasm upon Vico's central idea that civilization is the collective product of humanity, with its revolutionary implications for literature, religion, law, politics and economics. In June, 1824, he began to translate the *Scienza nuova*. On August 17 his zeal spilled over into an address to the winners of school prizes at Ste. Barbe. "Let disaster befall the man who would try to isolate a single branch of knowledge. He might observe facts, but he could not grasp the spirit giving them life. . . . Knowledge is one. Languages, literature and history; physics, mathematics, philosophy, kinds of learning apparently the farthest apart, really meet, or rather, all form a single system." [5] The history of thought, as well as of action, is an indissoluble continuity. "The individual appears for an instant, joins the community of thinking, modifies it and dies; but the species, that dies not, reaps the fruit of his ephemeral existence." [6]

Only a month after finding the reference to Vico, Michelet had learned of Herder through a Scotch acquaintance. While he was spelling him out in newly acquired German, he met, in May, 1825, Edgar Quinet, who had already begun to translate *Thoughts on History*. The young men, who were to be friends for life, exchanged their enthusiasms. To the insights of Vico, Herder added, for Michelet, the intimate relation of man to his geographical setting, which was to inspire some of his most brilliant pages. Through the translations by Michelet and Quinet, the French learned of Vico and of Herder simultaneously in 1827. As a reward for his revival of Vico, Michelet was called in that year to teach history at the École Normale Supérieure, center of the most advanced teachers' training in France.

Herder was Michelet's gateway to the literary, linguistic, and historical achievements of Germany, to collections of popular ballads and Northern antiquities, to Winckelmann and Goethe, to Creuzer's interpretation of myths, and thence to the *Nibelungenlied* and to Niebuhr's *Rome*. While on a month's visit to Germany in 1828, he heard of Jakob Grimm, whose works pointed to Savigny, to Indo-European linguistics, and to Otfried Müller. In 1830 he was sufficiently steeped in these matters to criticize Niebuhr for insufficiency of "the delicate and profound sense of the mythic and religious epochs" [7] and for neglect of Vico. Already he was far advanced with a *History of the Roman Republic*, which would complete Niebuhr's plan of joining hands with Gibbon.

Rome attracted Michelet as the basis of the history of his native France and of the generalizations of Vico. Niebuhr's discoveries, modified by Vico and by Müller's interpretation of Etruscan myth and knowledge in *The Etruscans* (1828), could be made attractive to French readers by orderly arrangement and by the narrative dress Thierry had adopted from Scott and Chateaubriand. And for the final centuries of the Republic, including Hannibal and Caesar, Niebuhr was not a rival.

Six weeks' strenuous travel in Italy, where Michelet sought out Alessandro Manzoni, whose great historical novel *I Promessi Sposi* (1825) had infused Scott's form with Vico's philosophy, provided material for an opening chapter describing the geology and geography of the Italian peninsula, to account for the strategic situation of Rome. Its first inhabitants Michelet studied as peoples, not as individuals. Vivid details from Müller introduced the almost forgotten agricultural Pelasgians, with their awesome mystery-religion, and the historic, but almost equally strange Etruscans, who left to the more prosaic Roman religion the legacy of augurs, larves, penates and lares. The Latins, who established the Republic after driving out their Etruscan kings, were revealed by the vocabulary of their language as an Indo-Germanic people, who originally were shepherds and brigands. Michelet compared the allied Sabines to Scotch Highlanders living by blackmail. Following Vico, Savigny, and Niebuhr, he read the Laws of the Twelve Tables as an accumulation from different stages of civilization: the barbarous primitive, the stern, exclusive patrician, and the expansive, cosmopolitan plebeian. Roman interpretation of law long remained archaic, holding to its letter rather than its spirit, as in the evasion of the terms of surrender at the Caudine Forks and in the destruction of Carthage. Reading the Roman character thus, Michelet has reservations concerning Niebuhr's theory of poetic traditions.

Few nations seem to me to have been in circumstances less favorable to poetry. Heterogeneous populations, shut within the same walls, borrowing from neighboring nations their customs, their arts and their gods; an artificial society, recent, without a past; continual war, but war of cupidity rather than enthusiasm; a character avid and miserly. The Klept,[8] after battle, sings upon his lonely mountain. The Roman, returned to the city with his booty, overreaches the senate, loans at usury, litigates and disputes. His habits are those of a lawyer; he interrogates the letter of the law grammatically, or tortures it by dialectic, to draw advantage from it. Nothing less poetic than all that.[9]

What was picturesque in early Roman annals was the clash with other civilizations. In the vein of Scott, Michelet recounts "the terrible epic of the Samnite War, the combat of the city against the tribe, of the plain against the mountain. It is the history of the Saxons and Highlanders of Scotland, the former disciplined in large battalions, the latter assembled as irregular militia. But Nature takes sides; the mountains hide and protect their children. Dark defiles, aerial peaks, raging torrents, snows and hoar frost of the Apennines. The elements are for the sons of the earth against the sons of the city. . . . This atrocious war peopled with fugitives all the Apennine caves. Less fortunate than the English outlaws, these refugees have left no monument, not a war cry, not a lament."[10] The vanquished Greek colonies of Italy are impressive even in their ruin: "The coast of Tarentum (and this feeble vestige is more eloquent than all the rest) is red from the debris of vases which the great city piled up there." The Punic Wars decided "to which of two races, the Indo-Germanic or the Semitic, was to belong the domination of the world. . . . On the one side, the heroic genius of art and legislation; on the other, the spirit of industry, navigation and commerce." [11] Carthage in defeat struck the imagination. "Rome annihilated her. There took place something found nowhere else in history, an entire civilization disappearing suddenly, like a falling star. The *Periplus* of Hanno, some medals, about twenty verses in Plautus, these are all that remains of the Carthaginian world." [12] Seeing like Niebuhr the downfall of the Roman Republic in the harshness and inequity of its property laws, Michelet hailed Caesar as "the man of humanity," whose assassination left to Augustus "the great labor of the Empire, the leveling of the world."

Rereading his *History of the Roman Republic* (1831–1832) thirty years after its publication, Michelet characterized it fairly: "One makes oneself a historian little by little, but already I was a writer." [13] The predominance of the writer's interest is obvious in the later centuries, when he could no longer lean on Niebuhr. He lavishes his skill on the war of Carthage with her revolted mercenaries, which had little bearing on world history, yet offered irresistible temptation to the artist. "In this world of Alexander's successors, in this iron age, the sanguinary war of the mercenaries nevertheless horrified all peoples, and was called the *implacable war*." [14] The maturing of the historian began when he entered upon his life's work, a *History of France* (1833–1867).

Appointment in 1831 as Chief of the Historical Section of the National Archives opened to Michelet an enormous mass of documents hitherto untouched by historians, just at the time when he was moved to patriotic faith in the destiny of the French people to lead humanity in its aspiration toward social justice. The Revolution of 1830 had seemed to confirm Vico by presenting "the first model of a revolution without heroes, without proper names. . . . Society did everything. No one planned; no one led; no one eclipsed the others." [15] In three July days the populace of Paris, though without police, committed no theft, no assassination, while it was ridding itself of its reactionary Bourbon King and dealing a mortal blow to the landed aristocracy. The French people must be taught to understand this self-discipline as the culmination of its long history, to see France as "a soul and a person," growing toward justice and culture. Other historians had observed aspects of this development, Thierry the clash and amalgamation of races, Guizot (who had appointed Michelet to the Archives), the foundation of institutions. Michelet aspired to present its totality, to envisage France as a complex and delicate organism, in which every organ affected every other.

Nor would France be shown in isolation. She was part of the great movement of the human spirit to emancipate itself from the tyranny of matter, outlined in Michelet's *Introduction to Universal History* (1831). Antiquity had been in bondage to climate and race. France was born after Christianity had begun the struggle to control brute force, and she had participated in the first triumph of the Church, the Crusades which enlisted military force for spiritual ends. "In a thousand years was accomplished the long miracle of the Middle Ages, that marvelous legend whose trace is daily being effaced from the earth, and whose very existence would be doubted a few centuries hence, were it not fixed and crystallized for all time in the spires, the steeples, the rose windows and the innumerable arches of the cathedrals. Each of these spires which would fain throw itself upward is a prayer, an impotent wish arrested by the tyranny of matter." [16] The Middle Ages accomplished only part of the liberation of the human spirit, for they left man exploited by his fellow man. In the struggle of modern times for social equality France had become the standard bearer. Her history illustrated Vico's theme of humanity creating itself.

Michelet made the test of his ability as an interpreter the establishment of an unbroken continuity of growth from the origin of the French nation to his own time. For the "resurrection" of the life of the past he would draw upon geology, geography, ethnology, linguistics, coins and monumental inscriptions, architecture, chronicles and memoirs, political and economic documents, literature, theology, and scientific theory. He would obey "the new condition imposed upon history: not only to narrate, but also to evoke, remake, resuscitate the ages. To have flame to rekindle ashes so long cold." [17] Looking backward in 1869 upon the completed labor of over thirty years, Michelet smiled sadly: "In the brilliant morning of July, its vast hope, its potent electricity, this superhuman enterprise did not frighten a young heart." [18] He was thirty-five when he published Volume One in 1833.

The first six volumes eclipsed in scope and penetration all previous attempts to restore the Middle Ages as a bridge between the ancient and the modern worlds. After the overthrow of Roman power in Gaul there emerges, in spite of conflicting races, Celtic, Latin, Germanic, and in spite of political fragmentation promoted by geographical barriers, a French people which gradually makes for itself a common language and a common social life. It passes through a cosmopolitan phase in which the ideals of a Universal Church and a Holy Roman Empire compete for its allegiance, until conflict with the English invader arouses national consciousness in the fifteenth century. A multitude of details give the reader the sense of a thousand years without wearying him, so surely does Michelet enlist sympathy for each medieval ideal: feudal loyalty, Christendom, chivalry, scholasticism. France, from her central geographical, cultural, and political position, largely epitomizes the Europe of those centuries. The English reader learns what international issues were at stake in the conflict between Becket and Henry the Second; the German can more easily forgive the ruinous intervention of his emperors in Italian affairs. Yet Michelet never distracts attention from his main theme: the French masses, oppressed, inarticulate, growing toward self-consciousness and self-defense.

In the controversial issue of the racial origins of the French, Michelet takes no side in favor of Latin, Celt, or German, but accepts a mixed race. The opening chapter of Volume Two, *Picture of France*, which in the spirit of Herder but with greater art reveals the role of geography and climate in the production of the rich variety of human character in the feudal divisions which were to become the Departments of modern France, although resplendent in local color, is not a plea for separatism. The racialism and localism dear to Thierry and Müller, though they contribute flavor to the national character, must be subordinated to the higher organisms of the nation and the yet unrealized world-state. The opinion of the biologist Dugès, that centralization increases as organisms mount in scale from mollusks and insects to man, introduces Michelet's fervent statement of the logic of history:

The local spirit has been disappearing every day; the influence of soil, climate, race, has yielded to social and political influence. The fatality of environment has been overcome; man has escaped from the tyranny of material circumstance. . . . Society, liberty have conquered nature; history has effaced geography. . . . Barbarous eras present almost nothing but the local, the particular, the material. Man still clings to the soil, is involved in it, almost part of it. Little by little man's own power will detach him, uproot him from the earth, . . . will lead him . . . to the idea of the universal fatherland, to the city of Providence.[19]

The French language, the first sign of nationality, appears in the ninth century. Two centuries later the Normans, by their conquests of England and Sicily, are a force drawing France, with her feudal divisions still largely a mere geographical expression, into the destinies of Northern and Southern Europe. Between the eleventh and the fourteenth centuries the Church makes a magnificent effort to unite Europe under a single spiritual power. At the height of its strength with Innocent III, the Papacy bends the mightiest kings, Philip Augustus of France and John of England, to its will, stamps out the Albigensian heresy and puts a momentary end to the schism of the Eastern and Western Churches by organizing a Crusade which captures Constantinople. Medieval Christianity, in those centuries of its youthful vigor, civilized the common man in more ways than the nineteenth century knew. It protected him from excesses of arbitrary feudal force; it fed the indigent and educated the gifted poor; it offered the naves of its churches as the true home of a populace housed in miserable huts, as the center for transaction of daily business without prudish supervision. And yet it did not fail to elevate the popular mind to spiritual matters.

Michelet's power of resurrection first comes into full play in explaining how the Middle Ages, especially France of the Middle Ages, "expressed in architecture its most intimate thought." [20] He repeoples the great churches. "Try to imagine the effect of lights in these prodigious monuments, when the clergy, circulating by aerial ramps, animated the dark masses with fantastic processions, passing and repassing along balustrades, on bridges of lacework, in rich costumes, with candles and chants; when lights and voices turned in circle after circle, while from below, in the shadow, the ocean of people responded. That was for this era the true drama, the true mystery play; the representation of the journey of humanity across the three worlds, that sublime initiation which Dante took from transitory reality to fix eternally in his *Di-*

vine Comedy. This colossal theater of sacred drama has returned, after the long festival of the Middle Ages, to silence and shadow. The feeble voice one hears there, the voice of the priest, is impotent to fill the arches whose amplitude was designed to embrace and contain the thunder of the people's voice. The church is widowed, empty. Its profound symbolism, which then spoke so loud, is mute; now an object of scientific curiosity, of Alexandrian interpretations. The church is a Gothic museum, visited by the sophisticated. They move about, gaze irreverently, praise instead of praying." [21] The very stones of these churches illustrated the philosophy of Vico by the sublime anonymity of the masons who shaped them. "To know with what care they toiled, obscure and lost in their guild, with what abnegation, you must go over the most retired, least accessible parts of the cathedrals. Mount to those aerial deserts, to the ultimate points of those spires where the roofer fears to venture. There you will often find, buffeted by eternal wind, some masterpiece of art and sculpture upon which the poor workman lavished his life. He worked for God only, *for the cure of his soul*." [22] Tombs told the same story. "In the first Christian ages, in the time of lively faith, sorrows were patient. Death seemed a brief divorce; it separated, but only to reunite. A sign of this belief in the soul, in the reunion of souls, is that, up to the twelfth century, the body, the mortal remains, seems to have less importance. It does not yet ask for magnificent tombs. Hidden in a corner of the church, a simple slab covers it; enough to mark it for the day of resurrection: *Hinc surrectura*." [23]

The absence of self-consciousness in these early centuries, the scorn of hypocrisy, which charmingly reveal so large a portion of our common humanity, tested to the utmost Michelet's sympathy and understanding. His narrative, colored by vivid phrases from contemporary chronicles, passes unperturbed from mysticism and naïve goodness to equally naïve violence and vice. Loyalty to feudal ties has never been described more attractively to modern readers than in his account of the Suabian Emperors. His championship of the anonymous masses does not tempt him to slight great personalities, the Angevin kings and their rival Philip Augustus, Becket, Abelard, Saints Francis, Dominic, and Thomas Aquinas. In portraying Louis the Ninth, the King of France who was also a saint, Michelet reaches the summit of the medieval ideal.

As Louis confesses to the chronicler Joinville his moments of doubt, Michelet asks: How many others doubted in silence, or uttered doubts that have not been recorded? All things human are in flux; even ideals are mortal. Twenty years after Louis' death, the irremediable loss of the Holy Land ends the age of Crusades. Less than ten years more, and in 1298 Marco Polo,

the Christopher Columbus of Asia, dictates the account of a journey, of a sojourn of twenty years in China and Japan. For the first time, it is learned that at twelve months' travel beyond Jerusalem, there are kingdoms, civilized nations. Jerusalem is no longer the center of the world,of human thought. Europe loses the Holy Land, but she sees the Earth. . . . The new religion of riches, of faith in gold, has its pilgrims, its monks, its martyrs. Like their prototypes, they dare and suffer, they fast and abstain.[24]

The other-worldly Middle Ages, the subordination of secular to spiritual power, chivalry, even feudalism, are now logically dead. But they take an unconscionably long time dying. In the Hundred Years' War of France with England, commercial and chivalric motives are intertwined: "The whole era is double, ambiguous. Contrasts dominate; everywhere prose and poetry giving each other the lie, mocking each other."[25] Prose wins decisively in France with Louis the

Eleventh (Michelet's portrait of this most unkingly king surpasses its fictional predecessors in *Quentin Durward* and Hugo's *Notre Dame de Paris*), but the ground beneath it is already mined by a new kind of poetry, patriotism. In reaction against the English invasions, the phrase, "a good Frenchman," begins to be used in the fourteenth century. Michelet is deeply moved by accounts of the long-suffering populace resorting to self-defense when its feudal superiors fail to protect it, such as the story of the peasant leader called the Grand Ferré:

> It is difficult not to be touched by this naïf tale. These peasants who defend themselves only after having asked permission, this humble strong man, the good giant who obeys willingly like Saint Christopher of the legend, all this presents an attractive picture of the people. The populace is obviously simple and brutish as yet, impetuous, blind, half man, half bull. It does not know how to defend its gates or to protect itself from its own appetites. When it has beaten the enemy like wheat in a barn, where it has hacked him up sufficiently with its axe and got overheated at the job, it drinks cold water and lies down to die. Patience! Under the rude education of the wars, under the English rod, this brute will make a man of himself. Very soon, pressed more closely, squeezed, he will escape by ceasing to be himself, by transforming himself. Jacques will become Jeanne, Jeanne the Virgin, the Maid.[26]

Joan of Arc is the climax of Michelet's medieval portraits, and also the first great portrait of this heroine saint whom, a century before, Voltaire had been applauded for making in *La Pucelle* a besmirched figure of anticlerical jest. Aided by Quicherat's opportune publication in 1840 of the official record of her trial, Michelet was able to avoid both the outworn caricature and the recent tendency to embellish. "What legend is more beautiful than this incontestable history? But we must take care not to make a legend of it. We should try to preserve piously all the traits, even the most human, to re-

RESURRECTION OF THE PAST

spect its touching and terrible reality." [27] Steeping himself in the atmosphere of her time through chronicles and documents, Michelet created, against a background of power politics, commercial intrigue, superstition and moral callousness, a bright womanly figure who lifts the ideal of a united France above popular fanaticism and feudal self-seeking. "This last figure of the past was also the first of the time that was beginning. In her appeared the Virgin . . . and already the Fatherland." [28]

Up to this climax, Michelet's sympathy with each successive phase of his country's history had been sustained opportunely by a similar phase in his personal life or beliefs. He had described the early Middle Ages while he was convinced that the Church was the best friend of the French people. When he wrote of the decline of medieval ideals, he understood "the somber monotony, . . . the waiting without hope, without desire except for death," by recalling the last days of Napoleon's Empire: "I knew, in my dark den, what the Jew dreamed while he was building the Pyramids, . . . what the man of the Middle Ages thought as he plowed his furrow under the shadow of the feudal tower." [29] The death of his first wife plunged him into obsessions and sensual debauch just as he turned to describe the nadir of French fortunes: the madness of Charles the Sixth, civil war, devastation by English armies, gaiety born of despair, dances of death in cemeteries. Love for Madame Dumesnil restored his peace of mind and increased his respect for womanhood at the moment when he must tell the story of Joan of Arc.

But as he turned with Louis the Eleventh to the absolute monarchy which would culminate in Louis the Fourteenth, the series of coincidences was broken. One winter day as he was writing at a table in his comfortable study—in 1838 he had reached the summit of professional success by being appointed to the Collège de France—a discordant memory arose. He was back in 1814. Napoleon had been defeated at Leipzig, and an invading army was approaching Paris. After Michelet's parents had made every sacrifice to pay his tuition at the Charlemagne Lycée, his fellow students had jeered at the plebeian clothes and manners of the miserable boy. He was trying to study one bitterly cold morning "without fire (snow covered everything), not sure I would have bread to eat that night; everything seemed about to finish for me." But with a supreme effort of will, "I struck with my fist, chapped with cold, on my oak table (which I have always kept) and I felt within me a manly joy of youth and hope."[30] Ashamed to find himself now, after thirty years, so comfortable while others shivered outside, Michelet vowed in expiation to write the story of the hitherto unavailing aspiration of the French people to economic justice.

The Revolution of 1830, which had once given him ardent faith in the future, had done less for the masses than the original Revolution. Its liberalism had proved merely political. In freeing the common man from the enfeebled landed aristocracy, it had delivered him into the firmer hands of the capitalistic middle class of a machine age. Michelet resolved to tell where and why the two Revolutions had missed their goal. The future of the nation depended upon this knowledge. He could not wait for the chronology of his History to take him from 1500 to 1789. He must plunge at once into the story of the first Revolution, which no Frenchman had yet written from the standpoint of the populace as distinct from its leaders, and which Carlyle, for all his economic radicalism, had studied with the too great detachment of a foreigner.[31] While writing history, Michelet would be making history, by demonstrating the necessity of a third, and economic, Revolution.

Investigating events only fifty years past, he could supplement written records with oral tradition. His father had seen the Bastille stormed and Louis the Sixteenth walking in the yard of the Temple prison. His uncle had felt the widespread fraternal enthusiasm of the Festival of Federation, which Carlyle dismissed as mere Gallic ebullience. The popular mind, which for the Middle Ages had to be pieced out from fragmentary records, he could here recapture with something approaching completeness. Michelet recalled thousands of conversations among the common people of Paris concerning the Revolution, which had been their own work. A largely unconscious work, however, like all popular creations. The task of the historian would be to restore "to the morning the forgotten dream of the night." If that could be done, the people would appear as the protagonist of the Revolution, whose fruits had largely been thrown away by its middle-class leaders. "This bourgeoisie, saturated with Voltaire and Rousseau, was more humanitarian, more disinterested and generous than industrialism has made it today, but it was timid. Its habits, its character, formed under the detestable *ancien régime*, were necessarily weak. The bourgeoisie trembled before the revolution it had made, retreated before its work. Fear misled, ruined it, much more than self-interest." [32] The vision of generations thus cheated of their opportunity, of countless men who had not been able to live to their full capacity, haunted Michelet. He would be their poet, their prophet.

In *The History of the French Revolution* (1847–1853), Michelet's lyrical identification of himself with his themes reached its greatest intensity. It engaged alternately his hopes and his fears, forced emotional outbursts more fervent even than Carlyle's. "Holy, holy Revolution! how slow you are in coming! . . . I, who waited for you a thousand years in the furrow of the Middle Ages, must I wait still?"[33] When it came, the Revolution brought him doubtful satisfaction. "This History is full of fatigue," he wrote to a friend in 1846, "not only because of the multitude and violence of its crises, but also because of the feeling that always comes when one suspends reading and reflects, the feeling of useless effort, of immense sacrifices without result. Results no doubt will come, but in the future."[34]

Before Michelet's History had reached the triumph of Valmy, the third Revolution he had been working for broke out in February, 1848, reinstating him in his post at the Collège de France from which he had been dismissed in January for introducing into his lectures advocacy of economic reform and attacks upon ecclesiastical control of education. Economic depression had precipitated the downfall of the limited monarchy of Louis-Philippe. Care for the unemployed was the first concern of the new Republic. It launched the experiment of providing work at public expense. The cost soon brought disagreement between those supporters of the new government who desired the widening of the suffrage and other political liberties only, and those determined to provide economic security for the masses also. The politically minded prevailed. In June, 1848, the closing of the National Workshops was announced. The hundred thousand unemployed who had come from all parts of France to government-subsidized work in Paris were offered the choice of enlisting in the army or of returning to their homes, where work was promised. Their suspicious refusal of both offers was supported by the workingmen of Paris, employed as well as unemployed. In rage against what they thought a betrayal of the cause for which they had taken up arms in February, they again barricaded the streets. This time, it was the government which proved the stronger. In four bloody days, its regular troops stamped out the insurrection.

Civil strife thus shattered Michelet's dream of fraternity, of a united people accomplishing internal reforms by free consent. "*Excidat illa dies* (may that day be blotted out)," he wrote in his diary at news of the revolt. The results of granting universal suffrage unaccompanied by economic reforms came swiftly. Louis-Napoleon, elected President largely because of the reflected military glory of his uncle the Emperor, made himself Emperor by seizing dictatorial power in 1851, on the anniversary of the battle of Austerlitz.

Rather than swear allegiance to the usurper, Michelet resigned his positions in the Archives and the Collège de France. Although doubtful whether any publisher would accept a volume so discordant with the temper of the times, he entered with inflexible resolution upon the final episode of the first Revolution, the Terror: "I am persevering, and will still persevere on the ruins of the world." [35] Having pronounced final judgment on the Revolution: "It changed the ownership of property, but left it a monopoly," he turned back to fill the gap he had left between the Renaissance and the Revolution in volumes published between 1855 and 1867. Their unfavorable picture of the absolute monarchy gave occasion for oblique attacks upon Napoleon the Third, who had destroyed Michelet's confidence in the uninterrupted progress of the French nation toward social justice. He lived to see Napoleon overthrown, and the Third Republic begin its precarious life.

"Let this be my part in history, not to have attained but to have marked, history's goal; to have named it with a name no one had mentioned. Thierry called it *narration*, and Guizot, *analysis*. I have called it *resurrection*, and this name will abide."[36] Where Michelet succeeded in approaching this almost impossible goal, it was by consummate literary tact reflecting a protean personality, which permits his readers to share in the experience of many generations of men. His letters meet literary problems with a precision which anticipates Flaubert. "I hope," he wrote Mme. Dumesnil as he approached Joan of Arc, "to have decidedly sloughed off my first form, to have mastered the petty details, so that they appear subordinate to a great and general harmony. That is to say, I believe I have found, by dint of concentration and reverberation, a flame intense enough to melt down the apparent diversities, and to restore to them the unity in history which they had in life."[37] In 1850 he explained the problem of the inarticulateness of the revolutionists: "I am buried in the catacombs where I have exhumed the Convention. Its very bones have perished. I pick a bit of dust up in the hollow of my hand, and breathe on it to revive it. There are an infinity of men of whom nothing remains but their acts. They did not care to write memoirs or apologies. And I try to; I restore their memory."[38] He adjusted his manner to the tempo of events in the Revolution. "Already I have begun by changing the rhythm of my History. There are no longer large chapters; there are small sections, hurried, darted one upon the other. The prodigious acceleration of the pulse is the dominant phenomenon of the Terror."[39] With utter naturalness his style adapts itself to every historical situation. Even in the most romantically mannered of his works, *The French Revolution*, it can assume the dry irony of the eighteenth century, as in analyzing the degeneration of the Church: "In the Middle Ages she had two things, her property and her functions, of which she was very jealous. More equitable in modern times, she has made a partition. She has kept the property; the functions, hospitals, chantries, patronage of the poor, all the things that involved her too much in the cares of this world, she has generously given back to the secular power." [40]

Appropriateness of tone came from Michelet's willingness to give himself completely to every demand, however painful. "I am accomplishing a hard task," says a letter of 1849, "that of reliving, remaking and suffering the Revolution. I have just passed through September and all the horrors of death: massacred at the Abbey, I am going before the Revolutionary Tribunal, that is, to the guillotine." [41] Those who have passed with Michelet through a thousand years of the life of the French people with such unreserved participation understand his melancholy conception of his profession: "Harsh necessity of the historian, to love and to lose so many things, to recommence all the loves, all the sorrows of humanity. I who have excuses for so many things, regrets for so many diverse ages, I for whom all life is precious and who feel all humanity as my family and my blood, I move across history like the Greek actor who, when playing Electra, bore the funeral urn of his son." [42]

VII

HISTORY AS ART: RENAN, BURCKHARDT, GREEN

THE three years following 1848 dealt European faith in collective humanity blows from which it has never recovered. Liberal hopes had mounted high when revolution spread rapidly from France: when the King of Prussia was forced to grant a Constitution, and a Parliament representing the smaller German States met to establish a National Federation; when the flight of the Emperor of Austria and his Minister Metternich, who had led the forces of reaction since the fall of Napoleon, left Vienna in the hands of a Committee of Public Safety and the Austrian Empire on the verge of dissolution from nationalist uprisings in Hungary and Italy; when Rome, wrested from the temporal power of the Pope, seemed about to become the capital of a united Italy; when the Chartists threatened a proletarian revolt in England. Hopes dropped to the depths with the rapidly receding tide of revolution. Prussia crushed the democratic aspirations of the German States. Autocratic Russia intervened to help Austria reabsorb Hungary and her Italian possessions. In England, Chartism dribbled away. Finally in 1851 France herself yielded to the dictatorship of Napoleon III, supported by big business and the Church. Only in England was absolutism not in the saddle; and there capitalism was supreme.

The masses, except in Paris, had lacked cohesion, discipline, steadfastness of purpose. Even in France, the peasants failed to see their common cause with the industrial workers of the cities, and had been dazzled by the name of Napoleon.

HISTORY AS ART

The poet Leconte de Lisle, after campaigning fruitlessly in Brittany for socialistic ideas, expressed a disillusion shared in varying degrees by liberal minds: "How stupid the populace is! A race of slaves who cannot live without rod or yoke. Let it die of hunger, then, this populace easy to dupe!" Michelet, admitting reluctantly that the masses must pass through a long process of education, addressed the readers of his 1855 volume on the Renaissance: "Generations too confident in the collective forces that make the greatness of the nineteenth century, come, see the live spring from which the human race recruits its strength, the spring of the soul, which when alone feels itself greater than the world, and does not wish to borrow from its neighbor aid for its salvation." [1]

Faith in the exceptional individual tended to replace faith in the group, in the nation, in the mass of mankind. Among men of letters, this revulsion of feeling was reinforced by growing awareness that increased literacy and cheap printing, instead of enlightening the masses, encouraged books with diluted or distorted thought and without art. Unwilling to stoop to meet the demand for literature as a mere commercial product, most of the ablest writers held themselves to exacting standards of art and thought. The extreme of this scorn of popular taste was the doctrine of art for art's sake proclaimed by Gautier, Flaubert, and Baudelaire in France, by Swinburne, D. G. Rossetti, and Pater in England. "Let the Empire run along," was the celebrated counsel of Flaubert, "let us climb to the top of our ivory tower, to the last step, the one nearest the sky. It is cold there, sometimes, isn't it? But what does that matter? You see the stars shine clear, and you do not hear the geese cackle any longer." [2]

Disgust with the present, with the spectacle of ignorant masses deluded and exploited by a vulgar plutocracy, with the ugliness of crass industrialism, turned many eyes to the past for refuge, for refreshment. In this mood Leconte de Lisle produced *Poèmes antiques* (1852) and William Morris *The Earthly Paradise* (1868–1870); in this mood Flaubert, Thackeray, and Morris each composed a historical novel— *Salammbô* (1862), *Henry Esmond* (1852), and the historical romance *A Dream of John Ball* (1888). "I am going to write a novel whose action will take place three centuries before Christ," Flaubert explained, "for I feel the need of escaping from the modern world, . . . which fatigues me as much to reproduce as it disgusts me to observe." [3] His theme was the "implacable war" of Carthage with her mercenaries brilliantly sketched by Michelet, a savage and remorseless struggle in which neither side engaged his sympathies. For, however refreshing a change from the present, the past was seldom idealized by authors who came to maturity after 1848. They contemplated both past and future with what Matthew Arnold called a "sad lucidity of soul." Darwinism reinforced this mood by emphasizing the lowliness of man's origin, his long subjection to a ruthless struggle for existence, by casting doubt not only on the Providential guidance of his destiny but also on Nature's plan, or on her beneficence if she had a plan. Darwin did great service to history by demonstrating continuity and development in all creation, and the unity of man with nature. But the vision he gave of the lowly beginnings of mankind discouraged hopes of rapid improvement in the future, and seemed to counsel immense patience while man worked out the beast in himself for aeons to come.

Intimate participation, like Michelet's, in all the travail of man's past became intolerably painful in view of the uncertainty of the future, the indefinite postponement of human perfection. But the wounds of the heart could be made endurable if history were regarded as a grandiose spectacle, as the greatest drama man is privileged to witness, and if it were clad in the utmost beauty of form and style which the quickened artistic conscience of the time could achieve. Aesthetic detachment, like scientific objectivity, gave scope to intellectual curiosity, to the sheer desire to know, whatever the consequences, which is perhaps the noblest, as well as the rarest, of human traits. There was no discarding of sympathy; but it was tempered by an alert critical intellect that had regard for the immense body of fact amassed by a century of zealous historical investigation. Scientific and philosophical ideas, literary and artistic masterpieces, intrinsic values independent of man's social destiny, assumed an importance in historical writing neglected since Voltaire, and were treated, as a result of the Romantic revolution in taste, with a flexibility and a delicacy beyond his reach.

These international tendencies are best represented by Ernest Renan, Jakob Burckhardt, and John Richard Green.

Abrupt changes in environment and in studies brought Renan early to maturity. Born in 1823, the son of a Breton sailor, he passed his first fifteen years in the small port of Tréguier, in a primitive environment of fishermen's superstitions and Celtic saints' legends. Renan's brilliance attracted the head of a Parisian school which was giving worldly polish to students for the priesthood by educating them together with sons of the aristocracy. From these school fellows in Paris the raw provincial youth acquired ease of speech and manner and at the same time met with models of graceful writing, including contemporary writers like Lamartine, Hugo and Michelet, in the largely literary training which succeeded the Latin and mathematics taught in the seventeenth-century manner by Breton priests. The Seminary of St. Sulpice then turned him away from letters to theology and philosophy. A born scholar, Renan was never content until he reached primary sources; and the candid, secure piety of his teachers permitted him to read far beyond the bounds of Catholic orthodoxy. In order to know the Old Testament thoroughly, he learned Hebrew; in order to consult Biblical critics, he learned German. Eichhorn's *Introduction to the Old Testament* and Ewald's recent *History of the People of Israel* (1843) posed questions concerning the authorship and the inspiration of the Scriptures. Natural science, notably Lyell's *Principles of Geology* (1830–1837), presented the picture of a world in flux, in perpetual becoming, hard to reconcile with fixed dogma. But Herder, Goethe, and Kant's school of idealistic philosophers offered a faith in harmony with such a world and with a historical view of the Scriptures, faith in spirit immanent in man and nature, and developing through them. Renan regretted deeply that he had not, like Herder, been reared as a Protestant, to remain a clergyman while accepting these views. After two years of inner struggle, he decided he could not take priestly vows.

Renan left the Seminary at twenty-three, well stocked with learning, but lacking money and worldly experience. Teaching was the only occupation he was prepared for, but it required secular academic degrees, achieved after three years of privation. His joy in free intellectual adventure, however, was never dampened. At the Collège de France he studied Sanskrit with Eugène Burnouf, who introduced him to Bopp's comparative linguistic method. Lectures at the Sorbonne on medieval literature kindled enthusiasm for popular, anonymous writing, which recalled the legends and superstitious lore of his Breton childhood. Friendship with the young Marcellin Berthelot, later an illustrious name in organic chemistry, widened and deepened Renan's knowledge of natural science, moving in the eighteen forties toward the solution of the greatest problem of origins, the origin of species. In a notebook of 1845 or 1846 Renan wrote: "The law of continuity, or more simply the law of rudimentary degradation (such and such a member in rudiment, and then developing), which recurs throughout comparative anatomy, comparative linguistics, comparative psychology, . . . comparative ethnography (races of men joined by insensible transitions), proves the unity of all systems of things whatsoever, their common generation."[4] Berthelot won him also to democratic opinions, and he went to hear Michelet lecture on the French Revolution in the stirring year 1848. Though there were holes in his shoes, he could write in his Journal: "I am nothing but fire, hope, life and future."[5]

At the close of three years crowded with study and tutoring he found time to expound his enthusiasms in *The Future of Science*, which deserves to stand beside Herder's *Journal of 1769* among the most learned, thoughtful, and high-minded books written by young men. Its inspiration, Renan said, was "the happy combination of poetry, erudition and philosophy" made by German writers, especially Herder and Goethe, "a combination which in my mind constitutes the true thinker."[6] The title would have been *The Future of Philosophy*, Renan tells us, if that word had not become technical and narrow. Science must be understood in its widest sense as systematic knowledge of every sort; but there was no word to "express that intellectual state in which all the elements of human nature unite in a superior harmony, and which, realized in a human being, would constitute the perfect man. I am willing to call it synthesis."[7]

The impulse to this confession of faith in the power of knowledge to perfect mankind had come when in February, 1848, he found the way to his Sanskrit class unexpectedly barred by revolutionary barricades. "That day I asked myself more seriously than ever whether there was anything better to do than to devote every moment of one's life to study and thought. After having consulted my conscience and affirmed my faith in human intellect, very resolutely I answered: 'No.' " [8] Renan believed that relieving the masses from economic exploitation and giving them leisure would open to them the accumulated results of thought: "There will be no happiness until all are equal, but there will be no equality until all are perfect. What sorrow for the scholar and the thinker to see themselves, because of their very excellence, isolated from humanity, having their world apart, their belief apart!" [9] The zeal of his reluctantly renounced priestly calling breathes through this reflection.

Man must know nature and know himself, was Renan's thesis, if he is to realize his full possibilities. The sciences were teaching him to control his environment and to banish his fear of the supernatural. Less known was the recent advance in the supremely difficult technique of understanding human nature. "The science of a being who is in a perpetual state of becoming can only be his history. The science of languages means the history of languages; the science of literature and religion means the history of literatures and religions. The science of the human intellect means the history of the human intellect. To attempt to seize a given moment, only, of these successive existences in order to dissect it, to examine it fixedly, is simply to falsify their nature." [10] Historical studies made a great leap forward when they broke away from the static, rigid conceptions of mathematics, physics, and religious dogma. The history of humanity is not only the story of its enfranchisement, as Michelet told it; it is above all the story of its education, which Hegel has described most clearly as "the story of a being developing itself by its own inner force, creating itself and arriving by diverse stages at full possession of itself." [11] That process begins with the primitive mind, best represented by the ancient religions. "Open the sacred books of primitive peoples, and what do you find? All the suprasensible life, all the soul of a nation. There is its poetry; there are its heroic memories; there is its legislation, its politics, its ethics; there is its history; there is its philosophy and science; there, in a word, is its religion." [12]

Only recently had it been possible to trace the growth of the human mind out of such beginnings; for hitherto languages and literatures, its chief records, had not been read properly. "The ancients knew no language but their own, and only the classical and settled form of that language.... They did not have the experience of a sufficient number of literary revolutions. They could not compare enough literatures to rise very high in aesthetic criticism." [13] The realization that languages had a history had come only in the fifteenth century, the comparative study of language only in the nineteenth. Comparative literature appeared tardily near the close of the eighteenth century, after a literary revolution had shattered faith in an absolute standard of taste. Acceptance of relativity in taste encouraged relative appraisal of states of civilization. Renan reviewed the triumphs of the historical revival initiated by linguistic and literary study, all that is associated with the names of Vico, Herder, Eichhorn, Wolf, Niebuhr, Jakob Grimm, Bopp, Müller, Chateaubriand, Scott, Thierry, and Michelet.

He proclaimed his faith in its future. "To construct the history of the human mind, one must be soaked in literature. Here the laws are exceedingly delicate, and do not present themselves to us directly, as in the physical sciences. The necessary faculty is that of the literary critic: delicacy in the turn of expression (it is the *turn* which usually expresses most), tenuity of perception, the contrary of the geometric spirit.... Delicate and subtle minds alone are equipped for the truth in the historical and moral sciences, as exact minds in mathematics. The truths of criticism are not on the surface; they have almost the air of paradoxes."[14] But delicacy and subtlety must be founded upon learning and thought. The perfect historian has himself investigated original documents minutely, and knows how to extract value from the minute researches of others, even when they have the appearance of useless pedantry. For he has also striven after the widest general knowledge, after the universality of a Herder. "I feel," said Renan, "that if I had ten human lives to live simultaneously, so as to be able to explore all the worlds, I being at the center, sniffing the perfume of everything, judging and comparing, combining and making inductions, I should get at the system of things."[15] The essence of this union of exact and universal knowledge with subtle evaluation is philosophy, in the true sense of the word. "Philosophy is not a science apart; it is one side of all the sciences."[16]

Still largely unexplored by subtle and profound philosophy was the greatest human achievement, the Christian religion. The setting of Christianity apart from things human has done it injustice.

It is time to proclaim the fact that one sole cause has wrought everything in the domain of intellect: the human mind, operating according to identical laws, but in different environments. . . . A history of philosophy that devotes one volume to Plato should, it seems, devote two to Jesus; and nevertheless this name will perhaps never be mentioned once. It is not the historian's fault. It is the fault of the position of Jesus. Such is the fate of everything that has arrived at religious consecration. How much Hebrew literature, so admirable, so original, has suffered in the eyes of learning and taste in becoming the Bible![17]

Renan announced that, in his maturity, he would attempt to write "the most important book of the nineteenth century,"[18] a history of the origins of Christianity.

All is to be divined. Neither Christians, Jews nor Pagans have handed down to us anything *historical* concerning its first appearance or concerning its principal hero. But criticism can rediscover the history beneath the legend, or at least re-draw the characteristic physiognomy of the epoch and its products. . . . Religions must be criticized in the same way as primitive poems.[19]

Such a book would crown the century's study of origins. It would make Europeans conscious of the nature of their own spiritual and mental culture, and would redeem for the masses their greatest heritage, the social gospel of Jesus. "My lot," Renan declared, "will always be with the disinherited." [20] After having seen the shooting in cold blood of insurgent prisoners taken in the street fighting of June, 1848, he had written to his sister: "No doubt they are guilty, these poor fools who shed their blood without even knowing what they want: but those are even more guilty, in my eyes, who have kept them in Helotism, systematically brutalizing their human feelings, and, to serve their selfish interests, have created a class of men whose interest is in disorder and pillage." [21]

Distinguished essays on the Semitic languages and on Greek during the Middle Ages won for Renan a commission from the Ministry of Public Instruction to make a census of the Semitic manuscripts in Italian libraries. He traveled in Italy from October, 1849, to June, 1850. Observation of the enthusiastic welcome the populace of Rome gave the Pope whom it had driven from the city only two years before made him reflect bitterly on the fickleness of the mob. On the way to the Doric temples at Paestum he encountered "real savages, almost without religion, barely clothed, with no cultivation, mere herds clad in skins of beasts" and speaking a horrible local jargon. "I have seen the limits of civilization," he wrote Berthelot, "and have been frightened, like a man striking his foot against a wall when he thought infinite space was ahead. That experience gave me the most melancholy feeling in my life. I trembled for civilization, seeing it so limited, so insecure, resting on so few individuals even in the country where it prevails. For how many men are there in Europe who really belong to the nineteenth century? And what are we, the scouts, the vanguard, before this inertia, this herd of brutes that follows us? Ah, if one day they should throw themselves at us and refuse to follow!" [22] But the Italians, who had awakened such fears, had much to give. A race with taste, they derived great pleasure simply from being alive. "The populace here says: beautiful, very beautiful. At home the word beautiful rarely issues from the mouth of a common man." [23] Entire cities, Siena, Pisa, Florence, were works of art. The long history of the Italian peninsula had taught a certain detachment from the anxieties of the present. "One of the most charming qualities of the Italian character is . . . a sort of *alibi*, that keeps despair from ever becoming extreme." [24]

Renan had need of this ability to observe life as an aesthetic spectacle when he returned in the summer of 1850 to a France which, after choosing Louis-Napoleon as President by universal suffrage, had seen him moving steadily toward the suppression of democratic institutions. Augustin Thierry warned that the time was not propitious for so bold a book as *The Future of Science*, and advised its publication piecemeal as magazine articles. Renan accepted this advice the more readily because his feeling for art, fully awakened in Italy, made him conscious of the heaviness of his style. The nation's acquiescence in Louis-Napoleon's *coup d'état* of December, 1851, completed his disgust with public opinion. The masses had evident need of a long period of education. He could not applaud Michelet's sacrifice of his posts rather than take the oath of allegiance, for this implied that "everything that is done and everything that happens ought to be taken seriously. . . .

It is clear that for a very long time we must stand aside from politics."[25] Yet the social situation saddened him profoundly. Late in life he retained vivid memory of "those gloomy years 1849, 1850, 1851, when the human mind was governed by its enemies, and the first ten years of the Empire, when everything not mediocre or frivolous was considered dangerous."[26]

Supported by a curatorship of Oriental and medieval manuscripts at the National Library, he employed those years in gathering materials for his life's work on the origins of Christianity, and in preparing an attractive presentation to a wide public by writing for periodicals. His marriage in 1856 to a niece of the Dutch painter Ary Scheffer brought him into a circle of artists and musicians and fostered his interest in style.

Renan's periodical writings, collected in two volumes, *Studies in the History of Religion* (1857) and *Ethical and Critical Essays* (1859), develop and refine the point of view of *The Future of Science*, which was not to appear in its original form until 1890. A memorial to his recently deceased friend Thierry examines the reasons why history has been "the characteristic and original creation" of recent years.

The amplitude of the events which signalized the end of the last century and the beginning of our own, the number and variety of incidents that followed, the great exercise for our reflection in grasping the play and laws of human revolutions, all this forms an excellent condition for understanding the past. . . . Nowhere before our time do I find the immediate feeling for the life of the past. . . . Our century was the first to have that kind of finesse which grasps, within the apparently colorless uniformity of ancient accounts, traits of manners and character which no longer have analogues in the present state of society.[27]

Renan defended warmly Thierry's innovations.

Every generalization is open to attack, and the only way to write history which escapes criticism is the flat manner which limits itself to insignificant particulars. But what am I saying? That is the falsest way of all, and the pretended exactitude of which it is so proud is at bottom only a lie. The imagination, which exclusively erudite historians proscribe with so many anathemas, has often more chance of finding truth than a servile fidelity, content to reproduce the original accounts of chroniclers. . . . History is not one of those studies antiquity called *umbratiles,* for which a calm mind and industrious habits suffice. It touches the deepest problems of human life: it requires the whole man with all his passions. Soul is as necessary to it as to a poem or work of art, and the individuality of the writer should be reflected in it.[28]

But Romantic practice receives an emphasis and a qualification which are Renan's own: "History is as much an art as a science; perfection of form is essential to it. . . . There is no exaggeration in saying that a badly arranged sentence always corresponds to an inexact thought."[29] In an essay on *The Religions of Antiquity* he remarks: "To write the history of a religion, it is necessary not to believe in it any longer, but also necessary to have believed in it."[30] Sympathy must be balanced by detachment.

Religion, like all living products of humanity, is subject to change; but the change has been so gradual as often to have escaped observation. "Christianity brought at first so little alteration in domestic and social life that it remains uncertain, in the case of a great body of men of consequence in the fourth and fifth centuries, whether they were pagans or Christians."[31] To make widely known the results of the historical study of religion, was to benefit religion. "In our day, religion cannot separate itself from spiritual delicacy or intellectual culture. I believe I have been doing it a service in endeavoring to transport it into the region of the unassailable, beyond particular dogmas and supernatural beliefs."[32] Religion should be the prime interest of the historian because it endures. "Possibly all we love, all that adorns life for us, may be destined to endure only for an age. But religion will not die. It will be the eternal protest of the spirit against organized or brutal materialism, which would imprison man in the lower region of vulgar life. Civilization has its intermittences, but religion has none." [33]

In 1860, Napoleon the Third began to conciliate the intellectual and the working classes by allowing considerable freedom of the press and the formation of an opposition party. Renan felt free to respond by accepting the leadership of an official expedition to explore the archeology of Phoenicia. As a rest from the strenuous task of supervising excavation on the torrid seacoast, he visited Palestine. The contrast of the fruitful region about the Sea of Galilee with the stern barrenness of the environs of Jerusalem provided an explanation of the preaching of Jesus which set him at length to writing his long-meditated *History of the Origins of Christianity*. Among the mountains of Lebanon, he composed rapidly a first volume, *The Life of Jesus*. "Delicious hours, and too soon sped, oh! may eternity resemble you! From morn to eve I was intoxicated by the thoughts unrolling before me. With them I went to sleep, and the first ray of sun behind the mountain gave them back to me clearer and more vivid than the day before." [34]

How Renan worked to give this volume its final form on his return to Paris, we see through the eyes of the disapproving but fascinated historian Hippolyte Taine.

He read me a large portion of his life of Jesus. He is remaking this life delicately, but arbitrarily. The documents are too much altered, too uncertain. For the period of Nazareth he puts together all the gentle and agreeable ideas of Jesus, removes the gloomy ones, and makes a charming mystical pastoral. Then, in another chapter, he gathers every threat, every bitterness, and attaches these to the journey to Jerusalem. . . . In vain Berthelot and I tell him that this is putting a novel in place of the legend; that he is spoiling the parts that are certain with an admixture of hypothesis. He will hear nothing, sees his idea only, says that we are not artists, that a merely positive and dogmatic treatise will not restore the life Jesus lived and must be made to live again. . . . Above all, he is a passionate man, obsessed with his ideas, obsessed nervously. He walked up and down my room as in a cage, with the gestures, the laconic, jerky tone of half-somnambulist invention. He is strikingly different from Berthelot, who is tranquil as a patient laboring ox, chewing the cud of his idea and dwelling upon it. Renan is completely incapable of precise formulas, does not move from one precise truth to another. He tastes, he feels about, he has *impressions*, a word that expresses everything.[35]

The Life of Jesus was published in 1863, when Renan was forty. Six other volumes completed the *Origins* within eighteen years. In those years of celebrity he was a familiar figure to Parisians as he crossed the Seine from his home on the Left Bank: a short, fat, stooped figure with impressive, deep-set eyes, who sometimes hurried along, sometimes stopped short to gesticulate, fist in air, at an unseen controversialist.

His original plan of a systematic account of the development of Christian doctrine had vanished at the sight of Palestine and its people. "All that history which, at a distance, seems to float in the clouds of an unreal world," thus took on "a body, a solidity," which strengthened his conviction that "history is not a simple play of abstractions, that men are more important in it than doctrines."[36] The personality of Jesus, minimized by liberal Christian theologians out of fear of including him among the Jewish believers in a Messiah and an Apocalypse, and reduced by the German scholar David Strauss' *Life of Jesus* (1835) to a philosophical conception, assumed the central position. "His glory does not consist in his being put apart from history; we render him a truer worship by showing that all history is incomprehensible without him."[37] He was greater than the Gospels tell; for his disciples must often have reduced him to their compass, often misunderstood him. Above all, he was "a man of charm," and his charm ensured his survival in the hearts of those who loved him. Renan interpreted Jesus' conception of his mission in terms of the Romantic theory of genius. Jesus never professed to be God in a wholly superhuman sense, but "the idea he has of man is not the humble idea introduced by a cold Deism. In his poetic conception of nature, a single inspiration pervades the universe; the inspiration of man is the inspiration of God. God lives in man, lives by man, just as man lives in God, lives by God." [38] The propitious moment in history lifted Jesus to sublimity unparalleled.

Each branch in the development of humanity, art, poetry, religion, meets, in traversing the ages, a privileged epoch, in which it attains perfection without effort by virtue of a sort of spontaneous instinct. What the beautiful ages of Greece were for secular arts and letters, the century of Jesus was for religion. . . . It was one of those divine hours when great things come about by the spontaneous conspiracy of a thousand hidden forces, when fine spirits find a flood of sympathy to sustain them.[39]

This sustaining environment Renan recreated for his readers out of diverse materials: out of knowledge of Semitic languages, literatures, customs and thought; out of parallels with the revolutionary times in France, where the Saint-Simonians and Lamennais had recently revived the social gospel of Jesus; out of memories of simple fisher folk in his native Brittany; out of impressions of Galilee and Judea, which he describes with an eye for local color rivaling Chateaubriand's. The first hearers of the Beatitudes are characterized in terms of the Romantic doctrine of the beneficence of nature.

The fine climate of Galilee made the existence of those honest fishermen a perpetual enchantment. Simple, good, happy, rocked softly on their delightful little sea or sleeping at night on its banks, they offered a true prelude to the Kingdom of God. It is hard to imagine the intoxication of life thus flowing under the open sky, the soft and vital flame engendered by this perpetual contact with nature, the dreams of those nights passed under the brilliant stars, beneath a blue dome of infinite depth. . . . The world perhaps unveiled its secret to the divinely lucid conscience of those happy children, who by the purity of their hearts merited one day to see God face to face.[40]

Such men loved Jesus' precepts because he gave them a poetic form they lacked in the Mosaic Law and in the sayings of the rabbis.

His preaching was suave and soft, full of nature and the perfume of the fields. The birds of the air, the sea, the mountains, passed into his teaching. . . . But the feeling, the image, the style, are essentially Jewish. He descends in direct line from Isaiah, the Psalmists, the Prophets of the time of the Captivity, from the author of the Song of Songs, and sometimes from the author of Ecclesiastes.[41]

His demand for community of goods met favorable response from men whose few wants were easily satisfied by a bountiful nature.

But in Jerusalem, Jesus preached at a disadvantage: "his imagination, his love of nature, were cramped within those walls." [42] There his artistry found vent in satire. "That Nessus shirt of ridicule which the Jew, son of the Pharisees, still wears in tatters after eighteen centuries, Jesus wove with divine artifice. Masterpieces of high raillery, his epithets are written in lines of fire on the skin of the hypocrite and the false bigot. Incomparable epithets, worthy of a son of God! Only a god could slay thus. Socrates and Molière merely strip off the skin. This man carries fire and rage to the very marrow of the bones. But it was just that this great master of irony should pay for triumph with his life." [43]

The originality of Jesus lay in his bringing the finest insights of the Prophets to their logical conclusion in "absolute religion"; religion without restriction of race, without holy places, without priests, without ritual, a religion of brotherhood, of liberty, of spirit and truth. He gave no fixed dogma, but symbols susceptible of interpretation indefinitely. His demand for nothing short of perfection has made the true Christian never content with the existing state of society; the perfect injustice of his crucifixion casts eternal suspicion on the infallibility of Church and State. His life encourages mankind by showing how close to perfection man may come. "Humanity, taken in the mass, is an assemblage of low egoists, superior to the animals only in the greater rationality of their egoism. Nevertheless, in the midst of this uniform vulgarity, columns rise toward the sky to bear witness of a more noble destiny. Jesus is the loftiest of those columns which show man whence he comes and whither he is going." [44]

Jesus left nothing in writing. For a generation after his crucifixion his disciples were so convinced of the imminent end of the world that they did not think of recording their memories. The authorship of the Gospels is uncertain and much of the record of the early Church anonymous. The Gospels are the earliest written examples of popular, colloquial Greek, as distinguished from classical. But Greek was not the first language in which the story of Jesus was set down. As an international tongue, it had been adopted for proselyting purposes by writers who, like Jesus, spoke Aramaic, or Syro-Chaldaic, as Renan called it, which as a consequence of the Captivity had replaced Hebrew as the spoken language of the Jews. Thus the New Testament offered Renan the supreme example of popular literature and of the growth of legend out of oral tradition.

It is in an obscure dialect, without literary culture, that was traced the first sketch of the book which has charmed souls. . . . Thus was begun by an unconscious genius this masterpiece of spontaneous art, the Gospel; not one or another of the Gospels, but that kind of unfixed poem, that unwritten masterpiece, in which every fault is a beauty, and whose very indefiniteness has been the principal condition of its success. A finished portrait of Jesus, fixed, classic, would not have had so much attractiveness.[45]

From the classical point of view the Greek text has neither style, plan nor beauty; the mental processes are those of men who thought in another tongue, Aramaic. But that invisible Semitic idiom carried into Europe an intoxicating Asiatic literary flavor. "Those absolute expressions, stiff, without shading—that tongue in which everything is black or white, sun or darkness, which in order to say: 'I love Jacob more than Esau,' says, 'I love Jacob, I hate Esau'—have seduced the world with their harsh grandeur. Our races are not accustomed to this Oriental amplitude, to this energetic decisiveness, to this way of presenting everything of a piece and by leaps. They were conquered, overwhelmed by it. Even today, this style is the great force of Christianity, that which charms souls and wins them to Jesus."[46] The Gospels, too, told a story completely to the taste of the masses, a story "in which the priest is always wrong, in which respectable people are all hypocrites, in which lawful authorities exhibit themselves as scoundrels, in which all the rich are damned."[47] The New Testament introduced into the world "a novel idea, that of popular beauty."[48]

What had been learned about the general characteristics of popular literature and the growth of legend guided Renan in his interpretation of Christian origins. When New Testament authors draw from the Prophets and from the Messianic ideal a framework and coloring for the real life of Jesus, he knows that they are "no more impostors than the authors of the Homeric poems, than Chrétien de Troyes";[49] for they are merely writing in a literary tradition. The account in the Acts of the Apostles of completely harmonious cooperation between Peter and Paul reminds Renan of the popular legend of the French Revolution, which reconciles Danton with Robespierre, Voltaire with Rousseau.

Nowhere have the complementary historical laws of change and continuity been displayed more perfectly than in Renan's six volumes which trace Christian origins for the century and a half after the death of Jesus. Gradually, almost imperceptibly, Christianity breaks its ties with Judaism. Gradually, almost imperceptibly, it acquires a theology, chiefly from Paul, who never heard Jesus preach, and from Greek philosophy; it acquires a ritual, notably from the Gnostic heretics; it establishes a canon of sacred books; it reconciles itself to the possibility that the end of the world may be delayed considerably, and begins to tolerate private property; its iconoclastic hatred of pagan art turns into a tendency to develop an art of its own. Commemoration of martyrs sows the seed of worship of intercessory saints; Mary the Mother of Jesus gains importance in Christian tradition. Slowly, almost imperceptibly, Christianity organizes itself into a Church, in which an original democracy yields to the absolute authority of bishops. Gradually its uncompromising detachment from the State yields to a desire for governmental recognition. The administrative divisions of the Church follow the political subdivisions of the Empire as decreed by Augustus. "The Empire became the mold in which the new religion coagulated." [50] By the end of the reign of Marcus Aurelius in 180 A.D., paganism was doomed. But Christianity, about to triumph, had become something Jesus would scarcely have recognized as his own. Nevertheless, his authentic message was preserved in the Gospels; and it still has a great work to do in the world. "What makes Christianity live is the little we know of the words and the personality of Jesus. The ideal man, the divine poet, the great artist, alone defies time and revolutions." [51]

Throughout the *Origins* runs Renan's warning to contemporary Europe that culture confined to an élite is too fragile to survive, that no idea can long endure if it does not strike root in the masses. Christianity triumphed because antique culture neglected the spiritual, emotional, intellectual and material needs of the people. Science, philosophy, and the graces of life suffered a great setback; for the early Christian "will have the defects of his qualities. He will declare vain and frivolous many things that are not so. He will make the universe small; he will be the enemy or scorner of beauty. A system in which the Venus of Milo is only an idol is a false or at least a partial system, for beauty has almost as great worth as goodness and truth." [52]

Contemplative, more interested in ideas and taste than in action, Renan was perturbed by the great gulf between the ideal harmony of truth, beauty and virtue, and the behavior of mankind as history reveals it. *The Origins of Christianity*, one of the supreme histories of ideas, showed that "humanity is a diverse thing, changing, pulled about by contradictory desires." [53] When accepted by it, ideas pure and logical in themselves undergo such strange transformations that historical trends are almost impossible to predict. How quickly Christianity detached itself from the Ebionites, who preserved Jesus' gospel of poverty and community of goods. "A law of this world decrees that every founder rapidly becomes a stranger, an excommunicate, then an enemy, in his own school, and that, if he persists in living long, those who derive from him are obliged to take measures against him as a dangerous man." [54] The tragic failure of the saint and sage Marcus Aurelius, though clothed with the absolute power of a Roman Emperor, to do much good or to prevent much ill, drew from Renan the reflection: "The great inconvenience of real life and that which renders it unbearable for the superior man is that, if one transfers to it the principles of the ideal life, qualities be-

HISTORY AS ART

come defects; so much so that often the accomplished man has less success in it than he who has for motives egoism or ordinary routine." [55] In view of the small encouragement the human race gives to virtue and industriousness in its rulers, he was surprised that the functions of king and emperor still found conscientious men to fill them.

With so many high hopes shattered in the France and in the Europe of his time, Renan had come to protect himself against heartbreak by accepting this division between the ideal and the real, and by looking upon history with aesthetic detachment. Writing the Preface to his fourth volume, *Anti-Christ*, in 1873, while France was being "consumed in a slow agony" after defeat by Germany, he confesses: "I will not hide the fact that the taste for history, the incomparable pleasure felt in seeing the spectacle of humanity unroll, has especially drawn me on in this volume." A volume in which the main stage is occupied by Nero, a monstrous caricature of the artist, and by fanatic Jewish nationalists who defend Jerusalem until it is utterly destroyed, while the future belongs to the obscure Christian martyrs. With incomparable pliability Renan enters the mind of the Jew, the Roman, the Greek, the Christian proselyte, seeing the world momentarily with the eyes of each and thereby becoming the more convinced of the relativity of his own opinions, of the possible truth of opposites. He reproaches Saint Paul with having been so completely a man of action as apparently never to have doubted himself, never to have opened the delightful book of Ecclesiastes; whereas his master Jesus "possessed to a superlative degree what we consider the essential quality of a distinguished person, the gift of smiling at his work, of being superior to it, not letting it obsess him." [56]

In 1890, two years before his death, Renan at length published *The Future of Science*. He made no revisions, for he desired it to show "in his uncorrupted state . . . a young man living solely with his own mind and believing fanatically in the truth. . . . Like Hegel, I made the mistake of attributing too confidently to mankind a central part in the universe. The whole of human development may be of no more consequence than the moss or lichen that covers every moist surface."[57] The logic of relativity could no further go. Nevertheless, he reiterates the faith of his youth, now dissociated from social hopes. "To us idealists a single doctrine is true, the transcendental doctrine according to which the goal of humanity is a loftier consciousness of the universe, or, as we used to say, the greatest glory of God. . . . Such an aim . . . must be carefully dissimulated. Men would revolt if they knew they were being thus exploited."[58]

The Swiss city of Basel, which in the eighteenth century had produced Iselin, with his zeal for world culture, a century later produced in Jakob Burckhardt a historian of similar zeal, but without confidence that it was toward culture that the world was moving. German-speaking, he attended the Universities of Berlin and Bonn. The Germany he found in the eighteen thirties and forties was turning away from philosophy and poetry to politics, economics, and applied science, and giving historical writing a decidedly political and scientific cast. At Berlin, where he studied for three years, Leopold Ranke ruled in history, followers of Hegel in philosophy and in the history of art. A comparison of the portraits of Louis the Eleventh and Charles the Bold in Scott's *Quentin Durward* and in the *Memoirs* of Commines had given Ranke so strong a preference for the latter that he had resolved to "avoid all invention and imagination" and "stick to facts." He was now putting extraordinary energy into the attempt to make of history an objective science. His seminar taught the young Swiss to criticize source materials and sent him to Paris to study diplomatic documents; but it failed to satisfy him. "History is still in large measure poetry to me," he wrote to a friend. Turning to the history of art, he found that cluttered with the technical vocabulary of Hegelian aesthetics. Hegel and Ranke agreed in representing history as a providential process, in which every event and circumstance was justified in the light of the whole. Burckhardt balked at this blanket acceptance of the past, and especially at acquiescence in the present course of Europe. Great cities, London, Berlin, Paris, were threatening to extinguish the distinctive culture of old towns like his native Basel.[59] Prussia was winning the smaller German States to the worship of military and economic power. His heart was with the older culture, with Winckelmann, Gluck, and Mozart, with Schiller and Goethe, with Boeckh and with his Berlin teacher, Jakob Grimm. He was happier in transferring his studies to Bonn, with its Rhineland atmosphere of Teutonic legend and the Middle Ages. But a post on a Basel newspaper dragged him back to the discouraging problems of modern life.

Release from the confines of German civilization and of the contemporary world began with his visit to Italy in 1846. From there, Burckhardt wrote to a friend: "You bookies wager yourselves ever deeper into this incurable epoch—I on the contrary have very quietly but completely fallen out with it and so have escaped into the beautiful lazy South, which has become dead to history, and as a quiet, wonderful monument should refresh me, tired of modernity, with its antique awe." [60] The events of 1848, which seemed to offer Europe a choice between outworn aristocracy, crass plutocracy, and a socialistic bureaucracy, confirmed this attitude. Holding with Goethe that the only conflict in which it was worth taking sides was the conflict between culture and barbarism, he resolved to uphold culture as an individual, even if it were no longer the concern of a considerable group. The seventh volume of Michelet's *History of France* (1855), which defended the Renaissance against the charge of having produced nothing but skepticism by emphasizing its "discovery of the world, discovery of man" and its figures of heroic stature, like Michelangelo, encouraged Burckhardt's individualism. In 1860 he published *The Culture of the Renaissance in Italy*, an investigation into the origins of the self-sufficiency of the modern European man of distinction.

The opening chapter, "The State as a Work of Art," emphasized continuity. It was the loosening of feudal ties which brought into power in thirteenth-century Italy illegitimate rulers, rulers having need to enlist in support of their usurpation men of talent without regard for birth or rank. Rending the "veil" of the Middle Ages, "woven from faith, childish trust and illusion," [61] these men rationalized administration, finance, the arts of war and diplomacy. Latin literature and the ruins and remnants of Roman architecture and art woke Italians to remembrance of the greatness that had once been on their soil, the greatness of men who were neither soldiers nor saints. Recognition of new kinds of distinction added artists and men of letters to the men of talent drawn to the illegitimate courts, in which the example of classical antiquity had aroused thirst for glory of every sort. Literature felt the impulse to individual distinction before the other arts. Dante's *Vita nuova* is the first example since antiquity of self-conscious artistry which joins form and content in indissoluble perfection. Form was developed so highly that those without artistic nature are incapable of judging Ariosto, however intelligent and learned they may be.

At the courts, social life became an art. Manners, conversation, language were refined; amateurism in all the arts was encouraged. From the courts, the art of living spread to the middle class. Women were accepted as equals, as individuals. Children were encouraged to a self-respect which prompts Burckhardt to a sneer at the preoccupations of the Ranke school of historians: "A history of whipping among Germanic and Latin peoples, carried out thoroughly and in a philosophic spirit, should indeed be worth as much as a few volumes of despatches and negotiations. When, and through what influence, has corporal punishment become a daily practice in German families? It must have been long after Walter sang, *Nieman kan mit gerten Kindes zuht beherten.* [Walther von der Vogelweide, "No one can improve a child's training with the rod."] In Italy, at least, striking stops very early; a child of seven is no longer struck." [62] In the Renaissance, dress expressed individuality, whereas "our era, which at least in men's clothing respects inconspicuousness as the highest law, thus renounces something greater than it realizes. But it spares itself much time, which (according to our business standard) outweighs every disadvantage." [63]

The all-embracing art of life included revenge; the imaginativeness that gave Italians the virtues of gratitude and sociability made them gamblers and feudists; the individualism allowing full scope to genius also fostered monsters whose egoism regarded neither man nor God. Burckhardt never concealed the dark side of the Renaissance nor refrained from moral judgment, as did his younger friend Nietzsche. He stresses the lingering of astrology beside the new science, the wavering between humanism and other-worldliness, as characteristics of an era of transition. But the era gave a foretaste of what is best in modern man. "This worldliness was serious, uplifted by poetry and art. It is a noble necessity of the modern spirit, that it cannot shake these things off, that it is drawn irresistibly to investigate men and nature, and considers this its vocation." [64] Pico della Mirandola declared that the individual man could not only draw God down to him in prayer; he could also rise, through love, to God's infinity in the universe.

In its form, *The Culture of the Renaissance* illustrates the individual flavor, the harmony and balance it extolls in life. In protest against recent German insistence upon printing every detail of evidence as a guarantee of thoroughness, Burckhardt is suggestive rather than exhaustive, content to choose those aspects of his subject of the greatest interest to himself and leave the rest to others. Where tangible evidence on some important topic is scanty, he vindicates his right of conjecture in terms that recall Niebuhr and Renan: "The substantiating phenomena to which we refer are few. Here, if anywhere in this delineation, the author has the feeling that he has entered into the precarious realm of conjecture, and that what floats before his eyes as delicate yet clear shading in the spiritual history of the fourteenth and fifteenth centuries may scarcely be recognized as fact by others. This gradual clarification of the soul of a people is a phenomenon which may appear different to each observer. Time will sift and judge." [65]

England, almost alone among Western nations, escaped revolution in the eighteenth and nineteenth centuries. This escape her ruling classes attributed largely to the conservative influence of Evangelical Christianity upon her lower classes, and historians have found abundant evidence to support this belief. The masses had so much reason for revolt that "a panic fear of change" reigned in Britain long after the crowning victory of Waterloo. As the chance of contagion from French revolutionary principles passed, this fear transferred itself to the subtler danger that German historical scholarship might unsettle the minds of the British people by removing the Bible from among things fixed and immutable. As early as 1799,

HISTORY AS ART

Niebuhr was amazed to find that, in Edinburgh, Germans had the reputation of atheists. The English translation in 1828–1832 of his *History of Rome*, although the work of the Anglican clergymen Hare and Thirlwall, was reprehended vigorously because its criticism of Roman origins might suggest similar criticism of Christian origins.[66] This state of public opinion discouraged British historians from study of primitive societies, of origins and development. Developmental studies in science were conducted with the utmost caution. The geologist Lyell took care not to suggest the wide implications of his uniformitarian theory.

The unhistorical conception of the Scriptures to which the majority of educated Englishmen clung, even in the middle of the nineteenth century, is illustrated in its extreme form by what Edmund Gosse has recorded concerning his father, a zoologist of repute, and his mother.

For her, and for my Father, nothing was symbolic, nothing allegorical or allusive in any part of Scripture, except what was, in so many words, proffered as a parable or a picture. Pushing this to its extreme limit, and allowing nothing for changes of scene or time or race, my parents read injunctions to the Corinthian converts without any suspicion that what was apposite in dealing with half-breed Achaian converts of the first century might not exactly apply to respectable English men and women of the nineteenth. . . . This was curiously exemplified in the very lively interest they both took in what is called "the interpretation of prophecy," and particularly in unwrapping the dark sayings bound up in the Book of Revelation. In their impartial survey of the Bible, they came to this collection of solemn and splendid visions, sinister and obscure, and they had no intention of allowing these to be merely stimulating to the fancy, or vaguely doctrinal in symbol. When they read of seals broken and of vials poured forth, of the star that was called Wormwood that fell from Heaven, and of men whose hair was as the hair of women, and their teeth as the teeth of lions, they did not admit for a moment that these mental pictures were of a poetic character, but regarded them as positive statements, in guarded language, describing events that were to happen, and could be recognized when they did happen.[67]

The belated unloosing of the historical spirit was like the bursting of a dam. The almost simultaneous impact upon the British public of *The Origin of Species* (1859), of Huxley's *Man's Place in Nature* (1860) and of *Essays and Reviews* (1860) by Anglican clergymen who accepted many of the conclusions of Continental Biblical scholarship, resembled that of Voltaire upon readers of Bossuet. As battles a century old were fought over again on English soil, there was danger that the moral authority of the Scriptures might be undermined, their beauty and greatness as literature lost. To prevent this disaster Matthew Arnold intervened between the contending parties. He had inherited the historical point of view from his father, the distinguished clergyman and teacher Thomas Arnold, whose *History of Rome* (1842) accepted Niebuhr's conclusions. Personally acquainted with Michelet and Renan, the son had read the German Biblical scholars upon whom Renan leaned. Although feeling keenly Renan's gibes at the backwardness of the English mind in history, he was even more concerned with the menace of its literal habit to poetry. For poetry could not thrive where symbol, allegory, myth, and legend were not understood; and the chief source of misunderstanding was the Bible, when taken wholly as scientific fact and fixed dogma.

Matthew Arnold's *Literature and Dogma* (1873) contrasted two approaches to the Scriptures: the dogmatic, which was static, arid, mechanical, and the literary, which upheld their authority as the best record of the growth of religious and moral consciousness. Arnold's niece, Mrs. Humphry Ward, a student of Spanish Christianity before Charlemagne, brought his point of view to a wider public. In her novel, *Robert Elsmere*, a young English clergyman comes upon the historical criticism of the Bible, accepts it after inner conflict, and feels obliged to leave the Anglican ministry in order to present the modern view of Christianity to the working classes. The sale of almost a million copies of this work of fiction in English-speaking countries during the twenty years following its publication in 1888 shows the rapid spread of an historical sense at the close of the nineteenth century.

The story of Robert Elsmere had a parallel in the decision of the author's friend, John Richard Green, to leave the ministry in order to write history. Born and educated at Oxford, the most beautiful survival of the English medieval city, Green early became interested in local antiquities, which went back to Roman and Celtic times. As he was completing his studies at the University, Darwin, geology, and the historical view of the Bible were putting human origins immensely farther back than the 4004 B.C. of Archbishop Usher's chronology. Green's well-known letter to his fellow student Dawkins, later a teacher of geology, describing Thomas Huxley's crushing retort to the attempt of the Bishop of Oxford to "smash Darwin," hails the discovery of mammal remains in Triassic deposits near Bath as "an ordinary link in the common series of animal life. Strongly Darwinian, eh? and strongly common-sense too." [68]

The discovery of human remains the next year in a Somersetshire cave opened exciting vistas of prehistory. Green wrote to Dawkins in a charming mixture of banter and seriousness:

Barrows, I myself think solemn humbugs—pretending to an antiquity which reaches no farther back than the later Roman Empire. But the Cave, with its Celts, if rightly worked, might really throw a flood of light on the field which science will have to delve in for the next half century, the period of man's origins. . . . I don't suppose that word of mine would influence your arranged plans, but interesting as "the anticlinal axis of old Red," "the flexions and dips" of the Mendip range may be, Man and Man's history to my mind is worth them all. . . . *Nihil geologicum a me alienum puto*, but still Trilobites and Echini are only king crabs and starfishes, while Man is Man.[69]

With this warm regard for humanity and with the realistic understanding of a poor tailor's son, Green felt the appeal of the Christian Socialism of Maurice and Kingsley. He entered the Anglican Church, although he confessed to reading "Goethe and Schiller instead of Paley and Pearson—I know from which one learns the *truest* theology." But a few months' experience as a curate in East London began to discourage him about the influence of the Church among the masses. "I had come to London full of hopes and ideals only to see them foiled, and myself utterly alone and without a friend in all this Babylon, and then came darkness and misery until I raised myself and fled to the British Museum, and fairly got into my historical reading again, which I had given up in the fit of religious enthusiasm which led me to take orders, and from that moment I never gave it up again."[70] Writing about legends of Saint Patrick and other Celtic topics, which led him to Thierry and Michelet, went on simultaneously with study of Christian origins in Renan, whose *Life of Jesus* he read the year of its publication,[71] and in the Germans Ewald and Baur. Convinced of the entire humanity of Jesus, and suffering from ill health aggravated by zealous parish work, he decided in 1869 to leave the Church in order to devote himself to writing a history of England.

This undertaking had grown out of an original design of a history of the Church of England.

The prospect widened as I read and thought. On the one hand, I could not fetter the word "Church" down to any particular branch of the Christian communion in England; after the Reformation, therefore, all historical unity would have been gone. . . . On the other, I could not describe the Church from the purely external and formal point of view taken by the general class of ecclesiastical historian; its history was, with me, the narrative of Christian civilization. And to arrive at a knowledge of this, it was necessary to know thoroughly the civil history of the periods I had passed through; to investigate the progress of thought, of religion, of liberty, even the material progress of England. No existing history helped me; rather, I have been struck with the utter blindness of all and every one as to the real subjects which they profess to treat—the national growth and development of our country. I should then have had to discover the History of England, only after my investigations to throw them aside and confine myself to a narrower subject—a subject whose treatment after the seventeenth century becomes (artistically) impossible and unhistorical.[72]

Green planned his history in opposition to his elder Oxford-trained contemporaries Freeman, Stubbs, and Gardiner, who were full of admiration for Ranke and the new school of "pragmatic" German historians. But it was an amicable opposition, for he respected their honesty and thoroughness within their restricted scope, and sought to benefit from their criticism.

He was on especially friendly terms with Freeman, the most Germanic of them all, whose *History of the Norman Conquest* (1867–1879) combated Thierry by minimizing the Celtic and French contributions to English blood and history. Their intimacy began with Freeman's admiration for Green's paper on Roman Somersetshire, read at a meeting of the Somersetshire Archeological Association in 1862. Green wrote in his diary: "Freeman is the Philistine of these meetings, but nothing has been of so much use to Archeology as the Archeological Philistine." Yet he urged against a school manual Freeman was preparing:

What we want to know in history is to know which are the big facts and which are the little ones. I am afraid you are making all your [pupils] till the mint and anise and cummin, and neglect the weightier matters of the Law. . . . Where is a word about Howard or prison reform, or the Wesleyan movement, or the discoveries of Captain Cook, or Brindley's canals, or Watt's steam engine, or the revival of art under Reynolds and Gainsborough, or that of poetry under Burns and Wordsworth, or the colonisation of Australia, etc.? [73]

He objected as frankly to Freeman's combination of overemphasis on political affairs with excessive admiration of the Germanic. "Florentine democracy was a democracy of men. Teutonic freedom is too often a development of man on one side only, the political, while Italian *was* (I feel all the answer that lies in that 'was') a development of the whole man—political, intellectual, religious, artistic. . . . To my mind a crowd of Florentines shouting themselves hoarse in the Piazza is a greater and nobler thing than all the Emperors that ever breathed." [74] As his own work neared completion, he defended its "suppression or omission of facts which appear to me to have no historic value. . . . I give English history in the only way in which it is intelligible or interesting to *me*, but it does not follow that others will find it interesting or intelligible." [75] He made up in breadth and variety for any arbitrariness of choice. As early as 1861 he wrote to Dawkins concerning an article on Glastonbury: "I found the references at the bottom of the opening page would be to Deuteronomy, Michelet's *France*, the *Iliad*—a collection worthy of my *omnium gatherum* reading." [76]

The threat of death from tuberculosis forced postponement of Green's design of a history in several volumes until, in a race against time, he had composed a Short History. But urgency never weakened his resolve to make his "Little Book" a work of art. During his curacy in East London the ugliness of long rows of monotonous houses had weighed on his spirits; he re-

HISTORY AS ART

joiced in Ruskin's zeal for the aesthetic education of the poor. After seeing Verona and Venice the year of his leaving the Church, he returned to England "with a new sense of the world's beauty . . . and a resolve to go to Italy every year until I die. The land has cast its spell upon me as it did on Theodoric and the Ottos." [77] Michelet and Renan showed how beautiful in form, style, and imaginative glow historical writing could be. To Freeman's objections to his reconstruction of British origins, he replied: "You will have to forgive my 'fancies' now and then. But even at the risk of fancies one must strive to get something like order out of that mere chaos of early history as your Lappenbergs write it." [78] He confessed: "Like Gibbon I have a hatred, a sort of *physical* antipathy, to notes. There is something to me in the very *look* of a page." [79] Accordingly, when the Short History was completed, he offered a section for advance publication in a periodical. "I shall never judge its readability (*the* thing I care about) till I see it in type. Cook [the editor of *The Saturday Review*] thinks that sort of anticipation of oneself bad—but I am wholly French in the question, as I am in most literary questions. It seems to me that on all points of literary art, we have to sit at the feet of French Gamaliels." [80]

The *Short History of the English People* appeared in 1874, with a Preface stressing its unlikeness to previous histories of England. Green proposed to write, "not of English Kings and English Conquests, but of the English People" and to dwell upon constitutional, intellectual, and social advances. "Figures little heeded in common history—the figures of the missionary, the poet, the printer, the merchant or the philosopher" would stand beside the soldier and the statesman. Thus, while the word "people" in the title suggests Michelet, Green's affinity is rather with Renan's balance of individual with collective achievement. Great personalities represent and embody social manifestations. Chaucer is English medieval culture in its flower, Queen Elizabeth the Renaissance character, Francis Bacon the new science, and Milton, Puritanism at its best.

Immune to invasion since 1066, England is the classic modern example of historical continuity, of a great people pursuing the logic of its own character. Green traced unbroken political development from Magna Carta to the Commonwealth, the Revolution of 1688 and the Reform Act of 1832, and similar religious evolution from Wyclif to the Latitudinarians and the Evangelicals. That England should have been the first nation to achieve domestic comfort and convenience was not so much a result of security from invasion as an expression of the practical and material bent which provoked Louis the Fourteenth, before Napoleon, to call it "a nation of shopkeepers," and made it the birthplace of the industrial and commercial revolutions. Patriotic pride in the "inborn political capacity of the English mind," [81] in the compromise and toleration that permitted movement toward social equality and freedom of worship with a minimum of violence and revolution, did not blind Green to its deplorable incapacity to deal with minds as different from itself as the Irish, and the complacency, the "timid content" which was the pitfall of even the profoundly philosophic Burke. He warned of "war of classes, . . . social severance between rich and poor, between employers and employed," [82] a legacy of the fatal juncture of the Industrial Revolution with the reaction against the French Revolution. Green was happiest in describing literature and science as the highest expressions of the national mind. The Anglo-Norman literature revealed the spirit which demanded the Great Charter. Spenser and Shakespeare are the summit of England's emergence as a world power.

For Green, as for Thierry, the essence of history is narration. It sweeps into its unflagging course even complex political

HISTORY AS ART 185

forms and economic statistics. Characteristic and telling quotation from the mouths of a multitude of historical figures was welcome relief from Green's chief rivals, from Hume's abstract analysis and reporting, from Macaulay's translation of his sources into his own flashy, monotonous style. With a subject less picturesque and violent than the history of France, Green provided drama in the contrast of social types, of Elizabethan and Puritan, and in brilliant portraits of individuals, of Bede, Dunstan, Sir Thomas More, Queen Elizabeth, Bacon, the younger Pitt. There could be no fuller realization of the young Herder's conception of history as pictures and action.

In haste to publish, Green narrowed the scope of his concluding chapters. After Milton, literature almost vanishes. The Industrial Revolution is merely glanced at. But he cheated death long enough to write a more detailed *History of the English People* (1877–1880), bringing the full design of his work up to Waterloo. This expansion introduces Dryden as "the first to impress the idea of literature upon the English mind," [83] and extolls Pope's championship of standards of art against the vulgarization of literature to meet increasing popular demand. Primacy in industry and commerce ensures England's victory over Napoleon, and leaves her the mightiest power in the world. Green glances forward to his own time, when the rebellious American colonists have become "the main branch of the English people," whose example of independence will probably be followed by the British in the Pacific. The story of a people that developed its character in long centuries of isolation has swollen into world scope. "English institutions, English speech, English thought, will become the main features of the political, the social, and the intellectual life of mankind." [84]

Despite this climax of widened vision, the expanded version failed to surpass the *Short History*. Green recognized this possibility in his diary for 1877: "There is a fire, an enthusiasm in one's first book that never comes again. I felt as if I were a young knight challenging the world with my new method, and something of the trumpet ring is in passage after passage." [85]

PART THREE

TOWARD A NEW SYNTHESIS

VIII

HISTORY AS SCIENCE

THE victories over Denmark, Austria, and France culminating in the coronation of a German Emperor at Versailles in 1871 were a cultural, as well as a political, disaster to Europe; they gave Germany a delayed cultural prestige no longer deserved. The deaths of Goethe and Hegel in 1832, of Niebuhr in 1831 and of Müller in 1840 mark the close of a great creative period in literature, philosophy, and history. "Original and bold views, characteristic of men of genius who open new paths to the human spirit and transform knowledge, those beautiful discoveries or, more precisely, those revelations and initiations that distinguished the century, seem to be exhausted," [1] admitted Karl Hillebrand in 1864, at the close of a survey of literary and historical scholarship. Lamenting that specialized studies had piled up a mass of factual detail so vast that no one dared complete Müller's enterprise of a general history of Greece, Karl Dilthey found himself looking back in 1897 upon "the spring-time of our scholarship from a period of overripeness, cheated of its golden summer." [2] Nietzsche warned his countrymen that their victories had been due to "strict military discipline, natural valor and endurance, superior leaders, unity and obedience among the led—in short, to elements which have nothing to do with culture." [3]

The imposing mass and organization of German scholarly production masked this emptiness from less discerning, and far more numerous eyes. In historical writing, mass and organization were personified in Leopold Ranke, whose publications extended over sixty-two years. Ranke had won national recognition, and the chair of history at Berlin, by his first book, *Histories of the Latin and Germanic Peoples* (1824), which opened the way to mass production by the illusory simplicity of its celebrated statement of aim: "To history has been attributed the function of judging the past, of instructing contemporaries for the profit of the future. To such lofty functions the present essay does not presume. It merely undertakes to show how things really took place." [4] This could be done, he explained, by subjecting the written sources of information concerning past events to certain tests, resembling those established for cross-examination of witnesses in courts of law. Were the historian to conduct these tests with the objectivity and the impartiality of a natural scientist, historical truth should emerge. Ranke's ironic modesty, resting as it did upon the assumption of exact knowledge where it is notoriously difficult, if not impossible, to obtain, might have recoiled upon him, had his reputation depended upon more worldly-wise judges than German professors. Indeed, he himself in practice found solid ground only in diplomatic reports and other official documents (which his Teutonic reverence for State and Church spared from thoroughgoing questioning). But his method spread rapidly because it proved so useful in the training of teachers and writers of history, by its simple, tangible exercises in the criticism and accumulation of historical evidence within the capacity of conscientious and moderately intelligent students. Too late, Mommsen warned in 1874 that the historian "is not made, but born; not educated, but educates himself." [5] From the strategic position of his seminar in the University of Berlin during a long tenure from 1825 to 1871, Ranke succeeded in placing his pupils, to the number of over one hundred, in almost all the important historical chairs in Germany. The uniformity and bulk of their writing, another manifestation of the systematic efficiency that had been the secret of German military success, became the envy and model of historians in other countries. Admirers of German methods, Stubbs and Freeman, held the Regius Professorship of Modern History at Oxford between 1867 and 1892; at Cambridge, Seeley, Lord Acton, and Bury set historical training in a similar mold from 1869 to 1927. On its founding in 1884, the American Historical Association elected Ranke, then almost ninety, as its first, and only, honorary member.

The prestige of Germany merely accelerated a general tendency of Europeans to revert to the Enlightenment. And for the cause that had produced the Enlightenment, an increased vogue of science. Now science was doubly impressive: because of the triumph of Darwinism over the opposition of organized religion, and possibly even more because of the technical applications of physics: the mechanized factory, the ironclad and the machine gun, the railroad, the telegraph, the telephone, which were transforming the material environment and even the organization of society. There was strong temptation for the historian to draw its aura about his work, to claim to be producing "scientific" history. The method historians borrowed was still essentially that of physics, for the newer sciences of biology and psychology considered life, even human, as merely a more complex physical mechanism obedient to the laws of matter and motion. According to Darwin, man was the result of a long process of natural selection, in which nature, not man, had done by far the greater part. Consequently, historians sought material causes of human behavior and represented mankind as ruled by blind, impersonal "forces" of geography, of economics, of racial heredity. British "classical" economics, with its "iron laws" deduced from the theoretical behavior of a pseudo-scientific abstraction, "economic man," motivated solely by the pursuit of material gain, together with the Malthusian-Darwinian conception of the "struggle for existence," served the German exile Karl Marx as the foundation for the most systematic and influential of materialistic interpretations of history, *Capital* (1867). In France, Taine prefaced his study of the *Ancien Régime* (1876) by saying: "The historian may be permitted the privilege of the naturalist; I have observed my subject as one might observe the metamorphosis of an insect." Fustel de Coulanges, maintaining that the skeptical and mathematical method of Descartes could make of history an objective science, admonished enthusiastic hearers: "Do not applaud me. It is not I who address you, but history that speaks through my mouth." [6]

Yet the new Enlightenment differed from that of the eighteenth century in the important respect that both scientists and historians had fallen under the sway of a subsequent creation of science: mechanical mass production through division of labor. For the ends of thoroughness, accuracy, and technical skill the individual scientist tended to concentrate his attention upon an ever diminishing segment of nature, and the historian to place inordinate emphasis upon minute factual information. Ranke had set the fashion in the eighteen thirties by requiring members of his seminar to investigate details of German medieval history, and by collecting their essays for publication in a cooperative volume. Historians lost sight of the qualitative difference between such agglomerations of raw material and the survey of an entire field by a single mind. Through contributing special articles to learned journals, which grew in number as history was subdivided, they acquired an almost pathological fear of making generalizations that might be contradicted by facts dredged up by rivals with even more limited interests.

Before long, this atmosphere began to affect even distinguished minds. The revolutions of 1848 had wrenched Theodor Mommsen from the collecting of Latin inscriptions to plunge him into the struggles of liberal journalism. Fresh from this experience in the actual making of history, he published in 1854–1856 the opening volumes of a brilliantly narrated *History of Rome* interpreting the downfall of the Republic in vividly intelligible terms of nineteenth-century political life. The work scandalized academic historians by the modernity of its phrasing, its partisanship for Caesar, and its lack of references and footnotes. In its defense, the author wrote: "I wanted to bring down the ancients from the fantastic pedestal on which they appear, into the real world. . . . Those who have lived through historical events, as I have, begin to see that history is neither written nor made without love and hate." [7] But after the Prussian Academy had invited him to Berlin to direct and edit the collection of all extant Latin inscriptions, Mommsen began to regard his masterpiece as a youthful indiscretion. Always convinced that he needed to learn more, he scattered his phenomenal energy over more than a thousand technical publications, and never executed his plan to complete his Roman history with the aid of impeccable information. Even more disintegrating was the effect of a German education on the widely cultured Lord Acton, who read and annotated enormously for a life's work on the History of Liberty, without writing a line of it, and is remembered chiefly for his planning the *Cambridge Modern History*, prepared by many historians on the principle of the division of labor. John Morley, who could not be accused of bias against science, lamented in 1878 that history "threatens to degenerate from a broad survey of great periods and movements of human society into vast and countless accumulations of insignificant facts, sterile knowledge, and frivolous antiquarianism." [8] Looking backward from 1925, the scientific philosopher Whitehead described the widespread results of this professionalization of learning: "In its last twenty years the century closed with one of the dullest stages of thought since the time of the First Crusade. It was an echo of the eighteenth century, lacking Voltaire and the reckless grace of the French aristocrats. The period was efficient, dull, and half hearted. It celebrated the triumph of the professional man." [9]

What flourished best in these decades was archeological excavation, which requires a matter-of-fact mentality that concerns itself with the purely material remains of humanity. Diggers must be patient, orderly, and cautious, for they run constant risk of destroying the evidence before describing it adequately. Lively, imaginative minds are at a disadvantage, since they find it hard to collect evidence for a long time without drawing any conclusions.[10] Appropriately, it was a German, Schliemann, who in 1871, the year of German triumph, gave archeology its great impetus by putting the historical truth of Homer to the material test of excavation at a legendary site of Troy. Later at Mycenae, at Tiryns, and at Orchomenos, where he uncovered the treasure house of Minyas, he confirmed Otfried Müller's surmise of a pre-Homeric civilization. Art objects preserved abundantly in the dry air of Egypt disclosed successive artistic styles which permitted Flinders Petrie to give orderly sequence to a long vista of Egyptian annals. His work was soon rivaled by discoveries in Mesopotamia. Before the end of the century, the spade had unearthed in Crete and Asia Minor two civilizations, the Minoan and the Hittite, of whose existence there had been only the faintest hints in tradition. But these exciting discoveries, like the somewhat earlier discoveries of skeletons of prehistoric races and the marvelous art of the "cave man," though expanding the length of man's earthly sojourn and casting salutary doubt upon the physical and cultural superiority of modern men, evade the questions we are most eager to ask. For material objects, where we are unaided by intelligible writing (the Cretan script, for instance,

HISTORY AS SCIENCE

is not deciphered), are tantalizingly difficult to interpret. We know what prehistoric man ate and how he dressed, but not the expression on his face, the impulses of his heart, or his conceptions of the world.

The dehumanizing of the humanities spread to language and literature. Sir John Sandys recorded complacently in his *History of Classical Scholarship* (1908):

> In the generation next to that of Wolf, the two great scholars, Gottfried Hermann and August Boeckh, were conspicuous as the heads of rival schools of classical learning. The first was the grammatical and critical school, which made the texts of the classics, with questions of grammar and metre and style, the main object of study. The second (already represented by Niebuhr) was the historical and antiquarian school, which investigated all the manifestations of the spirit of the old classical world. . . . The first was concerned with words, the second with things; the first with language and literature; the second with institutions, and with art and archeology. The adherents of the first were twitted by their opponents with a narrow devotion to notes on classical texts; those of the second were denounced as *dilletanti*. It is now, however, generally agreed that, while in theory, the comprehensive conception of the wide field of classical learning formed by Boeckh is undoubtedly correct, in practice a thorough knowledge of the languages is an indispensable foundation for the superstructure.[11]

In the name of thoroughness there came about an abstracting of words from what they signify, an overemphasis on the mechanics of grammar, which developed habits of mind incapable of rearing the superstructure; and this impoverishment of Latin and Greek occurred at the unfortunate moment of their serving as models for the innovation of training in modern languages and literatures.

Literary creation was explained in mechanical terms. Taine's *History of English Literature* (1863) described works of genius as the product of the race, the physical environment and the age in which they appeared. Inspired chiefly by Taine and by Claude Bernard's *Introduction to Experimental Medicine* (1865), Emile Zola conceived the idea of conducting an experiment in heredity by means of a series of novels concerning a fictitious family. In the Preface of the first of these, *The Fortune of the Rougons* (1871), he stated his deterministic thesis:

> I wish to explain how a family, a little group of beings, comports itself in a society, expanding by giving birth to ten, to twenty individuals, who at first glance appear profoundly unalike, but whom analysis shows intimately linked to one another. Heredity has its laws, like gravitation. I shall endeavor to find, and to follow, while solving the double question of temperaments and environments, the thread that conducts mathematically from one man to another. And when I get hold of all the threads, when I have in my hands an entire social group, I shall display that group as an actor in an historical epoch; I shall create it in action with the complexity of its effects; I shall analyze at the same time the sum total of the will of each of its members and the general pressure of the whole.

Here, in what purports to be biology and psychology, mathematical and physical terms are conspicuous. From Zola stemmed the international literary movement called Naturalism, from its aping of natural science, which included the English novelists George Moore and Arnold Bennett. The choruses of Thomas Hardy's great historical drama, *The Dynasts* (1903), represent nations as puppets in the hands of "the Prime Mover of the gear." Being true artists, Zola and Hardy fortunately did not adhere rigidly to their Naturalistic and deterministic theories in their creative works.

Enlightenment history had consorted amicably with literature and speculative ideas—Voltaire and Gibbon were *philosophes* and stylists—but the new scientific history suspected philosophy and literary form as distorters of the plain, unvarnished truth. In imitation of the inductive method of science, it produced thousands of pages crammed to the margins, presenting the work itself rather than its results. Formlessness and tepidity were worn as the outward and perceptible signs of thoroughness and impartiality, and their opposites regarded with suspicion, even with moral indignation. In Germany, which had never succeeded in developing a standard prose, the change was not so apparent as in the land of Gibbon, of Hume, of Carlyle, Macaulay, and Green when the pedestrian Stubbs, Freeman, and Gardiner appeared as champions of historical orthodoxy. The brilliant narrative and portraiture of James Anthony Froude, after the manner of Carlyle, provoked Freeman to repeated charges of gross inaccuracy, of ignorance, of lack of calm and judicial intellect, even of deliberate misrepresentation. In vain Froude offered the offending pages of his *History of England* to the test of an impartial committee of judges, provided that the *Saturday Review*, which had published Freeman's strictures, would agree to report their decision. The legend of Froude's "chronic inaccuracy" was spread by Langlois and Seignobos in France, by James Ford Rhodes before the American Historical Association.[12] Likewise to no avail did Green, similarly attacked in *Fraser's Magazine*, appeal to a higher standard of judgment: "There are slips, careless and discreditable slips, and I am sorry for them. But they are not blunders which affect the work itself; they do not show a real misreading of this period or that period; they are not the sort of errors which betray an unhistoric mode of looking at the course of things as a whole." [13] "Literary historian" remained a term of reproach or of deprecation.

"The last fifty years have witnessed great changes in the management of Clio's temple," wrote George Macaulay Trevelyan in 1913, "Her inspired prophets and bards have passed away and been succeeded by priests of an established church; the vulgar have been excluded from the Court of the Gentiles;

doctrine has been defined; heretics have been excommunicated; and the tombs of the aforesaid prophets have been duly blackened by the new hierarchy. While these changes were in process the statue of the Muse was seen to wink an eye. Was it in approval or in derision?" [14]

While a Cambridge undergraduate, Trevelyan had heard his great-uncle, Macaulay, and Carlyle dismissed by Professor Seeley as uninformed "literary" historians. He broke silence a decade later, when J. B. Bury, on succeeding to the chair occupied by Seeley and Acton, published the magisterial pronouncement: "It has not yet become superfluous to insist that history is a science, no less and no more. When [Ranke's well-known statement] is fully taken to heart, there will no longer be divers schools of history." [15] To Bury's "intolerance" Trevelyan retorted bluntly in an article, "The Latest View of History," in *The Independent Review* for 1904: "The question, in its broader aspect, is this: Whether starting from the twentieth century, mankind shall banish literature, emotion, speculative thought, from the examination it accords to its own past." [16] This youthful protest matured into the suave and philosophic essay, "Clio, a Muse" (1913), which joined urbane raillery with grave concern for the future of historical writing, now rapidly and for the first time losing its influence. Once widely read because produced by "persons moving at large in the world of letters or politics," it had become the exclusive preserve of specialists, chiefly academic, who chose to write for other specialists, in disdain of "the common reader of books." [17] The analogy with physical science responsible for this specialization was false. False because it is impossible to isolate completely any historical event from its circumstances, or to test its cause or effect by repetition, as in laboratory experiment: for a historical event "is itself a set of circumstances, none of which will ever recur." With the amassing of facts and the testing of evidence the scientific function of the historian ends. Until interpreted, facts are inert, meaningless; and interpretation can never take the form of rigorous induction or deduction of laws: it must remain "an imaginative guess at the most likely generalizations." That historian is the best who has the widest and most comprehensive mind and soul. In an important sense, Carlyle's *French Revolution* is "more true than the cold analysis of the same events and the conventional summings up of the same persons by scientific historians who, with more knowledge of the facts, have less understanding of Man." The wide compass of human nature includes humor. How refreshing the comic scenes in Carlyle, in Gibbon, after the prim solemnity of writers concerned for "the dignity of history."

History's true value is educational, stimulating men to reflect upon the past, to enlarge their minds to the understanding of great events and sympathy with the infinite variety of human nature. Its usefulness will increase with the number of its readers;[18] and they should be attracted by the art of narrative, by the glow of enthusiasm and intellectual passion. "Life is short, art is long, but history is longest, for it is art added to scholarship." Not resting with the statement of this ideal, Professor Trevelyan has illustrated it by distinguished and eminently readable histories, fortunately still coming from his pen. His succession to Bury as Regius Professor of Modern History in 1927 marked a revolution in the teaching of history at Cambridge; and his confidence in the value for history of the amateur, of the man of letters, was justified by Lytton Strachey's *Elizabeth and Essex*. "What was the use of his writing on that topic? All the facts were known," grumbled a highly reputed professor of English literature on the appearance of Strachey's book in 1928. Such were the Philistines who had infiltrated into the teaching of the humanities in the guise of "scientific" scholars.

Philosophical speculation in history found a champion in one of the subtlest and most profound thinkers of our time, Benedetto Croce. Provocatively, he chose to publish his book, *History: Its Theory and Practice* (1915), in Germany before bringing it out in Italian. To demand that facts be permitted to speak for themselves, to fall spontaneously, or by mechanical induction, into patterns undisturbed by philosophic thought, was to mistake, Croce insisted, the nature of historical facts and the nature of philosophy. Facts long known have had a way of lying dead or dormant until a stage in the development of human consciousness has stirred them into life.

The Romans and Greeks lay in their sepulchres, until awakened at the Renaissance by the new maturity of the human spirit. The primitive forms of civilization, so gross and barbaric, lay forgotten, or little regarded, or misunderstood, until that new phase of the human spirit, which was known as Romanticism or Restoration "sympathized" with them—that is to say, recognized them as its own proper present interest. Thus great tracts of history which are now chronicle for us, many documents now mute, will in their turn be traversed with new flashes of life and will speak again. These revivals have altogether interior motives, and no wealth of documents or narratives will bring them about.[19]

Philosophy is identical with this growth of insight. It is no closed system, fixed and finite, but the process of thinking itself, in which every attainment opens a new prospect, presents new problems. To the saying of Fustel de Coulanges that there are certainly "philosophy and history, but not the philosophy of history," Croce retorts that "there is neither philosophy nor history, but history which is philosophy and philosophy which is history and intrinsic to history." [20] From the time of the

Greeks, "historical understanding has always been enriching and deepening itself, not because abstract causes and transcendental ends of human things have ever been recovered, but only because an ever increasing consciousness of them has been acquired." [21] There is no "definitive" history, no "definitive" philosophy; but history and philosophy "progress together, indissolubly united." [22]

Croce's chapter on "The Historiography of Positivism," inquiring into the pretensions of three recent schools of history to eschew philosophy, is a masterpiece of good-humored polemic, so closely knit that it would deserve quotation entire. It exposes the inadequacy of Taine's mechanical categories to deal with the living process of history, and "the device of half-words, of innuendos, of prudent silences" upon which Ranke's "diplomatic" school bases its vaunted objectivity and impartiality. Croce observes caustically that

the ambition of altogether rejecting the admission of thought into history, lacking to the diplomatic historians (because they were without the necessary innocence for such an ambition), was, on the other hand, possessed by the philologists, a most innocent group. . . . In Germany every mean little copier of a text, or collector of variants, or examiner of the relations of texts and conjecturer as to the genuine text, raised himself to the level of a scientific man and a critic, and not only dared to look upon himself as the equal of such men as Schelling, Hegel, Herder or Schlegel, but did so with scorn and contempt, calling them "anti-methodical." . . . They remembered and were ever ready to repeat five or six anecdotes concerning errors in names and dates into which celebrated philosophers had actually fallen, easily forgetful of the innumerable errors into which they fell themselves (being more liable as more exposed to danger); they almost persuaded themselves that philosophy had been invented to alter the names and confuse the dates which had been confided to their amorous care, that it was the abyss opened by the fiend to lead to the perdition of serious "documentary history." [23]

But such protests, however cogent and incisively phrased, would scarcely have availed against the potent name of science, had not science begun to modify its own methods and assumptions.

IX

TWENTIETH-CENTURY THOUGHT IN SEARCH OF A HISTORIAN

SCIENCE has turned another face to the twentieth century. Nowhere is this so apparent as in physics and mathematics, upon which, as fixed and immutable, scientific historians had reposed their trust. Newton no longer is the symbol of absolute truth. No longer must we think in terms of a single geometry, that of Euclid and Descartes. The conceptions of matter, substance, mass and weight have been profoundly altered, and determinism has been called into question by new conceptions of cause and scientific law.

Investigations into electricity and magnetism set in motion these revolutionary changes. The reader will recall that electrical phenomena, when barely discovered, seemed to Herder and others strangely like those of life. But even then, mechanical conceptions had become so established in physics that scientists did not hesitate to assume that electricity could be explained mechanically. For a century, investigations followed this course, though meeting with increasingly awkward difficulties. Just as Ptolemaic astronomy had been driven to the invention of complicated epicycles, so the ether was invented as a material medium for the transmission of electromagnetic occurrences throughout space. In 1873 Clerk Maxwell, although starting with the usual mechanical assumptions, arrived at equations which made the ether unnecessary and proved the identity of electricity, light, and radiant heat as waves of different length but identical speed, the speed already established for light. When distinguished physicists like Lord

Kelvin refused to accept these conclusions because they could not be made visible and palpable in terms of a mechanical model, Clerk Maxwell presented an illuminating defense: "If . . . cultivators of science . . . are led to the study of the singularities and instabilities, rather than the continuities of things, the promotion of natural knowledge may tend to remove that prejudice in favor of determinism which seems to arise from assuming that the physical science of the future is a mere magnified image of that of the past." [1]

But orthodox habits were so strong that it was not until 1905 that a genius in his twenties, Albert Einstein, in his first paper on Relativity, showed the implications of Maxwell's hint that light is not to be explained in mechanical terms. In 1907 Einstein presented his well-known theory that the velocity of light seems always the same, whether the observer be approaching or receding from its source; for the reason that our measures of time and space vary with our motion. The next year another young man, Minkowski, produced the mathematical explanation of this theory: time is one dimension of the four-dimensional continuum of the universe, which can be represented only by a form of geometry unknown to Euclid and Descartes.

Since the eighteen thirties, mathematicians had been constructing, as mere play of the mind, geometries based upon axioms other than Euclid's. Among these, Einstein, following Minkowski's hint, found a special kind of spherical geometry, published by Riemann in 1867, which not only corresponded exactly to the physical reality of such a four-dimensional universe but also served to explain a problem left unsolved by Newton: why gravitation works instantaneously at any distance and is impeded by no intervening object. Gravitation turned out to be not a force, but a quality of this new geometry of the universe. Planets merely follow their easiest path in space-time. Likewise mass, hitherto regarded as absolute, proved relative, increasing with a body's velocity; and this led Einstein to equate mass with energy, something bordering on the immaterial.

While the grand outlines of the universe thus were changing shape, orthodox notions were even more upset at the opposite end of the scale of magnitudes. Up to the threshold of the twentieth century, the atom had retained its etymological meaning of the ultimate, indivisible particle of matter, hard and impenetrable. It was again the phenomena of electricity, light, and heat, expanded by the discovery of X rays and radioactivity in the eighteen nineties, which made the word a misnomer, and led to Bohr's now familiar picture of each atom as a miniature solar system of electrons in orbits of vast distances relative to the size of the central nucleus. Matter is thus mostly empty spaces. Stranger still, electrons were found to have no weight distinct from their electric charge; which supports Einstein's theory of the identity of mass with energy. The stability of the atom results from the equilibrium of positive and negative charges: were that disturbed, the atom would dissolve into pure energy, in quantities undreamt of. Already by 1911, Rutherford gave this theory laboratory confirmation. The devising of ever more potent means of breaking up the atom culminated, in the popular eye, with the atomic bomb of 1945. Newton's basic notions of matter and motion, of mass and force, although fecund in scientific discoveries for over two centuries, have been superseded or supplemented.

Even the fundamental notion of causal determinism is being questioned. Its insecurity dates from 1900, when a convinced determinist, Max Planck, tried to resolve the conflict of mathematical theory and experimental results as to which lengths of incandescent heat waves—all so long as to be invisible—carry the most energy. His reconciliation involved the observation that the atom does not radiate energy continuously, but by jerks or lumps, which he called "quanta." This observation fitted into the picture of the behavior of electrons within the atom. Electrons could not be forced to occupy the space between their regular orbits. Their leaps from orbit to orbit correspond to the jerks of quanta. Thus was contradicted the conception of continuity by infinitesimal changes, which goes back to Leibnitz. The infinitesimal calculus based upon it could not predict the position of electrons or photons, the irreducible quanta of heat or light. Another mathematical instrument, the calculus of probabilities devised to deal with games of chance or to construct tables of mortality or fire risk, will work well enough where very large numbers of electrons or electromagnetic waves are involved, but cannot predict the position of an individual wave or electron. Electromagnetic waves seem "as immaterial as the waves of depression, loyalty, suicide and so on that sweep over a country." [2] Schrödinger, one of the foremost investigators of quantum phenomena, speaks of 'the custom, inherited through thousands of years, of thinking causally. Whence? Why, from observing for hundreds and thousands of years precisely those regularities in the natural course of events which, in the light of our present knowledge, are most certainly *not governed by causality;* or at least not so governed essentially, since we now know them to be statistically regulated phenomena." [3] Such conclusions revive Hume's reduction of causation to invariably observed succession: "upon the whole," he wrote in his *Treatise of Human Nature*, "necessity is something that exists in the mind, not in objects."

The creative achievements of physics during the past fifty years, the greatest since the century of Galileo and Newton, contradict popular impressions of science and of scientists that have come down from the comparatively routine and orthodox physics of the eighteenth and nineteenth centuries. Science, we have learned, does not pretend to be an exact, unalterable copy of the external world. Scientific laws, even those of Newton, are working hypotheses, tools justified by their power to explain and to control nature until better approximations to truth are reached. Einstein has not discredited Newton; he has only given him more rigorous and more delicate expression. Nor does mathematics offer finality or even greater security. We know Descartes was mistaken in saying that the figure of a triangle "depends in no way on my mind." Mathematics need not be derived from experience of the external world; its relation with externality is a matter of chance, the same equation sometimes representing several quite different physical relations. The nature of the human mind imposes no single geometry. There may be as many as mathematicians can invent postulates for. Yet theoretical physics does not suffer from this condition of its mathematical tools, since it seeks only the highest degree of probability. Huxley's description of science as "organized common sense" has become obsolete as science has ranged far beyond the bounds of habitual human observation into the infinitely great and the infinitely small. "Mechanical representations and classical concepts," says d'Abro, "are no longer of much avail, except as props to a bewildered imagination which is unable to feel at ease in its new surroundings." [4] The universe, suggests the biochemist J. B. S. Haldane, is "not only queerer than we suppose, but queerer than we *can* suppose."

Those who have probed deepest into what the astronomer Sir James Jeans calls "the mysterious universe" are not made in the popular image of the impersonal, matter-of-fact man of science. Their ways of thinking are highly idiosyncratic; their minds make breath-taking leaps. Mr. J. W. N. Sullivan has remarked concerning Einstein's Theory of Relativity: "The extraordinary lack of comprehension with which the scientific world first greeted it was not due to its technical difficulties, but to the unfamiliarity of the outlook it assumed. It seemed the product of an alien mind. We could say of this theory what Einstein said of some of the work of Gauss, that if its author had not thought of it, there is no reason to suppose that it ever would have been thought of." [5] Between such creative mathematicians and mere patient logicians, between those with the rare gift of combining rules and those who merely follow them, lies an immense difference. "The creative mathematician needs imagination, or genius, or whatever we wish to call it. He must be an artist, not merely a worker with a one-track mind. The trained student may usually detect very easily by the form of the presentation whether a demonstration is due, say, to Riemann or to Weierstrauss. A similar situation arises of course in poetry and in music, but there it is so familiar that it scarcely warrants mention." [6] D'Abro, who made the above observation, followed it up with a chapter, "Psychological Differences among Physicists," explaining their division into two types: the patient experimenters, with great ingenuity in devising and great dexterity in operating apparatus, but with comparatively little skill in mathematics; and the theoretic coordinators, who with no equipment except pencil and paper synthesize the results of experiments in all branches of physics. Among the latter, for whom he revives the eighteenth-century term "natural philosophers," he distinguishes monistic temperaments like Einstein, eager to break down separate physical categories, and others like Eddington who are content with dualism or pluralism. Far from presenting a common front, physical science offers great variety of opinion and outlook among its leaders.

Less spectacularly but indubitably, the twentieth century has likewise altered the methods and results of scientific inquiry into the nature of man and of society.

In 1901, the year after Planck's discovery of quanta, appeared De Vries's parallel theory of mutations, indicating that biological evolution has proceeded by leaps rather than by infinitesimal variations. Almost simultaneously Mendel's laws of heredity, indicating prenatal evolution, were rescued from oblivion. While we still do not know the nature of the genetic changes which produce mutations, it seems certain that evolution has not taken the Darwinian path of environmental choice of chance variations. And the questions, Can a machine repair itself? reproduce itself? have not been answered. Those who would reduce human consciousness to the physiological functioning of the nervous system, and the behaviorists, who would reduce it to automatic response to material environment, have been outstripped in useful psychological discovery by the psychoanalysts, working with the impalpable stuff of dreams, which Freud found "not a somatic but a mental phenomenon,"[7] for which there is no objective evidence, anatomical, chemical or physiological.

Words were Freud's tools of investigation. "Words and magic were in the beginning one and the same thing," he declared, "and even today words retain much of their magical power."[8] By their magic, he overcame men's resistance to the uncovering of the unconscious content of their minds. And he found that content in the form of symbols, which go back to the prehistory of humanity, when images represented thoughts, when language was memory-pictures. "The era," he said, "to which dreams take us back is 'primitive' in a two-fold sense; in the first place, it means the early days of the individual—his childhood—and secondly, in so far as each individual repeats in some abbreviated fashion during childhood the whole course of the human race, the reference is phylogenetic."⁹ In the history of language he discovered corroboration for his interpretation of dream-work: identity of opposites in the Latin *altus*, meaning both high and deep, the Latin *sacer*, both sacred and accursed, the Egyptian *ken*, meaning strong and weak, and transformations, giving in English *boat* and *tub*. Hieroglyphic writing was a lingering form of the picture-thinking of symbolism.

Myths and literature gave Freud his most effective representations of the content of the unconscious mind, including the Oedipus complex. Although he misunderstood art in confining it to escape from reality, he was himself one of the most creative literary artists of our time, its greatest myth-maker. By uncovering the work of the censor, he illuminated the process of rationalization already noted by Romantic men of letters and historians, including Carlyle. He continued their work of reducing the sphere of conscious reason, placing the rational ego on the surface of the mind, and beneath it the far larger region of the unconscious ego and of the "id," that "obscure and inaccessible part of our personality" recognizing neither time nor space, wherein dwell the instincts, "mythical beings superb in their indefiniteness. . . . 'It flashed over me,' people say, 'it was something in me, stronger in that moment than I!' . . . The ego lies between reality and the *id*, the genuine soul-stuff." ¹⁰ It is impressive evidence of Freud's honesty that, although a convinced mechanist, rejecting religion and mysticism, he should have acknowledged that "certain practices of mystics may succeed in upsetting the normal relations between different regions of the mind, so that, for example, the perceptual system becomes able to grasp relations in the deeper regions of the ego and the *id* which would otherwise be inaccessible to it."[11] Against his conscious will, he enriched the tradition of Romanticism.

Freud and his followers have belittled the advance from savagery to civilization, the boast of the Enlightenment, by exhibiting the most cultured and refined modern Europeans as depositories of sinister and obscene impulses rarely admitted even to themselves. On the other hand, anthropological investigation has been raising the savage in esteem. "Boas and his school," writes Robert H. Lowie in his *History of Ethnological Theory* (1937), "revolutionized the outlook on savage life. What hitherto had been a static phenomenon now appeared instinct with the germs of change; automata obedient to custom gave way to human beings paralleling the gamut of emotional and intellectual values familiar in civilization."[12] Anthropologists find no justification for the alleged congenital inferiority or superiority of certain races; the physical improvement of individuals, they insist, could be better attained by social cooperation than by selective breeding or elimination of the "unfit." The genuine divisions of mankind are not races or nations, but societies, distinguished by common patterns of "values." The diversity of cultural patterns throughout the world contradicts the Enlightenment conception of universal principles of human nature, and also Freud's conception of the individual as rootedly antisocial. Anthropologists point out that Freud's observation, confined to Europeans in a highly competitive society, would have been reversed had he psychoanalyzed Pueblo Indians, for example, whose culture pattern discourages competition and puts a premium on mutual aid.[13]

Historical and anthropological investigation into the economic organization of societies has disproved the claim of "classical" economics to be a science deduced from immutable principles of human nature in relation to an inelastic material environment, by revealing it as merely an empirical description of the functioning of a certain stage of industrial society, local and already passing. Economics is becoming experimental and is taking into account the unprecedented fact that technology has given man mastery over his environment. No longer niggardly, as she seemed to Malthus, nature puts no obstacles in the way of an economy of abundance. The "struggle for existence," in countries of advanced technology, is almost wholly man-made, the result of obsolete thinking. Men are not helpless before economic or political "forces"; what they mistake as such are ideas in their own heads.

While twentieth-century thought was thus obliging historians to revise their conception of the working methods of science, while it was analyzing matter into something strangely akin to mind and spirit, and restoring the nature of man—no automaton but the creator of societies and the molder of his physical environment—to the central place in history, events were exhibiting the disastrous consequences of erroneous and obsolete ideas. The philosophy of materialistic determinism, of the fated struggle of races and the dominance of economic forces, the doctrine of "manifest destiny" and the right to "Lebensraum," led to the two most destructive wars the world has known. The allegedly free enterprise of classical economics belied its freedom by producing vast monopolies and involuntary unemployment, culminating in a world-wide depression between those wars. The "fated" historical evolution of the class struggle, whereby the theory of Marx had been promising ultimate economic freedom to the masses after their disillusion with narrowly political rights, likewise belied itself by denying ideal values. For when war broke out in 1914, the vast majority of Marxists found their loyalty to national cultures stronger than the international class solidarity supposedly dictated by their material interests. The victory of Marxism in Russia was not by materialistic evolution but by political revolution, which has developed in the direction of cultural nationalism. And the failure of Marx to allow for the irrational qualities of the human soul, especially in a lower middle class squeezed between monopoly capitalism and organized labor, is writ large in the demonic apparition of German National Socialism, which has brought Europe to the verge of material ruin.

Twentieth-century historians therefore have been preoccupied with the problems of the collapse of civilizations, in contrast to the Romantic preoccupation with their origin and growth. At the threshold of our present era of historical thinking stands the formidable and ambiguous figure of Oswald Spengler. His *Decline of the West,* begun in 1911, was ready for publication in 1914, when it was delayed by the outbreak of war. Accident, by timing it to appear first in July, 1918, and in amplified form in 1920-1922,[14] put behind its thesis the emphasis of the first World War and of the demoralized post-war era.

In the large outlines of his theme, Spengler had been anticipated by Flinders Petrie's little book, *The Revolutions of Civilization* (1911), and by the Count de Gobineau's four-volume *Essay on the Inequality of Human Races* (1853-1855). Gobineau, a French aristocrat, poet and sculptor, in alarm at the condition of Europe after the failure of the hopes of 1848, had pondered upon "the fall of civilizations, . . . the most striking and at the same time the most obscure of historical phenomena." [15] Disdained and hated by most men living under them, civilizations have been like "temporary islands pushed above the waves by submarine volcanoes." Sometimes "processes born of scientific discoveries have gone on perpetuating themselves by routine when the intellectual movement which gave them birth has stopped forever and let perish the secret of the theory from which they arose. . . . Who has heard of a society keeping alive merely because it knew how to go fast and how to clothe itself well?"[16] Some regions of the world, although offering no insurmountable obstacles of geography or climate, have never produced civilization. For what other reason than the congenital backwardness of the people inhabiting them? The highest civilization, civilization in the grand style, seemed to Gobineau the creation of a single race, the Aryan, which includes the Greeks, the Romans, and the dominant nations of modern Europe. But admixture with inferior races, that had sapped the creative energies of Greco-Roman civilization, was now threatening modern Europe with decline.[17] Pure Aryan blood was retained only by the dwindling remnant of the aristocracy, and complete absorption would bring universal mediocrity. From this fate there was no escape, for the laws of the decay of civilization belong to "the code of the universe, beside those other laws which, in their imperturbable regularity, govern animate and inanimate nature alike. . . . It is we moderns, we for the first time, who know that every agglomeration of men and their mode of culture must perish."[18]

Archeological discovery of the subsequent fifty years in Egypt, Crete, Asia Minor and Central America so extended knowledge of dead civilizations that the distinguished Egyptologist Petrie could survey in 1911 ten thousand years, with precise information concerning every single century of the latter seven thousand. He distinguished eight great periods of Mediterranean civilization, none deviating far from their average duration of 1330 years. Within each period he found culture attaining ripeness first in sculpture, then in painting, literature, music, mechanics and wealth, and thus could speak of civilizations widely separated in time and space as "contemporary," [19] in the special sense of being in the same phase of culture. Each phase seems to come to an end by the internal exhaustion of its possibilities, and as modern times approach, the phases are more widely separated, so that "the art is decadent before mechanical ability is free and wealth has grown." The maximum of wealth "must inevitably lead to the downfall." [20] Thereafter, civilization cannot revive of its own accord and repeat the cycle; for the reason, Petrie thinks, that the race which has built it has exhausted its potentialities. Salvation can come only from reinvigoration by the fresh blood of some people not worn out by civilization; not Aryan blood alone, as Gobineau thought, but the blood of any young race. Europe, now close to the end of the final phase, will soon need reinvigoration. But the chance of its taking place has become rare, since ease of travel has been fusing the blood of the entire world. In course of time civilization will be possible only by artificial breeding, which will "carefully segregate fine races and prohibit continual mixture, until they have a distinct type."

Spengler, though accepting in the main Petrie's and Gobineau's facts, did not share their belief in the saving virtues of race. Anthropology, notably the studies of Boas in America, stood in the way. Spengler defined peoples as "neither linguistic nor political nor zoological, but spiritual, units." [21] Their highest expression is a "Culture," closely knit by loyalty to distinctive values, as contrasted with a primitive condition of "fugitive and heterogeneous associations that form and dissolve without ascertainable rule," [22] and with a late state of "Civilization," which after values have exhausted themselves, lives on in immobility, like Egypt, like Byzantium, like the Chinese mandarins. Not mankind, therefore, but only cultures have a history; for true history is growth in time. All cultures, however dissimilar, pass through identical phases, comparable to the seasons, or to the various ages of man or any living organism. Spengler's chart of these regularly appearing phases in the great world cultures, the Egyptian, Classical, Chinese, Arabian, Western, using Petrie's special term "contemporary" to describe their parallelism, is his most brilliant and least debatable achievement. It places twentieth-century Europe in the phase of Civilization, European culture having spent itself by 1800. Civilization has no qualitative but only extensive possibilities, represented by imperialism, by Wagnerian opera with its taste for the grandiose, by the railroad, the telegraph, the wireless, the skyscraper. The grand style of life has given place to the "autumnal, artificial, rootless life of our great cities, under forms fashioned by the intellect"; [23] as in Imperial Rome, the populace exists only for *panem et circenses*, bread and amusement.

This would be self-evident, had not Civilization already so benumbed the minds of historians, that they apply the categories of matter and space to man, whose essence is life in time. A teacher of mathematics and in touch with the latest developments in physics, Spengler saw these sciences as themselves relative to the "style" of Western Culture: "The less anthropomorphic science believes itself to be, the more anthropomorphic it is. One by one it gets rid of the *separate* human traits in the Nature-picture, only to find in the end that the supposed pure Nature which it holds in its hands is —humanity itself, pure and complete." [24] But by dwelling in overgrown world-cities, surrounded by mechanical gadgets, historians of the present day have lost touch with organic processes, lost sight of "the difference between a feeling of life and a method of knowledge." [25]

Means of restoring the sense of historic growth Spengler found ready for his use, a legacy of the battle of eighteenth-century men of letters against the Enlightenment. He avowed having learned from Goethe that "sympathy, observation, comparison, immediate and inward certainty, intellectual *flair*" [26] were the means of research in history; and he employed Herder's verb *einfühlen* to describe the process whereby the organism of a culture is "intuitively seen, inwardly experienced, grasped as a form or symbol and finally rendered into poetical and artistic conceptions." [27] In resuming Herder's search for the logic of time, he found that its mysterious property of Direction, of "irreversibility," offered no problem, if we recall that *"we ourselves are Time,* inasmuch as we live." [28] The political and social forms of a culture, as Burke and Niebuhr had observed, grew and were not made; they arose after the fashion of biological mutations. To enter the soul of a culture, one must comprehend its signs and symbols, such as Faust, representative of the soul of the West. One of Spengler's signal achievements was to give refinement and precision to the conception of the *Zeitgeist* by disclosing family resemblance between apparently unrelated, disparate portions of a single culture: between the Greek city-state and Euclid's geometry, between the space-perspective of Western oil painting and Western mechanical conquest of space.

In his Preface of 1922 Spengler tells how he chose an appropriate language, one that "seeks to present objects and relations illustratively instead of offering an army of ranked concepts. It addresses itself solely to readers who are capable of living themselves into the word-sounds and pictures as they read." Racy idioms, words newly coined or refreshed by return to their root meaning, reproduce the pulse of daily existence which is the continuity of humanity, while in the grand style "the great Cultures accomplish their majestic wave-cycles. They appear suddenly, swell in splendid lines, flatten again and vanish, and the face of the waters is once more a sleeping waste."[29] Subtle psychological distinctions, novel and difficult speculations, Nietzschean transvaluations of values are made familiar and comprehensible by a variety of approaches, by the musical devices of incremental repetition and change of tempo. Curt sentences stress leading contentions: "All genuine historical work is philosophy, unless it is mere ant-industry."[30]

Spengler's imagination is equally at home with the primitive and with the sophisticated. Memorable are the opening sentences of his second volume:

Regard the flowers at eventide as, one after the other, they close in the setting sun. Strange is the feeling that then presses in upon you—a feeling of enigmatic fear in the presence of this blind dreamlike earth-bound existence. The dumb forest, the silent meadows, this bush, that twig, do not stir themselves, it is the wind that plays with them. Only the little gnat is free—he dances still in the evening light, he moves whither he will. . . . A vegetable is only a vegetable; an animal is a vegetable and something more besides. A herd that huddles together trembling in the presence of danger, a child that clings weeping to its mother, a man desperately striving to force a way into his God—all these are seeking to return out of the life of freedom into the vegetal servitude from which they were emancipated into individuality and loneliness.[31]

Equally felicitous his interpretation of culture that is past its noon:

The Baroque park is the park of the Late season, of the approaching end, of the falling leaf. . . . It is perspective that begins to awaken a premonition of something passing, fugitive and final. The very words of distance possess, in the lyric poetry of all Western languages, a plaintive autumnal accent that one looks for in vain in the Greek and Latin. It is there in Macpherson's "Ossian" and in Hölderlin, in Nietzsche's Dionysus-Dithyrambs, and lastly in Baudelaire, Verlaine, George and Droem. The Late poetry of the withering garden-avenues, the unending lines in the streets of a megalopolis, the ranks of pillars in a cathedral, the peak in a distant mountain chain—all tell us that the depth-experience which constitutes our space-world for us is in the last analysis our inward certainty of a Destiny, of a prescribed direction, of *time*, of the irrevocable.[32]

By turns lyrical and analytical, meditative and vigorous, Spengler transfers to us the sensation of intimate participation in man's incredible fertility in art and science, in economics and politics, in religion and philosophy. To accompany him is an exhilarating experience; even when the reader dissents from the conclusions, his mind is enriched, and bears something of Spengler's stamp.

Yet throughout *The Decline of the West* sounds a discord of anti-poetry. In his "venture of predetermining history," Spengler forgets his own insistence upon the purely symbolic nature of cultures, by assuming their absolute, not metaphorical identity with organisms, by stating flatly: "The immense history of the Chinese or of the Classical Culture is the exact equivalent of the petty history of the individual man, or of the animal, or the tree, or the flower." [33] He merely substitutes for physical determinism of cause and effect a biological determinism of *"pre-ordained* life-durations" [34] more mechanical and material than the Darwinism he rejects, and oppressive in its implications for the individual. "Henceforward," Spengler pronounces, "it will be every man's business to inform himself of what *can* happen and therefore of what with the unalterable necessity of destiny and irrespective of personal ideals, hopes or desires, *will* happen." [35] In adding his "hope that men of the new generation may be moved by this book to devote themselves to technics instead of lyrics, the sea instead of the paint brush, politics instead of epistemology," [36] he ignores the Promethean steadfastness of the artistic and philosophic temperaments, to whose highest achievements he elsewhere gives percipient and genuine homage. A man of exquisite feeling for nature, who says: "It is, to me, a sight of deep pathos to see how the spring flowers, craving to fertilize and be fertilized, cannot for all their bright splendour attract one another, or even see one another, but must have recourse to animals, for whom alone these colours and these scents exist," [37] nevertheless is so insensible to human suffering as to glorify war as "the creator of all great things." [38] Although Goethe's *Alles Vergängliche ist nur ein Gleichnis* (Everything mortal is merely a symbol) runs like an admonitory refrain throughout his book, he has faith in *Realpolitik*. To the relative and symbolic character of all historical interpretation, he makes his own the solitary exception. And that interpretation, by a mind that has ranged through universal history with amazing versatility, reveals at its core the arrogant provincialism of a German landed gentleman, writing in the bitterness of national defeat and employing intellect to disparage intellect, art to extinguish art.

Spengler lived to see the Caesarism he predicted, but Caesar was not the super-Bismarck of his imagining. He came as a proletarian demagogue, bearing the banner of racial theories for which Spengler had intellectual contempt. During the years when European civilization seemed defenseless before the insidious poison of Hitlerism, Arnold J. Toynbee was publishing *A Study of History* (1934–1939). "The contemporary atmosphere in which the present three volumes was produced," says his Preface of 1939, "was painfully appropriate to the themes of 'breakdown' and 'disintegration' which these volumes have for their subjects. There were moments when it almost seemed like tempting Fate and wasting effort to go on writing a book that must be the work of many years, when a catastrophe might overtake the writer's world within the next few weeks or days." [39] But Professor Toynbee fortified his mind by recalling the triumphant survival of Saint Augustine's *City of God*, begun soon after the sack of Rome by Alaric.

As to the present state of the world, Toynbee is not far from agreement with Spengler. Like him, he sees the greatest peril of our time in the "cancer" of the city proletariat, in "the stagnation of the masses." [40] Surveying the twenty-six civilizations of which there is record, he finds sixteen already dead and buried and every one of the rest apparently "broken down and in the process of disintegration, with the possible exception of our own" [41] (Western), which comparison with the life courses of other civilizations seems to place in what the Chinese call "a Time of Troubles," presumably leading to a petrified Universal State. Yet Toynbee will have none of Spengler's determinism. Exhaustive analysis of historic instances of breakdown and disintegration has convinced him that "the dead civilizations are not 'dead by Fate'; and therefore a living civilization is not doomed irrevocably in advance." [42] Spengler's strict analogy of societies with plant and animal organisms is erroneous, since their vital force lies in individuals, the sum of whose efforts may vary to an incalculable degree. And the human race, larger and more enduring than any civilization it has brought forth, may preserve and hand down the fruits of individual endeavors to all times and places. Thus there is still ground for hope in the creative leadership of exceptional men: "The divine spark of creative power is instinct in ourselves; and if we have the grace to kindle it into flame, then the stars in their courses cannot defeat our efforts to attain the goal of human endeavors." [43] But even such leadership will fail if it resorts, as Spengler wished, to constraint of the masses by force and drill. It must win them, must charm them, into imitation. The greatest leaders have withdrawn from the world for self-conquest, like Jesus in the wilderness, like Buddha, in order to return to redeem the world by service and self-sacrifice. The immortal myths of Proserpine, of the Dying God, point the way.

Not only in this faith in salvation through ideal and religious values, but also in its form, *A Study of History*, which will extend to thirteen volumes, is the antithesis of Spengler. The English tradition of cautious empiricism and the example of scientific induction have encouraged Mr. Toynbee's bent toward profuse illustration and leisurely bypaths,[44] in contradiction to the sense of urgency that breathes from the mottoes prefixed to his *Study*. Although liberal in culture, copious and various in his quotation from world poetry, he seems indifferent to artistic means of power over readers, which are nevertheless part of the charm which he rightly sees as the essence of leadership. Here Spengler has shown more wisdom than the children of light.

In prisons and in concentration camps, among the perils, the monotony, the anxieties of warfare, and now among the ruins of historic cities, the best minds of Europe have been meditating with unexampled intensity. They have seen Western civilization brought low, not by barbarous aliens, but by pseudo-scientific notions exploiting the intellectual and moral backwardness of neglected, rootless masses. They face the possibility that the center of civilization may pass to some other continent. Yet brooding over the mistakes of yesterday need not exclude from their minds the possibility of reestablishing civilization more firmly upon the best thought of today, which frees man from bondage to theological, material, or biological necessity. Centuries of probing into the meaning of history have brought forth the considered judgment that humanity has no single goal, fixed and ultimate, upon the attainment of which it must rest in a routine which is death in life. The future is ours to devise and revise endlessly, as time discloses fresh possibilities. Only our mistaken ideas of ourselves can bind us, only our relinquishment of standards undo us. These are tidings of great joy; but they must be for all people, not the private possession of an enlightened class. They must be spread to the politicians and to the masses, lest they turn again and rend what remains of civilization. The thought of the twentieth century, in its audacity, grandeur and liberating power, awaits a historian with consummate artistic skill. Perhaps he is among those reborn to the spirit in Europe's agony.

NOTES

I. VOLTAIRE SHATTERS TRADITION

(*Unless otherwise noted, translations are by the author.*)

1. See James Shotwell, "The Discovery of Time," *Journal of Philosophy*, XII (1915), Nos. 8, 10, 12.
2. The translations from *Discours sur l'histoire universelle* follow the text of *Oeuvres complètes de Bossuet* (Paris, 1864; Vol. XXIV).
3. The translations from the *Essai sur les moeurs et l'esprit des nations* follow the text of *Oeuvres complètes de Voltaire* (Paris, 1878; Vols. XI, XII, XIII).
4. Compare Gibbon's account in his *Autobiography* of the inception of his *Decline and Fall of the Roman Empire*.
5. The translations from Iselin's *Geschichte der Menschheit* follow the 2-volume text published in Zürich in 1768.

II. HERDER AND GOETHE: THE LIVING PAST

1. The translations from *Auch eine Philosophie der Geschichte* follow the text of *Herders Sämmtliche Werke*, ed. B. Suphan (Berlin, 1877–1909; Vol. V).
2. This is the first appearance of the verb *einfühlen*, which has had so wide a currency.
3. Cited by Preserved Smith, *A History of Modern Culture* (New York, 1930), II, 404.
4. Vorrede, *Ideen zur Philosophie der Geschichte der Menschheit*, in *Herders Sämmtliche Werke*, ed. Suphan, XIII, 7.
5. Edward Young, *Conjectures on Original Composition* (London, 1759.)
6. J. Blackwell, *An Enquiry into the Life and Writings of Homer* (London, 1735), p. 65.
7. Cited by Blackwell, *op. cit.*, p. 45.
8. *Ibid.*, p. 32.
9. Robert Wood, *An Essay on the Original Genius and Writings of Homer* (London, 1765), p. 141.
10. *Ibid.*, pp. 179–180.
11. See Emery Neff, *A Revolution in European Poetry* (New York, 1940), Chap. I.
12. *Oeuvres d'Alembert* (Paris, 1805), I, 292.

NOTES FOR CHAPTER II

13. See Jonathan Swift, *Proposal for Correcting, Improving, and Ascertaining the English Tongue.*
14. Observe the subsequent opposition to Wordsworth's poetic diction.
15. Blackwell, *An Enquiry*, pp. 60–61.
16. *Ibid.*, pp. 58–59.
17. Wood, *Essay on . . . Homer*, p. 279.
18. Blackwell, *An Enquiry*, p. 40 and note.
19. *Oeuvres philosophiques latines et françaises de Leibniz* (Amsterdam and Leipzig, 1765), p. 242.
20. Wood, *Essay on . . . Homer*, pp. 241–242.
21. Robert Lowth, *Lectures on the Sacred Poetry of the Hebrews*, tr. G. Gregory (London, 1787), II, 89, note 6 (by Michaelis).
22. Blackwell, *An Enquiry*, p. 45.
23. Lowth, *Lectures*, I, 113.
24. Leibniz, *Nouveaux essais*, p. 12 (in *Oeuvres philosphiques latines et françaises*, ed. Raspe, Amsterdam and Leipzig, 1765).
25. *Ibid.*, pp. 10–11.
26. *Ibid.*, pp. 267, 265.
27. The phrase is Herder's (in *God: Some Conversations*).
28. Leibniz, *op. cit.*, p. 441.
29. David Hume, *Essays: Moral, Political and Literary* (London, 1882), II, 331.
30. *Ibid.*, pp. 362, 359.
31. *Ibid.*, 361–362.
32. *Ibid.*, p. 363.
33. *Ibid.*, p. 339.
34. Emil Gottfried von Herder, ed., *Herders Lebensbild* (Erlangen, 1846), I, 386.
35. *Ibid.*, p. 390.
36. *Ibid.*, p. 377.
37. *Ibid.*, p. 126.
38. *Ibid.*, p. 125–126.
39. *Ibid.*, p. 108.
40. *Ibid.*, pp. 464–465, 467.
41. *Herders Sämmtliche Werke*, ed. Suphan, I, 152.
42. *Ibid.*, I, 159.
43. *Ibid.*, IV, 347.
44. *Ibid.*, V, 168–169.
45. *Ibid.*, IV, 439.
46. *Herders Lebensbild*, II, 348–349.
47. *Poetry and Truth*, Part II, Bk. 10.

NOTES FOR CHAPTER II

48. Heinrich Düntzer and Ferdinand von Herder, eds., *Aus Herders Nachlass* (Frankfurt-am-Main, 1856), I, 29. Letter from Goethe, dated September, 1771.
49. *Goethes Sämmtliche Werke* (Munich, 1909), I, 289.
50. See Chap. IV, p. 99, of this book.
51. *Herders Sämmtliche Werke*, V, 213.
52. *The Chief Works of Benedict Spinoza*, tr. Elwes (London, 1905), I, 135.
53. *Ibid.*, p. 133.
54. *Ibid.*, p. 182.
55. Richard Simon, *Histoire critique du Vieux Testament* (Rotterdam, 1685), pp. 3-4.
56. *Ibid.*, p. 29.
57. Johann Gottfried Eichhorn, *Einleitung ins Alte Testament* (2d ed., Reutlingen, 1790), I, vi.
58. *Ibid.*, II, 252.
59. *Ibid.*, p. 258.
60. Modern scholarship would augment, rather than decrease, the number of strands out of which Genesis was woven.
61. Eichhorn, *Einleitung*, II, 297.
62. *Ibid.*, p. 345.
63. *Ibid.*, III, 1-2.
64. *Ibid.*, p. 4.
65. *Ibid.*, p. 545.
66. *Ibid.*, p. 393.
67. *Ibid.*, p. 62.
68. Lowth, *Lectures*, I, 150.
69. *Ibid.*, p. 101.
70. *Ibid.*, p. 238, note 1; p. 332, note 11; p. 348, note 28. These notes are by Michaelis.
71. *Herders Sämmtliche Werke*, ed. Suphan, XI, 170.
72. *Ibid.*, p. 219.
73. *Ibid.*, XII, 287.
74. *Ibid.*, XI, 231-232.
75. *Ibid.*, p. 234.
76. *Ibid.*, XII, 15.
77. *Ibid.*, p. 52.
78. *Ibid.*, p. 23.
79. See Robert T. Clark, Jr., "Herder's Conception of 'Kraft,'" *Publications of the Modern Language Association of America*, LXXXI (September, 1942), 750 ff.
80. *God: Some Conversations*, tr. Frederick Burckhardt (New York,

Veritas Press, 1940), p. 172. Reprinted by permission of Oskar Piest.
81. *Aus Herders Nachlass*, I, 75.
82. Cited by Suphan, *Herders Sämmtliche Werke*, XIV, 665.
83. *Ibid.*, XIII, 9.
84. *Ibid.*, p. 8.
85. *Ibid.*, XIV, 244.
86. *Ibid.*, XIII, 11.
87. *Ibid.*, p. 16.
88. *Ibid.*, p. 172.
89. *Ibid.*, p. 23.
90. *Ibid.*, pp. 52, 156–157.
91. *Ibid.*, pp. 53, 54.
92. *Ibid.*, pp. 60, 108.
93. *Ibid.*, pp. 60, 61, 48–49. See also Goethe's prose *Hymn to Nature*, written about 1782–1783.
94. *Herders Sämmtliche Werke*, ed. Suphan, XIII, 147.
95. *Ibid.*, XIV, 85.
96. *Ibid.*, XIII, 304, 308.
97. *Ibid.*, p. 307.
98. *Ibid.*, XIV, 132.
99. *Ibid.*, p. 137.
100. *Ibid.*, pp. 144, 149.
101. *Ibid.*, p. 144.
102. *Ibid.*, p. 184.
103. *Ibid.*, p. 221.
104. *Ibid.*, pp. 237, 238.
105. *Ibid.*, p. 336.
106. *Ibid.*, p. 451.
107. *Ibid.*, p. 241.
108. *Ibid.*, XIII, 61.

III. GIBBON, VICO, AND THE MASSES

1. *Herders Sämmtliche Werke*, ed. Suphan, XIV, 330, note.
2. The *Autobiographies of Edward Gibbon*, 2d ed. (London, 1897), p. 267.
3. *Miscellaneous Works of Edward Gibbon* (Dublin, 1796), III, 67; entry for July 14 (1764). The original is in French.
4. *Ibid.*, II, 264. Written in military camp at Winchester, July 26, 1761.
5. Gibbon, *Autobiographies*, p. 278.
6. *Ibid.*, p. 308.

7. *Ibid.*, p. 311.

8. "Ancient civilizations were destroyed by imported barbarians: we breed our own." W. R. Inge, *The Idea of Progress* (Oxford, 1920), p. 13.

9. Gibbon, *Miscellaneous Works*, II, 225, 229.

10. Hamann mentioned the *Scienza nuova* to Herder in a letter of December 22, 1777, but without indicating its character or importance. Goethe, who was told of its value while in Italy, may have spoken of it on returning to Weimar in 1787, when three out of the four Parts of *Thoughts on History* had been published. Herder first mentions Vico in 1797, six years after the publication of the final Part, with the hope that his services to humanitarianism be kept in memory (*Briefe zur Beförderung der Humanität*, Brief 114). Herder's habit of full acknowledgment of his sources makes it improbable that he should have concealed a debt to Vico. See Benedetto Croce, *The Philosophy of Giambattista Vico*, tr. R. G. Collingwood (New York, 1913), Appendix II, and the Introduction to *The Autobiography of Giambattista Vico*, tr. M. H. Fisch and T. G. Bergin (Ithaca, N. Y., 1944).

11. *Principj di Scienza nuova . . . seconda la terza impressione del 1744* (Milano, 1836), pp. 288–289.

12. *Ibid.*, p. 99.

13. *Ibid.*, p. 486 ("essi popoli Greci furono quest'Omero").

14. *Ibid.*, p. 389.

15. *Ibid.*, p. 97.

16. *Ibid.*, p. 117.

17. *Ibid.*, pp. 617–618.

18. Niebuhr, *History of Rome*, tr. Julius Hare and Connop Thirlwall (London, 1855), I, ix.

IV. THE FASCINATION OF ORIGINS: NIEBUHR, OTFRIED MÜLLER

1. Friedrich Perthes, *Lebensnachrichten über Barthold Georg Niebuhr* (Hamburg, 1838), I, 35.

2. Chevalier (Christian) Bunsen, *The Life and Letters of Niebuhr* (New York, 1852), p. 247; letter to Jacobi, November 21, 1811.

3. Dietrich Gerhard and Wilhelm Norvin, eds., *Die Briefe Barthold Georg Niebuhrs* (Berlin, 1926), I, li; letter to Dore Hensler, September 18, 1812.

4. Niebuhr, *The History of Rome*, tr. Julius Hare and Connop Thirlwall (London, 1855), I, 1.

5. *Ibid.*, p. 147.

NOTES FOR CHAPTER IV

6. Niebuhr, *The History of Rome*, p. 209.
7. *Life and Letters of Niebuhr*, p. 250; letter to Perthes, December, 1812.
8. *History of Rome*, I, 259.
9. In 1842, the English historian Macaulay restored this and other incidents of Roman legend to the form of verse in his well-known *Lays of Ancient Rome*, with a Preface popularizing Niebuhr's theory.
10. *History of Rome*, I, 260.
11. *Ibid.*, p. 164.
12. *Ibid.*, p. 13.
13. In the year of Montesquieu's *Spirit of the Laws*, 1748, David Hume wrote in his *Enquiry Concerning Human Understanding*: "Would you know the sentiments, inclinations, course of life of the Greeks and Romans? Study well the temper and actions of the French and English: you cannot be much mistaken in transferring to the former most of the observations you have made in regard to the latter. Mankind are so much the same, in all times and places, that history informs us of nothing new or strange in this particular."
14. *History of Rome*, I, xxiv.
15. *Life and Letters*, p. 142.
16. *History of Rome*, II, 135.
17. *Ibid.*, p. 154.
18. *Ibid.*, III, 130.
19. *Ibid.*, p. 118.
20. *Ibid.*, II, 5.
21. *Ibid.*, I, ix.
22. *Life and Letters*, p. 389.
23. *Ibid.*, p. 503. This observation in Niebuhr's letter to Dore Hensler, July 1, 1827, anticipated Disraeli's famous phrase in his novel *Sybil* (1845).
24. *History of Rome*, III, 356.
25. *Life and Letters*, p. 526.
26. *History of Rome*, III, 349.
27. *Life and Letters*, p. 517; to Dore Hensler, December 20, 1829.
28. Jules Michelet, *Histoire de la république romaine* (Paris, n. d.), "Avant-propos," p. 18.
29. Otfried Müller, *Geschichten hellenischer Stämme und Städte* (Breslau, 1841), I, 18.
30. Ernest Tonnelat, *Les Frères Grimm* (Paris, 1912), p. 406, citing Jakob Grimm, *Deutsche Grammatik*, I^2, 584.
31. Tonnelat, *op. cit.*, p. 406.
32. *Ibid.*, p. 407, citing Jakob Grimm, Deutsche Grammatik, I^2, 588.

33. Otfried Müller, *Prolegomena zu einer wissenschäftlichen Mythologie* (Göttingen, 1825), p. 78.
34. *Ibid.*, p. 270.
35. *Ibid.*, p. 267.
36. *Ibid.*, p. 207.
37. *Ibid.*, p. 172.
38. *Ibid.*, p. 293.
39. Otfried Müller, *Geschichten hellenischer Stämme und Städte*, I, 13.
40. *Ibid.*, I, 139.
41. *Ibid.*, p. 151. See Vico's similar interpretation in Chapter III, above.
42. *Ibid.*, II, 457.
43. *Ibid.*, III, 396.

V. THE ROMANTIC GARB: CHATEAUBRIAND, SCOTT, THIERRY, CARLYLE

1. René de Chateaubriand, *Les Martyrs* (Paris, 1834), I, 146. *The Martyrs* was a sequel to his *Genius of Christianity* (1802), which had vindicated the grandeur and beauty of the Christian tradition against Enlightenment slurs.
2. *Ibid.*, I, 220.
3. Augustin Thierry, *Récits des temps mérovingiens* (Paris, 1856), I, 11-12.
4. Thierry, *Dix ans d'études historiques* (Paris, 1883), Preface, p. 9.
5. *Ibid.*, pp. 13, 10.
6. *Ibid.*, p. 13.
7. Thierry, *Histoire de la conquête d'Angleterre par les Normands* (Paris, 1846), I, 10. The first edition appeared in 1825.
8. Thierry, *Dix ans d'études historiques*, p. 9.
9. Thierry, *Histoire de la conquête d'Angleterre*, I, 10.
10. *Ibid.*, I, 11.
11. *Ibid.*, VI, 95.
12. Thierry, *Récits des temps merovingiens*, I, 4.
13. *Ibid.*, I, 5.
14. Renan, *Essais de morale et de critique*, 2d ed. (Paris, 1860), p. 115.
15. Carlyle, "Sir Walter Scott" (in *Critical and Miscellaneous Essays*).
16. Alexander Carlyle, ed., *Letters of Thomas Carlyle to John Stuart Mill* (London, 1923), pp. 82-83.
17. Thomas Carlyle, *Reminiscences*, ed. J. A. Froude (New York, 1881), p. 132.

18. Carlyle, *Sartor Resartus*, Bk. II, Chap. VIII.
19. *Past and Present*, Bk. II, Chap. I.
20. *Letters of Thomas Carlyle to John Stuart Mill*, p. 134; letter to Mill, July 22, 1836.
21. *History of the French Revolution*, Vol. III, Bk. II, Chap. VIII.
22. *Past and Present*, Bk. II, Chap. V.
23. Alexander Carlyle, ed., *New Letters of Thomas Carlyle* (London and New York, 1904), II, 50.
24. *Ibid.*, I, 244.
25. *Past and Present*, Bk. II, Chap. I.
26. Thomas Carlyle, *Oliver Cromwell's Letters and Speeches* (Centenary ed., London, 1897), I, 7.
27. *Past and Present*, Bk. II, Chap. IV.

VI. RESURRECTION OF THE PAST: MICHELET

1. Jules Michelet, *Le Peuple* (Paris, n. d.), Introduction, p. 17.
2. *Ibid.*, p. 22.
3. Michelet, *Ma jeunesse* (Paris, 1884), p. 45.
4. See *The Autobiography of Giambattista Vico*, tr. Fisch and Bergin, for the Introduction tracing Vico's reputation.
5. G. Monod, *La Vie et la pensée de Jules Michelet* (Paris, 1923), I, 23.
6. *Ibid.*
7. *Ibid.*, p. 229.
8. The reference is to Fauriel's *Popular Songs of Modern Greece*, which had influenced Thierry.
9. Michelet, *Histoire de la république romaine* (Paris, n. d.), pp. 311–312.
10. *Ibid.*, p. 183.
11. *Ibid.*, p. 209.
12. *Ibid.*, p. 210.
13. *Ibid.*, p. 5; "Avant-propos" of 1869.
14. *Ibid.*, p. 243.
15. "Introduction à l'histoire universelle," published in Albert Sorel, *Michelet, histoire et philosophie* (Paris, 1900), p. 91.
16. *Ibid.*, p. 32.
17. Michelet, *Histoire de France* (Paris, n. d.), Preface of 1869.
18. *Ibid.*
19. *Ibid.*, II, 100.
20. *Ibid.*, p. 490.
21. *Ibid.*, p. 489.

22. *Ibid.*, p. 495.
23. *Ibid.*, p. 127.
24. *Ibid.*, III, 210.
25. *Ibid.*, p. 218.
26. *Ibid.*, p. 334.
27. *Ibid.*, V, 157.
28. *Ibid.*, p. 158.
29. *Ma jeunesse*, p. 76.
30. *Le Peuple*, p. 17.
31. For Michelet's attitude toward Carlyle, see the first edition of his *Histoire de la révolution française* (Paris, 1847), III, Bk. II, Chap. III, 250, and Alan Carey Taylor, *Carlyle et la pensée latine* (Paris, 1937), p. 60.
32. *Histoire de la révolution française*, II, 240.
33. *Ibid.*, I, 129–130.
34. Paul Sirven, ed., *Jules Michelet: Lettres à Alfred Dumesnil et à Eugene Noël* (Paris, 1924), p. 96 (to Dumesnil, June 29, 1846).
35. *Ibid.*, p. 182 (to Dumesnil, 1852, no month).
36. *Le Peuple*, Introduction, p. 24.
37. *Jules Michelet: Lettres à Dumesnil*, p. 5; to Madame Dumesnil, 1841, no month.
38. *Ibid.*, p. 146; to Eugene Noël, March 25, 1850.
39. *Ibid.*, pp. 178–179; to Noël, July 2, 1852.
40. *Histoire de la révolution française*, I, Introduction, Sec. 2, par. 3.
41. *Jules Michelet: Lettres à Dumesnil*, pp. 136–137; to Auguste de Gérando, September 8, 1849.
42. *Ma jeunesse*, Preface, xvi.

VII. HISTORY AS ART: RENAN, BURCKHARDT, GREEN

1. Michelet, *Histoire de France*, VII, Introduction.
2. Gustave Flaubert, *Correspondance*, 2d ser. (Paris, 1925), p. 149; to Madame X, 1852, no month.
3. *Ibid.*, 3d ser. (Paris, 1925), p. 79; to Mlle Leroyer de Chantepie, March 18, 1857.
4. Ernest Renan, *Cahiers de jeunesse*, 1845–1846 (Paris, 1901), p. 280.
5. *Ibid.*, p. 257.
6. Renan, *Lettres intimes* (Paris, 1896), p. 301; to his sister Henriette, September 22, 1845.
7. *L'Avenir de la science* (Paris, 1890), p. 301.
8. *Ibid.*, p. 1.
9. *Ibid.*, Chap. XVI, pp. 323–324.

10. *L'Avenir de la science*, Chap. VIII, p. 131.
11. *Ibid.*, Chap. X, p. 173.
12. *Ibid.*, Chap. XVI, p. 302.
13. *Ibid.*, Chap. VIII, pp. 143-144.
14. *Ibid.*, Chap VIII, pp. 150-151, and Chap. XIII, p. 176.
15. *Ibid.*, Chap. VIII, p. 148.
16. *Ibid.*, Chap. IX, p. 154.
17. *Ibid.*, Chap. XV, p. 273.
18. *Ibid.*, Chap. XV, p. 279.
19. *Ibid.*, Chap. XV, pp. 281, 275.
20. *Ibid.*, Chap. XXIII, p. 491.
21. *Nouvelles lèttres intimes* (Paris, 1923), pp. 189-190; to Henriette Renan, June 26, 1848.
22. *Ernest Renan et M. Berthelot, Correspondance*, 2d ed. (Paris, 1898), pp. 75-76; letter of January 7, 1850.
23. *Ibid.*, p. 102; letter of February 17, 1850.
24. *Ibid.*, p. 122; letter of May 22, 1850.
25. Cited by Edmund Wilson, *To the Finland Station* (New York, 1940), p. 39.
26. Ernest Renan, *Mélanges d'histoire et de voyages* (Paris, 1898), p. xiii.
27. Renan, *Essais de morale et de critique*, 2d ed. (Paris, 1860), pp. 104-105.
28. *Ibid.*, pp. 129-130, 120.
29. *Ibid.*, p. 131.
30. Renan, *Études d'histoire religieuse*, 7th ed. (Paris, 1864), pp. 6-7.
31. *Ibid.*, p. 58.
32. *Essais de morale et de critique*, Preface, pp. ii-iii.
33. *Études d'histoire religieuse*, p. 71.
34. *Lettres intimes*, p. 60; "Ma Soeur Henriette."
35. H. Taine, *Sa vie et sa correspondance* (2d ed., Paris, 1904), II, 244-245; Notes of August, 1863.
36. Renan, *Vie de Jésus* (Paris, 1893), Preface, pp. xciii, ci.
37. *Ibid.*, p. ci.
38. *Ibid.*, p. 254.
39. *Ibid.*, p. 472.
40. *Ibid.*, pp. 171-172.
41. *Ibid.*, p. 172, and *Saint Paul* (Paris, 1869), III, 470.
42. *Vie de Jésus*, p. 350.
43. *Ibid.*, pp. 346-347.
44. *Ibid.*, pp. 473-474.

NOTES FOR CHAPTER VII

45. Renan, *Les Évangiles et la seconde génération chrétienne* (Paris, n. d.), p. 98.
46. Renan, *L'Église chrétienne* (Paris, n. d.), p. 116.
47. *Les Évangiles*, p. 213.
48. *L'Église chrétienne*, p. 115.
49. *Les Évangiles*, p. 89.
50. *Marc-Aurèle* (Paris, 1882), p. 412.
51. *Saint Paul*, p. 571.
52. *Les Apôtres* (Paris, 1866), p. 372.
53. *Ibid.*, p. 375.
54. *Les Évangiles*, p. 75.
55. *Marc-Aurèle*, p. 468.
56. *L'Antéchrist* (Paris, 1873), p. 102.
57. *L'Avenir de la science*, Preface, p. xiii.
58. *Ibid.*, pp. xvi–xvii.
59. In 1859 Burckhardt published a volume of poems in the local dialect.
60. Jakob Burckhardt, *Briefe und Gedichte an die Brüder Schauenberg* (Basel, 1923), p. 68; letter of February 28, 1846.
61. Burckhardt, *Die Kultur der Renaissance in Italien* (Berlin, 1930), V, 95.
62. *Ibid.*, p. 288, footnote 2.
63. *Ibid.*, p. 264.
64. *Ibid.*, p. 354.
65. *Ibid.*, p. 219.
66. Among the minority who welcomed Niebuhr's critical scholarship is the distinguished name of Thomas Babington Macaulay.
67. Edmund Gosse, *Father and Son*, 5th ed. (New York, Charles Scribner's Sons, 1925), pp. 70–72. Reprinted by permission of the publishers.
68. Leslie Stephen, ed., *Letters of John Richard Green* (London, 1901), p. 43; to W. Boyd Dawkins, July 3, 1860.
69. *Ibid.*, p. 74; to Dawkins, 1861.
70. *Ibid.*, p. 455.
71. The historian Stubbs, seeing the young curate reading the *Vie de Jésus* on a train journey, borrowed it in order to put harm out of his way. When Green asked for its return, Stubbs replied that unfortunately a maid had thrown it into a wastebasket.
72. *Letters of John Richard Green*, p. 103; to Dawkins, September 11, 1862.
73. *Ibid.*, p. 304; to A. E. Freeman, June 27, 1871.

74. *Letters of John Richard Green*, p. 309; to Freeman, November 17, 1871. Nevertheless, Greene's last works, *The Making of England* (1882) and *The Conquest of England* (left unfinished at his death in 1883), both on the Anglo-Saxon period, show a strong influence of Freeman and his school.

75. *Ibid.*, p. 357; to Freeman, September 16, 1873.

76. *Ibid.*, p. 84; to Dawkins, June 26, 1861.

77. *Ibid.*, p. 234; to Freeman, November, 1869.

78. *Ibid.*, p. 250; to Freeman, April, 1870. Johann Martin Lappenberg's *Geschichte von England* (1834–1837) had been translated as *History of England under the Anglo-Saxon Kings* (1845). Henry Adams wrote to Henry Cabot Lodge from London in 1880: "John Green is one of my intimate friends here, and how he objurgates you fellows for your German style. He says my Essay is bad enough, but you others are clean mad." *Letters of Henry Adams*, ed. Worthington Chauncey Ford (Boston, 1930), p. 323.

79. *Ibid.*, p. 179; to Freeman, March 2, 1867.

80. *Ibid.*, p. 384; to Freeman, c.1874.

81. John Richard Green, *A Short History of the English People* (London, 1882), p. 681 (Chap. IX, Sec. 4).

82. *Ibid.*, p. 771 (Chap. X, Sec. 4).

83. Green, *A History of the English People*. Bk. VIII, Chap. IV, Sec. 1383.

84. *Ibid.*, Bk. IX, Chap. II, final paragraph.

85. *Letters of John Richard Green*, p. 447.

VIII. HISTORY AS SCIENCE

1. Karl Hillebrand, *Étude sur Otfried Muller et son école historique de la philologie allemande* [introducing] *L'Histoire de la littérature grècque par Otfried Muller* (Paris, 1883), I, 90–91.

2. Karl Dilthey, *Rede zur Saekularfeier Otfried Müllers* (Göttingen, 1898), p. 40.

3. Friedrich Nietzsche, *Thoughts out of Season*, tr. A. M. Ludovici (New York, 1924), p. 4.

4. Leopold von Ranke, *Geschichten der romanischen und germanischen Völker*, 2d ed. (Leipzig, 1874), Foreword of the First Edition (October, 1824), p. viii.

5. Theodor Mommsen, *Reden und Aufsätze* (Berlin, 1905), p. 11; Rectorial Address for 1874.

6. Reported by G. Monod, in *La Rèvue Historique*, XLI, 278.

7. Cited by G. P. Gooch, *History and Historians of the Nineteenth Century* (London, 1935), pp. 457, 458.

8. John Morley, *Diderot and the Encyclopaedists* (London, 1914), II, 212.

9. Alfred North Whitehead, *Science and the Modern World* (New York, 1925), p. 148.

10. See the opening pages of Rhys Carpenter, *The Humanistic Value of Archeology* (Cambridge, Mass., 1933). Compare William James's remark: "Within a few years, what one may call a microscopic psychology has arisen in Germany, carried on by experimental methods. This method taxes patience to the utmost, and could hardly have arisen in a country whose natives could be *bored*." Chapter on "The Methods and Snares of Psychology" in *Principles of Psychology*, Vol. I.

11. Sir John Sandys, *A History of Classical Scholarship* (Cambridge, England, Cambridge University Press, 1908), III, 89. Reprinted by permission of the publishers.

12. Waldo Dunn, *Froude and Carlyle* (New York, 1930), Chap. XIII.

13. Leslie Stephen, ed., *Letters of John Richard Green* (London, 1901), p. 420; letter to Freeman, September 2, 1875.

14. George Macaulay Trevelyan, *Clio, a Muse, and Other Essays* (London and New York, Longmans, Green and Co., 1930), p. 140. Reprinted by permission of the publishers.

15. J. B. Bury, *Inaugural Lecture* (Cambridge, 1903).

16. George Macaulay Trevelyan, "The Latest View of History," *Independent Review*, I (1904) 395.

17. Trevelyan, *Clio, a Muse*, p. 140.

18. Professor Trevelyan has recently returned to the theme with *History and the Reader* (Cambridge, England, 1946).

19. Benedetto Croce, *History: Its Theory and Practice*, tr. Douglas Ainslee (New York, Harcourt, Brace, 1921), pp. 24–25. Reprinted by permission of the publishers.

20. *Ibid.*, p. 83.

21. *Ibid.*, p. 77.

22. *Ibid.*, p. 119.

23. *Ibid.*, pp. 292–294.

IX. TWENTIETH-CENTURY THOUGHT IN SEARCH OF A HISTORIAN

1. Cited by J. W. N. Sullivan, *Aspects of Science* (New York, 1925), p. 56.

2. Sullivan, *The Limitations of Science* (London, 1933), p. 102.

3. Cited by Robert Livingston Schuyler, "Indeterminism in Physics and in History," *Social Studies*, XXXI (December, 1936), 511.

NOTES FOR CHAPTER IX

4. A. d'Abro, *The Decline of Mechanism in Modern Physics* (New York, 1939), Preface.
5. Sullivan, *The Limitations of Science*, pp. 268–269.
6. D'Abro, *op. cit.*, p. 189.
7. Sigmund Freud, *A General Introduction to Psychoanalysis*, tr. Joan Rivière (Garden City, 1938), p. 90.
8. *Ibid.*, p. 19.
9. *Ibid.*, p. 177.
10. Cited by Egon Friedell, *Kulturgeschichte der Neuzeit* (Munich, 1928), III, 578.
11. Freud, *New Introductory Lectures on Psycho-analysis*, tr. Sprott (New York, 1933), p. 111.
12. Robert Lowie, *A History of Ethnological Theory* (New York, 1937), p. 266.
13. See Ruth Benedict, *Patterns of Culture* (New York, 1935), and Karen Horney, *The Neurotic Personality of Our Time* (New York, 1937).
14. T. S. Eliot's *The Waste Land* appeared in 1922.
15. M. A. de Gobineau, *Essai sur l'inégalité des races humaines* (Paris, 1853–1855), I, 1.
16. *Ibid.*, I, 280–281.
17. The superiority of the Aryans was moral and political. Artistic culture could come from the contact and mixture of diverse races.
18. Gobineau, *op. cit.*, I, 4.
19. W. M. Flinders Petrie, *The Revolutions of Civilization* (New York, 1941), p. 81. Note the reappearance of this technical sense of the word "contemporary" in Spengler.
20. *Ibid.*, p. 126.
21. Oswald Spengler, *The Decline of the West*, tr. Charles Travis Atkinson (New York, Alfred Knopf, 1926–1928), II, 169. Reprinted by permission of the publishers.
22. *Ibid.*
23. *Ibid.*, I, 353.
24. *Ibid.*, p. 427.
25. *Ibid.*, p. 119.
26. *Ibid.*, p. 25.
27. *Ibid.*, p. 56.
28. *Ibid.*, p. 122.
29. *Ibid.*, p. 106.
30. *Ibid.*, p. 41.
31. *Ibid.*, II, 3.
32. *Ibid.*, I, 241.

33. *Ibid.*, p. 104.
34. *Ibid.*, p. 109.
35. *Ibid.*, p. 39.
36. *Ibid.*, p. 41.
37. *Ibid.*, II, 115.
38. *Ibid.*, p. 363.

39. Arnold J. Toynbee, *A Study of History* (London, Oxford University Press, 1934–1939), IV, viii–ix; Preface dated March 31, 1939. Reprinted by permission of the publishers.

40. *Ibid.*, III, 342.
41. *Ibid.*, IV, 3.
42. *Ibid.*, p. 39.
43. *Ibid.*

44. These obstacles to literary effectiveness have been largely removed by D. C. Somervell's one-volume abridgment of *A Study of History* (London and New York, 1947); but even this falls short of Spengler's skill.

SELECTED REFERENCES

BACKGROUND READING

The History of Historical Writing

Shotwell, James T. The History of History. New York, 1939.
  The best introduction to the subject, but confined to antiquity.
Fueter, Eduard. Geschichte der neuren Historiographie. Munich, 1911.
  Good for the Renaissance and Enlightenment only.
Meinecke, Friedrich. Die Entstehung der Historismus. Munich, 1936.
  Useful in gathering scattered ideas of Goethe and Herder, but puts them out of focus by considering Ranke as their fulfillment.
Gooch, G. P. History and Historians of the Nineteenth Century. London, 1935.
  Well balanced and illuminating.
Thompson, James Westfall, and Bernard J. Holm. A History of Historical Writing. 2 vols. New York, 1942.
  Covers all periods, but is superficial and chaotic.
Croce, Benedetto. Teoria e storia della storiografia. 3d ed. Bari, 1927.
  Translated by Douglas Ainslee as *History: Its Theory and Practice* (New York, 1921).
Flint, Robert. Historical Philosophy in France. New York, 1894.
Black, J. B. The Art of History. London and New York, 1926.
  Voltaire, Hume, Robertson, and Gibbon as literary artists.

The History of Taste

Neff, Emery. A Revolution in European Poetry (1660–1900). New York, 1940.
Hazard, Paul. La Crise de la conscience européenne (1680–1715). 3 vols. Paris, 1935.
  The rise of the Enlightenment.
Chambers, Frank P. The History of Taste: the Revolutions of Art Criticism and Theory in Europe. New York, 1932.
Wellek, René. The Rise of English Literary History. Chapel Hill, N.C., 1941.

The History of Science

Whitehead, Alfred North. Science and the Modern World. New York, 1925.
  A philosophical and critical approach.

Smith, Preserved. A History of Modern Culture. 2 vols. New York, 1930.
A belated example of the Enlightenment point of view.
Nordenskiöld, Erik. The History of Biology. Translated from the Swedish by Leonard Bucknall Eyre. New York, 1929.
Giekie, Sir Archibald. Founders of Geology. London, 1905.
Penniman, T. K. A Hundred Years of Anthropology. London, 1935.
Lowie, Robert H. The History of Ethnological Theory. New York, 1937.
Stresses American contributions.
Carpenter, Rhys. The Humanistic Value of Archeology. Cambridge, Mass., 1933.

Old Testament History and Literature

Spinoza, Baruch. Tractatus Theologico-Politicus. Translated by R. H. Elwes. London, 1905.
Simon, Richard. Histoire critique du Vieux Testament. Rotterdam, 1685.
Margival, Henri. Essai sur Richard Simon et la critique biblique. Paris, 1900.
[Astruc, Jean]. Conjectures sur les mémoires originaux dont il parait que Moyse s'est servi pour composer le Livre de Genèse. Brussells, 1753.
Lowth, Robert. Lectures on the Sacred Poetry of the Hebrews. Translated by G. Gregory, with the Principal Notes of Professor Michaelis. London, 1787.
Eichhorn, Johann Gottfried. Einleitung ins Alte Testament. 2d ed. Reutlingen, 1790.
Bewer, J. The Literature of the Old Testament in Its Historical Development. New York, 1933.

The Homeric Question

Browne, Henry. A Handbook of Homeric Study. London, 1905.
An attractive introduction to the subject.
Vico, Giambattista. Principj di Scienza nuova. Milan, 1836.
A reprint of the 1744 edition with variants of the 1735 edition. See the chapter called "Scoperto del vero Omero."
[Blackwell, J.]. An Enquiry into the Life and Writings of Homer. London, 1735.
Wood, Robert. An Essay on the Original Genius and Writings of Homer. London, 1765.

Wolf, Friedrich August. Prolegomena ad Homerum. Halle, 1795.
Essays by Mark Pattison. Collected by Henry Nettleship. Oxford, 1889.
  Volume I contains an attractive essay on the life, teaching, and scholarship of F. A. Wolf.
Sandys, John Edwin. A History of Classical Scholarship. 3 vols. Cambridge, England, 1908.

Trends in Twentieth-Century Thought

Abro, A. d'. The Decline of Mechanism in Modern Physics. New York, 1939.
Sullivan, J. W. N. Gallio; or, The Tyranny of Science. New York, 1928.
—— The Limitations of Science. London, 1933.
Crowther, J. W., editor. Science for a New World. New York, 1934.
  Fifteen scientists survey the state of the sciences.
Jeans, Sir James. The Mysterious Universe. Cambridge, England, and New York, 1930.
Schuyler, Robert Livingston. "Indeterminism in Physics and History." *The Social Studies*, December, 1936.
Cole, Charles W. "The Relativity of History." *Political Science Quarterly*, June, 1933.
Freud, Sigmund. A General Introduction to Psychoanalysis. Translated by Joan Rivière. Garden City, N.Y., 1938.
—— New Introductory Lectures on Psycho-analysis. Translated by W. J. H. Sprott. New York, 1933.
—— Beyond the Pleasure Principle. Translated by C. J. M. Hubbach. London and Vienna, 1932.
Boas, Franz. "Anthropology." In *The Encyclopedia of the Social Sciences*. New York, 1930.
Malinowski, Bronislaw. The Dynamics of Culture Change. New Haven, Conn., 1945.
Benedict, Ruth. Patterns of Culture. New York, 1934.
Horney, Karen. The Neurotic Personality of Our Time. New York, 1937.
Fromm, Erich. The Escape from Freedom. New York, 1941.
  This book and that by Karen Horney (above) unite fruitfully the methods and conclusions of anthropology and of psychoanalysis.
Murray, Sir Gilbert. Five Stages of Greek Religion. New York, 1925.
Harrison, Jane. Prolegomena to the Study of Greek Religion. 3d ed. Cambridge, England, 1922.
  This book and that by Sir Gilbert Murray (above) use anthropology, archeology, psychology, and literature to illuminate the early history of religion.

Drucker, Peter. The End of Economic Man. New York, 1939.
Wootton, Barbara. Lament for Economics. London, 1938.
Hofstadter, Richard. Social Darwinism in American Thought (1860–1915), Philadelphia, 1944.
Barzun, Jacques. Race. New York, 1937.
The genesis and development of a modern myth.
—— Darwin, Marx, Wagner: Critique of a Heritage. Boston, 1941.
—— Of Human Freedom. Boston, 1939.
How twentieth-century thought supports the freedom and the dignity of the individual.

INDIVIDUAL HISTORIANS

Bossuet

Bossuet, Jacques Bénigne. Discours sur l'histoire universelle. Vol. XXIV of *Oeuvres complètes de Bossuet*. Paris, 1864.

Burckhardt

Burckhardt, Jakob. Die Kultur der Renaissance. In the Gesamtausgabe, Berlin and Leipzig, 1930.
Translated as *The Civilization of the Renaissance* by S. C. G. Middlemore (London and New York, 1944).

Carlyle

Carlyle, Thomas. Letters . . . to John Stuart Mill, John Sterling and Robert Browning. Edited by Alexander Carlyle. London and New York, 1923.
—— New Letters. 2 vols. Edited by Alexander Carlyle. London and New York, 1904.
—— Letters. Edited by Charles Eliot Norton. 2 vols. London, 1889.
Young, Louise Merwin. Thomas Carlyle and the Art of History. Philadelphia, 1939.
Neff, Emery. Carlyle. New York, 1932.
—— Carlyle and Mill. New York, 1924, 1926.

Chateaubriand

Chateaubriand, François René de. Les Martyrs. 2 vols. Paris, 1834.

Gibbon

Gibbon, Edward. Autobiographies. Edited by John Murray. 2d ed. London, 1897.

SELECTED REFERENCES

—— Miscellaneous Works. Edited by Lord Sheffield. 3 vols. Dublin, 1796.
Contains Gibbon's journals and letters.
Young, G. M. Gibbon. London, 1932.

Gobineau

Gobineau, Joseph Arthur, Count de. Essai sur l'inégalité des races humaines. Vols. I and II, Paris, 1853; Vols. III and IV, Paris, 1855.
Barzun, Jacques. Race. New York, 1937.
Contains an illuminating account of Gobineau and his ideas.

Green

Green, John Richard. A Short History of the English People. London, 1874.
This is available in many editions.
—— Letters. Edited by Leslie Stephen. London, 1901.

Herder

Herder, Johann Gottfried von. Sämmtliche Werke. Edited by B. Suphan. 32 vols. Berlin, 1877–1909.
The standard edition. None of Herder's historical works is readily accessible in English translation, but *God: Some Conversations* (tr. by Frederick H. Burckhardt, New York, 1940) gives philosophical and theological background for *Thoughts on History*.
Herder, Emil Gottfried von. Herders Lebensbild. 3 vols. Erlangen, 1846.
Düntzer, Heinrich, and Ferdinand von Herder, editors. Aus Herders Nachlass. 3 vols. Frankfurt-am-Main, 1856.
Haym, R. Herder nach seinem Leben und seinen Werken. 2 vols. Berlin, 1877.
The standard biography and fullest criticism.
Gillies, A. Herder. Oxford, 1945.
The easiest approach to Herder in English.
McEichran, F. The Life and Philosophy of Johann Gottfried Herder. Oxford, 1939.
The best analysis of Herder's ideas.
Nevinson, Henry. A Sketch of Herder and His Times. London, 1884.
The most intimate biographical account in English.

Among writings which influenced Herder's mind, see the following:

Hume, David. The Natural History of Religion. In Hume's *Essays, Moral, Political and Literary*, ed. by T. H. Green and T. H. Grose (2 vols. London, 1882).

Leibnitz, G. W. Oeuvres philosophiques latines et françaises. Edited by Rud. Eric Raspe. Amsterdam and Leipzig, 1765. (Contains *Nouveaux essais*, the reply to Locke.)

Sauter, Eugen. Herder und Buffon. Rixheim, 1910.

ISELIN

Iselin, Isaac. Geschichte der Menschheit. 2 vols. Zürich, 1768.

MICHELET

Michelet, Jules. Oeuvres complètes. Paris, c.1898.

—— The History of the Roman Republic. Translated by William Hazlitt. London, 1847.

This is the only historical work by Michelet fully translated into English.

—— Lettres à Alfred Dumesnil et à Eugene Noël. Paris, 1924.

Michelet has left interesting fragments of autobiography in *Ma jeunesse* (7th ed., Paris, 1884), *Mon journal* (Paris, 1888), and in his Introduction to *Le Peuple* (1846).

Monod, G. La Vie et la pensée de Jules Michelet. Paris, 1923.

The standard biography.

Halévy, Daniel. Jules Michelet. Paris, 1923.

An excellent brief introduction to the historian and his work.

MÜLLER

Müller, Otfried. Prolegomena zu einer wissenshäftlichen Mythologie. Göttingen, 1825.

—— Geschichten hellenischer Stämme und Städte. 2d ed. Breslau, 1844.

Hillebrand, K. "Etude sur Otfried Muller et sur l'école historique de la philologie allemande." In Vol. I of his translation, *Histoire de la littérature grecque par Otfried Muller* (Paris, 1883).

Dilthey, Karl. Rede zur Saekularfeier Otfried Müllers. Göttingen, 1898.

For the linguistic background of Müller's work see Ernest Tonnelat, Les Frères Grimm: leur oeuvre de jeunesse (Paris, 1912).

NIEBUHR

Niebuhr, Barthold Georg. The History of Rome. Translated by Julius Hare and Connop Thirlwall. 3 vols. London, 1855.

—— Die Briefe Barthold Georg Niebuhrs. Edited by Dietrich Gerhard and Wilhelm Norwin. 2 vols. Berlin, 1926.

Perthes, Friedrich. Lebensnachrichten über Barthold Georg Niebuhr. 2 vols. Hamburg, 1838.

Bunsen, Chevalier (Christian). The Life and Letters of Barthold Georg Niebuhr. New York, 1852.

PETRIE

Petrie, Sir William Matthew Flinders. The Revolutions of Civilizations. 2d ed. New York, 1941.

RENAN

Renan, Ernest. L'Avenir de la science. Paris, 1890.
  Translated as *The Future of Science*, by Albert Vandam and C. B. Pitman (London, 1891). Another translation with the same title but without the translator's name appeared in New York, 1891.

—— Etudes d'histoire religieuse. 7th ed. Paris, 1864.
  Translated as *Studies in Religious History* (New York, 1887).

—— Essais de morale et de critique. 2d ed. Paris, 1860.

—— Mélanges d'histoire et de voyages. Paris, 1898.

—— Histoire des origines du christianisme. 7 vols. Paris, 1863–1881.
  The French text has been published in separate volumes by Calmann-Lévy in Paris at various dates. Only the *Life of Jesus* is readily accessible in English translation.

—— Cahiers de jeunesse (Paris, 1906); Nouveau cahiers de jeunesse (Paris, 1907).
  Valuable for the genesis of his ideas.

—— Souvenirs d'enfance et de jeunesse. Paris, 1883.
  Translated as *Recollections*, by Isabel Hapgood (New York, c.1892), and as *Recollections of My Youth*, by C. B. Pitman (New York, 1883).

Renan, Ernest, and M. Berthelot. Correspondance. 2d. ed. Paris, 1926.

Renan, Ernest, and Henriette Renan. Lettres intimes (6th ed., Paris, 1896); Nouvelles lettres intimes (Paris, 1923).

Mott, Lewis Freeman. Ernest Renan. New York, 1921.
  A good introduction to the man and his work.

Darmsteter, Mary James. La Vie de Ernest Renan. Paris, 1898.
  Intimate glimpses of the man.

Soman, Marielle. La Formation philosophique d'Ernest Renan. Paris, 1914.

Spengler

Spengler, Oswald. The Decline of the West. Translated by Charles Francis Atkinson. 2 vols. New York, 1926, 1928.

Gauhe, Eberhard. Spengler und die Romantik. Berlin, 1937.

Thierry

Thierry, Augustin. Histoire de la conquête d'Angleterre par les Normands. 6 vols. 7th ed. Paris, 1846.

—— Récits des temps mérovingiens. 6th ed. Paris, 1856.

—— Dix ans d'études historiques. Paris, 1883.

Toynbee

Toynbee, Arnold J. A Study of History. 6 vols. London, 1934–1939.
A one-volume abridgment by D. C. Somervell was published in London and New York in 1947.

Trevelyan

Trevelyan, George Macaulay. Clio, a Muse. London, 1913.

—— History and the Reader. London, 1945.

Vico

Vico, Giambattista. Principj di Scienza nuova. Milan, 1844.
A reprint of the 1744 edition, with variants of the 1735 text.

—— Principes de la philosophie de l'histoire. Brussels, 1885.
A free translation of Vico's *Scienza nuova* by Jules Michelet.

—— Autobiography. Translated by Max Harold Fisch and Thomas Goddard Bergin. Ithaca, N.Y., 1944.
The Introduction traces the international influence of Vico.

Adams, H. P. The Life and Writings of Giambattista Vico. London, 1935.

Croce, Benedetto. The Philosophy of Giambattista Vico. Translated by R. G. Collingwood. New York, 1913.

Voltaire

Voltaire, François Marie Arouet de. Essai sur les moeurs et sur l'esprit des nations. In Vols. XI, XII, XIII, of *Oeuvres complètes de Voltaire*. Paris, 1878.
This has not been translated into English.

Tallentyre, S. G. Voltaire in His Letters. New York, 1919.

—— The Life of Voltaire. New York, n. d.

INDEX

Abro, A. d', 207, 208
Accounts of Merovingian Times (Thierry), 122
Acton, Lord, 191, 198; works planned by, 193
Aeneid (Virgil), 30, 99
Aeschylus, 110, 115
Age of Louis the Fourteenth, The (Voltaire), 17
Agrarian conditions and laws, 101 f.
Alembert, d', 18, 26, 45; quoted, 32
Alexander, 17, 19
American Revolution, 3, 96
Anatomy, comparative, 67, 69, 72
Ancien Régime (Taine), 192
Anthropology, 25, 26, 67, 72, 84, 211, 215
Anti-Christ (Renan), 171
Arabs, 12, 16, 22
Archeology, 194, 214
Architecture, Gothic, 24, 48, 77, 139
Aristotle, 7, 14, 15, 19, 22, 27, 43, 98
Ariosto, 16, 174
Arnim and Brentano, 49
Arnold, Matthew, 152, 178
Arnold, Thomas, 131, 178
Art for art's sake, 151
Astronomy, 6, 7, 25, 36, 76
Astruc, Jean, 54-55, 57
Atala (Chateaubriand), 131
Augustine, Saint, 4, 11, 54, 220
Augustus, 17, 135
Autobiography (Gibbon), 79

Bacon, Francis, 6, 25, 184
Ballads, popular, 29, 94, 120, 132
Baudelaire, Charles, 151, 218
Baur, Ferdinand, 180
Beaufort, Louis de, 97
Bennett, Arnold, 196
Bernard, Claude, 196
Berthelot, Marcellin, 154, 163
Bible, 8, 11, 27, 28, 34, 42, 61, 158, 179; "botanical" poetry: language a clue to writers, 35; inclusion of Hebrew history and literature in studies and translations of, 42, 51-64; the Gospels, 167 ff.; conception of, by English, 177; approaches to, 178; *see also* Old Testament *and its books*, e.g., Psalms
Biology, 13, 25, 69, 191, 196, 209, 219
Blackwell, James, 29, 43; quoted, 33, 34, 35
Boas, Franz, 211, 215
Boeckh, August, 106, 173, 195
Bohr, Niels, 205
Boileau, 19, 27, 43; quoted, 30
Bopp, Franz, 107, 154, 157
Bossuet, Bp. of Meaux, 11 ff., 18, 54, 59, 80, 81, 88, 131, 178; Herder's mediation between Voltaire and, 49
"Botanical" poetry of Jews, 35
Bruno, Giordano, 27
Buffon, Count, 24, 25, 38, 70; quoted, 65; research, and works by, 66 ff.
Burckhardt, Jakob, 153, 172-76; book on the Renaissance, 174-76
Burke, Edmund, 184, 217
Burnouf, Eugène, 154
Bury, J. B., 191, 198, 199
Buttmann, Philipp Karl, 95, 106
Byron, Lord, 131

Caesar, 17, 135
Cambridge Modern History, 193
Capital (Marx), 192
Carlyle, Thomas, 144, 145, 197, 198, 199, 210; writers influencing, 118, 122 f.; early work, 123; style: historical writing, 125-28
Carthage, 135, 152
Change and continuity, historical laws of, 169
Chardin, Jean, 9
Charlemagne, 12
Chateaubriand, René de, 118, 122, 131, 157; style and narrative art of his prose epic, 116 f.
Chaucer, 184
Chemistry, 13, 25, 69
China, 8, 12, 14, 15, 16
Christianity, 19; origins, 13; mythol-

Christianity *(Continued)*
ogy, 76; Renan's ideas about, and history of its origins, 158, 162 ff.; the Gospels, 167 ff.;
City of God (Saint Augustine), 4, 221
Civilizations, rise and fall of, 213-22 *passim*
"Clio, a Muse" (Trevelyan), 198
Coleridge, Samuel Taylor, 28, 131
Commines, 172
Conjectures on ... Memoirs ... Used by Moses in Compiling Genesis (Astruc), 55
Constantine, 15, 34
Copernicus, 16
Corneille, 43
"Correspondence about Ossian ..." (Herder), 49
Creuzer, 106, 132
Critical History of the Old Testament (Simon), 52, 54
Criticism, literary, 7; "higher" distinguished from "lower," 58 f.
Croce, Benedetto, 200 f.
Cromwell, Oliver, 126, 127
Crusades, 15, 76, 77, 80
Culture of the Renaissance in Italy, The (Burckhardt), 174-76

Dante, 16, 139, 174
Danton, 124, 169
Darwin, Charles, 69, 152, 179
Darwinism, 191, 209, 219
Daubenton, Louis, 67
Decline and Fall of the Roman Empire, The (Gibbon), 79 ff.
Decline of the West (Spengler), 213, 215-20, 221, 222; excerpts, 218
Descartes, René, 5, 6, 7, 10, 22, 70, 192, 203, 204, 207
Determinism, 196, 203, 205, 212, 219 221
De Vries, Hugo, 209
Diderot, Denis, 26
Dilthey, Karl, 189
Dissertation on ... Roman History (De Beaufort), 97
Divine Comedy (Dante), 140
Donation of Constantine, 15, 34

Dorians, 113-15
Dream of John Ball, A (Morris), 152
Dynasts, The (Hardy), 196

Earthly Paradise, The (Morris), 152
Ecclesiastes, 58
Economic struggles of Roman Republic, 101 f.
Economics, classical, 191, 211, 212; experimental, 212
Eddas, 22, 29, 31, 40, 46, 80, 94
Egypt, 9, 23; myths, 46
Eichorn, Johann, 51, 61, 154, 157; study of the Old Testament, 55 ff.
Einstein, Albert, 204 f., 207, 208
Electricity, 65, 203, 205
Elizabeth, Queen, 184
Elizabeth and Essex (Strachey), 199
Embryology, 68, 70 ff.
Émile (Rousseau), 43
Encyclopaedia, 18, 32
England, revolution escaped, 176; influence of Christianity, 176 ff.; change in historical method, 197 ff.
English language, 32 f.
English people, Thierry's histories of, 120-22; Green's, 180-86
English popular ballads, 29, 94, 120
Enlightenment, The, 6, 17, 26, 29, 41, 50, 83, 191, 196, 211, 216; the new, 192
Enquiry into the Life and Writings of Homer, An (Blackwell), 29
Epochs of Nature (Buffon), 67
"Essay on Criticism" (Pope), 43
Essay on Man (Pope), 25
Essay on the Human Understanding (Locke), 6
Essay on the Inequality of Human Races (Gobineau), 213 f.
Essay on the Manners and Character of the Nations (Voltaire), 4, 11, 17, 24, 131
Essay on the Original Genius and Writing of Homer (Wood), 30
Essays and Reviews, 178
Ethical and Critical Essays (Renan), 161
Ethics (Spinoza), 64
Etruscans, The (Müller), 133

Etymology, 35, 85, 100, 106-8; *see also* Languages
Euclid, 203, 204, 217
Ewald, Heinrich, 154, 180

Fabius Pictor, 97, 100
Fauriel, Charles, 121
Feudalism, 8, 141, 142
Flaubert, Gustave, 148, 151, 152
Folk poetry, 49
Folk songs, 26, 48
Folksongs . . . (Herder), 49, 99
Folk tales, 28
Fontenelle, Bernard de, 58; quoted, 6
Fortune of the Rougons, The (Zola), 196
Fragments of Ancient Poetry Collected in the Highlands of Scotland (Macpherson), 29
Fragments on Recent German Literature (Herder), 43, 62
France, Michelet's study, and histories, 135-49
Franklin, Benjamin, 65
Fraser, Sir James, 40
Frederick the Great, 32
Freeman, E. A., 181 f., 183, 191, 197
French language, 31 f., 43, 44, 138
French Revolution, 3, 82, 83, 84, 88, 93, 118, 130, 155, 169, 176, 184; *French Revolution* (Carlyle), 122-28 *passim*, 144, 199; Michelet's, 144 ff.; Carlyle's history, 122-28 *passim*, 144, 199; *History of the French Revolution, The* (Michelet), 145 ff.
French Revolution, Third, 146
French Revolution of 1830, 104, 136, 144
Freud, Sigmund, 209-11
Froissart, 130
Froude, James Anthony, 197
Fustel de Coulanges, Numa Denis, 192, 200
Future of Science, The (Renan), 155 ff., 160, 161, 171

Galileo, 5, 16, 124, 206
Gardiner, Samuel Rawson, 181, 197

Gauss, Carl, 208
Gautier, Théophile, 151
Genesis, 23, 26, 42, 53, 54; Eichhorn's study, 55 ff.
Geography, 7, 9, 67, 74, 111, 132, 137, 138, 191
Geology, 13, 24, 25, 69, 95, 179
Geometry, 6, 204; analytical, 7
German Character and Art (Herder and Goethe), 48, 50
German Grammar (Jakob Grimm), 107
German literature, 42 ff.
Germanic Architecture (Goethe), 48
Germanic languages, 35, 43, 44, 107
Germany, heroic poems, 97, 99; scholars' work in mythology, 106 ff.; political and cultural changes, 189 ff.
Gibbon, Edward, 5, 96, 104, 105, 133, 183, 196, 197, 199; history of Rome and influences that led to it, 79; its design and treatment, 81 f., 84
Gobineau, Count de, 213 f., 215; popular misunderstanding of his racial theory corrected, 238n
Goethe, 88, 93, 94, 117, 127, 132, 154, 155, 173, 180, 189, 217, 220; association with Herder, 48, 50, 51, 68, 69
Golden Bough (Fraser), 40
Gospels, the, 167 ff.
Gosse, Edmund, quoted, 177
Gothic architecture, 24, 48, 77, 139
Gottsched, Professor, 32
Götz von Berlichingen (Goethe), 48, 88
Gravitation, 204
Greece, 9, 17, 19, 23; civilization in, 74; decline of, 75
Greeks, language, 33, 35, 43, 111, 167; art, 35; literature, 44; myths, 46, 56, 106; poetry, 59; history of literature of, 62; history writing, 73; effect of Byzantine Christianity, 79; relation between myths and early history: scholars' investigations, 106-15 *passim;* religion, 113
Green, John Richard, 153, 197; early life and studies, 179 f.; histories of the English people, 180-86
Gregory of Tours, 122

INDEX

Grimm, Jakob, 99, 107, 108, 132, 157, 173
Grimm brothers, 110
Grimm's Law, 108
Guiccardini, 11
Guizot, François P. G., 136, 147

Haldane, J. B. S., 207
Haller, Albrecht von, 65
Hamann, Johann, 38, 41, 50; conclusions and influence of, 26 ff.
Hamburg Dramaturgy (Lessing), 43
Hardy, Thomas, 196
Heart of Midlothian, The (Scott), 118
Hebrew language, 43, 63
Hebrew poetry, 35, 42, 61-64
Hebrew Scriptures, *see* Bible
Hebrews, *see* Jews
Hegel, Georg, 156, 172, 173, 189, 201
Henry Esmond (Thackeray), 152
Herder, Johann Gottfried, 81, 82, 84, 94, 99, 108, 115, 123, 126, 127, 138, 154, 155, 157, 158, 185, 201, 203, 217; enlarged concept of history in his *Still Another Philosophy of History*, 21 ff., 47; pastorates, 24, 28, 50; early life, 24 ff.; sources of enlarged inspiration, 28; interest in the poetry and culture of primitive peoples, 29 ff., 49, 77; study of languages: opening of windows upon history, 34; philosophies in which he met acknowledgment of the limitations of pure reason, 36 ff.; appreciation and interpretation of Bible, 42, 51, 61 ff.; literary problem that gave opening for his novel views of history, 42; period of disillusionment, 45; sea voyage and its effect: fragments from *Journal* kept, 45 ff.; vision of history as his life work, 47; his masterpiece, 47, 69; essays, 48, 61; association with Goethe, 48, 50, 51, 68, 69; work on Hebrew poetry, 61-64; steps toward his synthesis of history, 64 ff.; the published work, 68 ff.; wide influence, 83, 88, 132; question of his indebtedness to Vico, 229*n*
Heredity, 196, 209
Hermann, Gottfried, 195
Herodotus, 7, 8, 56, 114
Hillebrand, Karl, quoted, 189
Hindus, 40
Historical novel, 48; Scott's, 116, 117 f., 119, 122
Historical spirit, effect of belated unloosing of, 178
Histories of the Latin and Germanic Peoples (Ranke), 190
History, effect of revolution in taste and literary creation, 3 f.; sacred and profane, 11 ff.; Voltaire's view, 4 ff.; his writings and their influence: the four great eras, 17; Herder's original and fresh valuation, 21 ff.; poetry the original language, 26 ff.; windows opened by language-study, 34; prehistory, 34, 40, 73, 86; literary problem that gave opening for Herder's novel views, 42; inclusion of Hebrew literature and history in works on the Bible and Hebrew poetry, 42, 51-64; men of action and their role: Herder's new concept of the stuff of history, 46; his vision of, and masterpiece on, 47; work that led to his writing, 48; synthesis of, 64 ff.; serious work of Greeks, 73; connection of ancient with modern, in Gibbon's Rome, 81; effect of French Revolution upon writing of, 83; Vico's conception, 83 ff.; prose appropriate to poetry of, 88; material embedded in legend and myth: recovered by historian, 97 f.; logic of, 138; Darwin's service to, 152; as science, 191 ff.; relationship of philosophy and, 200 f.; sense of historic growth lost, 216; judgment brought forth by probings into meaning of, 222
History: Its Theory and Practice (Croce), 200
History of Art in Antiquity (Winckelmann), 35

INDEX

History of England (Hume), 18, 123, 131
History of English Literature (Taine), 195
History of Ethnological Theory (Lowie), 211
History of France (Michelet), 135-49 *passim*, 174
History of Hellenic Races and Cities (Müller), 110
History of Oracles (Fontenelle), 58
History of Rome (Thomas Arnold), 178
—— (Mommsen), 193
—— (Niebuhr), 93-105 *passim*, 132, 177
History of Scotland (Robertson), 18, 123
History of the Anglo-Saxons (Turner), 119
History of the English People (Green), 185
History of the Metaphysical, Moral and Political Sciences (Stewart), 131
History of the Norman Conquest (Freeman), 181
History of the Norman Conquest of England (Thierry), 120
History of the Origins of Christianity (Renan), 163 ff., 170
History of the People of Israel (Ewald), 154
History of the Roman Republic (Michelet), 133, 135
Hitlerism, 220
Hittite civilization, 194
Hobbes, Thomas, 54
Homer, 7, 16, 45, 59, 86, 194; reason for misunderstanding of, 29; modern writings about, 29, 30; language of, 33, 35; as guide for Niebuhr, 94, 98 f.; Wolf's *Prolegomena* to, 98
Horace, 14, 43, 59
Hugo, Victor, 142, 153
Humanists, 4, 7, 34
Hume, David, 18, 23, 36, 38 ff., 79, 119, 123, 131, 185, 197, 206
Hurd, Richard, 23, 31
Hutton, James, 69, 95

Huxley, Thomas, 178, 179, 207

Iliad (Homer), 7, 16, 74, 98, 99, 111
India, 8, 12, 15, 16
Industrial Revolution, 3, 184, 185
Infinitesimals, 36 ff.
Introduction to Experimental Medicine (Bernard), 196
Introduction to the History of Denmark (Mallet), 80
Introduction to the Old Testament (Eichhorn), 55, 154
Introduction to Universal History (Michelet), 136
Ionians, 115
Iselin, Isaac, 18, 23
Italian Humanists, 34
Italy, 16, 17, 19, 173, 183; the Renaissance in, 174-76
Ivanhoe (Scott), 118, 119, 126

Jeans, Sir James, 207
Jerome, Saint, 53, 59
Jerusalem Delivered (Tasso), 16
Jesus, 158, 171, 221; Renan's *Life of*, 163 ff.; Strauss', 164
Jews, 12, 17, 49, 74; inclusion of literary and history of, in works on the Bible and the spirit of their poetry, 42, 51-64; disparagement of, 51, 63; genius stressed by Herder, 63; *see also* Hebrew
Joan of Arc, 15, 142, 143, 148
Job, Book of, 31, 59, 64
Johnson, Samuel, 32
Jones, Sir William, 107
Josephus, 59, 98
Journal of My Voyage in 1769 (Herder), 47, 155

Kant, Immanuel, 26; erudition and tutorship: influence on Herder, 25
Keats, John, 39, 106
Kelvin, Lord, 204
Kingsley, Charles, 180
Knaben Wunderhorn, Des (Brentano and Arnim), 49

La Bruyère, Jean de, 8
Lafitau, Joseph, 8

INDEX

Lamartine, Alphonse de, 131, 153
Lamennais, Felicité Robert de, 165
Languages, 21, 31-36, 43 f., 63, 111, 138; of scientists, 31; linguistics, 34, 100, 107 f., 157, 195; etymology, 35, 85, 100, 106-8; clue to the kinship of, 107; Grimm's Law, 108; of Gospels, 167; two schools of study, 195; Freud's use of, 209 f.
"Latest View of History, The" (Trevelyan), 198
Latin, language, 32, 34, 43
Latin poetry, 59
Latvian folk songs, 26
Law of Moses, ceremonial, 58
Laws of the Twelve Tables, 133
Leclerc, Jean, 54
Leconte de Lisle, 151, 152
Leibnitz, Gotthold Wilhelm, 9, 25, 32, 65, 108, 107, 206; quoted, 6, 35; infinitesimals, 36 ff.
Lessing, Gotthold Ephraim, 43
Letters and Speeches of Cromwell, The (Carlyle, ed.), 126, 127
Letters on Chivalry and Romance (Hurd), 23, 31
Life of Jesus, The (Renan), 163 ff.
Life of Jesus (Strauss), 164
Linguistics, 34, 100, 107 f., 157, 195; *see also* Languages
Linnaeus, 25, 38, 66
Literary criticism, 7
Literary revolutions, 3, 4, 157
Literature, 25, 130, 131; model for German, 42 ff.; youth of, 44; comparative, 48, 69, 157; history of Greek, 62; popular, 167; mechanical tendencies, 195; Naturalism, 196; *see also* Poetry
Literature and Dogma (Arnold), 178
Livy, 96, 99
Locke, John, 6, 25; conception of mind, 36
Louis IX, 141
Louis XI, 141, 143
Louis XIV, 11, 12, 54; era of, 17
Louis-Philippe, 146
Lowie, Robert H., 211
Lowth, Robert, 36, 59 f.
Lucretius, quoted, 55

Lycurgus, 19
Lyell, Charles, 154, 177

Mabillon, Jean, 81
Macaulay, Thomas Babington, 185, 197, 198
Machiavelli, 11
Macpherson, James, 29, 218
Mallet, 29, 80
Malthus, Thomas, 212
Man, relationship to the earth and living things, 64, 70 ff.
Man's Place in Nature (Huxley), 178
Manzoni, Alessandro, 133
Marat, Jean Paul, 124
Martyrs, The (Chateaubriand), 116, 118
Marx, Karl, 192, 212
Marxists, 212 f.
Masses, Vico's discovery of role of, 84; the main theme of Michelet's *History*, 138, 141, 142, 144; disillusionment about, 150 f.; Renan's philosophy, 156, 160, 170
Materialistic determinism, 196, 203, 205, 212
Mathematics, 6, 25, 37, 204, 207 f. 216
Matter and spirit, 64, 65
Maurice, Frederick Denison, 180
Maxwell, James Clerk, 203
Memoirs (Commines), 172
Mendel, Gregor Johann, 209
Merovingian times, 122
Metaphysics, 25
Michaelis, J. D., 26, 31, 35, 43, 51, 55, 56; quoted, 60
Michelet, Jules, 105, 118, 151-57 *passim*, 174, 178, 180, 182, 183; personal and literary qualities, 129; as teacher, 129, 131, 144, 146, 147; awakening of interest in past: education, 130 f.; writers influencing, 131 ff.; maturing of the historian in his life's work, 135; interest in, and history of, France, 135-49; sacrifice of his posts: oath of allegiance spurned, 147, 160; his opinion of Carlyle's *French Revolution*, 233*n*

INDEX

Middle Ages, 7, 10, 18, 19, 20, 27, 48, 49, 86, 96, 111, 136, 173, 174; scope and penetration of Michelet's resurrection of, 137-48 *passim*
Milton, John, 184, 185
Mind, conceptions of, 36; psychoanalysis, 209 f., 211
Minkowski, Hermann, 204
Minoan, civilization, 194
Minyae, 112
Miracles, 12
Molière, 7, 43
Mommsen, Theodor, 190, 192 f.
Montesquieu, Baron de, 9, 62, 101
Monuments of the Mythology and Poetry of the Ancient Scandinavians (Mallet), 29
Moore, George, 196
Morley, John, 193
Morris, William, 152
Moses, 55, 64; author of the Pentateuch? 52; Law of, 58
Motte, Houdar de la, 7
Müller, Otfried, 116, 132, 133, 138, 157, 189, 194; classical and other learning, 106; investigation and use of comparative mythology, 107, 108 ff.; history of ancient Greece, 110-15; death, 115
Muratori, Ludovico, 81
Mycenean civilization, 112, 114
Mythology, 29; Christian, 76; interest in, and work of, German scholars, 106 ff.; *see also* Eddas
Myths, 40, 46, 56, 73, 106, 210; how historical material could be recovered from, 97; Müller's conception and investigation of, 107-15 *passim*

Names, and symbols, 106, 107; place names, 110
Napoleon I, 93, 104, 118, 119, 143, 144, 185
Napoleon III, 147, 150, 160, 163
National Socialism, 213
Natural history, 24, 25, 64 ff.
Natural History (Buffon), 66
Natural History of Religion, The (Hume), 39

Naturalism, 196
Natural science, 154
Nature, laws of, 10
Nature religion, 113
Neo-Platonists, 27
New Essays on the Human Understanding (Leibnitz), 35, 36
New Testament, 167 ff.
Newton, Isaac, 5, 9, 22, 25, 36, 65, 203, 204, 205, 206, 207
Nibelungenlied, 97, 132
Niebuhr, Barthold Georg, 49, 89, 106, 116, 131, 132, 133, 134, 135, 157, 176, 177, 178, 189, 195, 217; quoted, 3; characteristics: learning, 93 f.; career, 94 f., 104; interest in, and knowledge of, Roman literature and history, 94, 96 ff., 101; found historical material in legend and myth, 97 ff.; writing of the *History of Rome*, 103; character of his achievement, 105; his ballad theory popularized by Macaulay, 230*n*
Nietzsche, Friedrich, 175, 189, 218
Norman conquests, 120, 138 f.
Northern barbarians, 14, 23, 80
Notre Dame de Paris (Hugo), 142
Novels, historical, 48; Scott's, 116, 117 f., 119, 122

Odyssey (Homer), 7, 16, 46, 74, 98
Old Testament, 8, 14, 42, 51, 154; inquiries into origin and transmission of, 52 ff.; first book on, as literature, 59; *see also* Bible; *and the chapters, e.g.,* Genesis
Optics (Newton), 65
Orchomenos and the Minyae (Müller), 110, 111
Origin of Species, The (Darwin), 178
Origins of Christianity, see History of the Origins . . .
Orlando Furioso (Ariosto), 16
Ossian, 29, 49, 94
"Ossian" (Macpherson), 46, 218

Palestine, 9
Pallas, Simon, 67, 68
Pascal, Blaise, 79

Past and Present (Carlyle), 125, 127
Pater, Walter, 151
Pentateuch, Moses author of? 52
Percy, Bishop, 29, 49
Periclean age, 17, 35
Persian Letters (Montesquieu), 9
Petrarch, 16
Petrie, Sir Flinders, 213, 214 f., 216
Phidias, 115
Philosophes, 9, 36, 42, 45, 58, 79, 196; defined, 5
Philosophical Speculations on the History of Humanity (Iselin), 18
Philosophy, 130, 131; Renan's ideas, 155 ff.; relationship of history and, 200 f.
Physicists, two types, 208
Physics, 6, 13, 25, 38, 191, 203 ff., 216
Pindar, 27, 44, 45, 59, 114
Planck, Max, 205, 209
Plato, 17, 28, 98
Playfair, John, 95
Plutarch, 100, 105, 131
Poèmes antiques (Leconte de Lisle), 152
Poetic Meditations (Lamartine), 131
Poetics (Aristotle), 43
Poetry, 4, 41, 46, 73; as mother tongue of the race, 26 ff.; effect upon German conception of: literary history reversed, 27; language for purposes of, 31 ff.; Hebrew, 35, 42, 61-64; Herder an inspired translator of primitive, 49; Greek and Latin, 59; prose appropriate for poetry of history, 88
Polybius, 8
Pope, Alexander, 7, 9, 25, 27, 33, 43, 185
Populace, *see* Masses
Popular movements, Gibbon's attitude, 82; Vico's, 84
Popular Songs of Modern Greece (Fauriel, ed.), 121
Pouilly, Levesque de, 10
Prehistory, 34, 40, 73, 86
"Preliminary Discourse" (d'Alembert), 18
Principles of Geology (Lyell), 154

Prolegomena to Homer (Wolf), 94, 98, 131
Promessi Sposi, I (Manzoni), 133
Psalms, 58, 59, 62
Psychoanalysis, 209 f., 211
Psychology, 191, 196

Quentin Durward (Scott), 118, 142, 172
Quinet, Edgar, 132
Quintus Curtius, 14

Racial theories, 211, 212, 214, 215, 220
Racine, Jean, 7, 19, 43
Ranke, Leopold, 172, 173, 175, 181, 189 f., 191, 192, 198, 201
Rask, Rasmus Christian, 108
Relativity, physical theory of, 204, 208
Religion, 11, 23, 41; comparative, 14, 69; wars of, 16; Gibbon's attitude, 80; *see also* Christianity
"Religions of Antiquity, The" (Renan), 162
Reliques of Ancient English Poetry (Percy), 29, 49
Renaissance in Italy, Burckhardt's work on, 174-76
Renan, Ernest, 122, 176, 178, 180, 183; characteristics: education: early life, 153 ff.; his *Future of Science*, 155 ff., 160, 161, 171; ideas about, and histories of, Jesus and Christianity, 158, 162-71; essays, 159, 162; journey in Italy, 159; periodical writings: ideas about history, 161
Revolt of the Netherlands (Schiller), 123
Revolution, cause of England's escape from, 176
Revolution in taste, 3, 4
Revolutions of Civilization, The (Petrie), 213
Revolutions of 1848, 150, 173
Riemann, Georg F. B., 204, 208
Robert Elsmere (Mrs. Ward), 179
Robertson, William, 18, 23, 79, 123
Robespierre, 124, 169
Robin Hood ballads, 120

INDEX

Roman folk poetry, 49
Romantic art in historical writing, 116 ff.
Rome, 9, 12, 17, 19; decline of, 75; Gibbon's enthusiasm for, and history of, 79-82; Vico's studies, discoveries, and history, 84; Niebuhr's, 93-105, 132, 177; Michelet's, 133-35
Rossetti, D. G., 151
Rousseau, Jean Jacques, 26, 43, 68, 88, 131, 145, 169
Ruskin, John, 183
Rutherford, Baron, 205

Sacra poesia Hebraorum (Lowth), 36, 59 f.
Saint-Simonians, 165
Salammbô (Flaubert), 152
Sandys, Sir John, quoted, 195
Sanskrit, 107, 155
Saussure, Horace B. de, 67
Savigny, Friedrich von, 95, 101, 132, 133
Schelling, Friedrich Wilhelm, 106, 201
Schiller, Friedrich, 94, 123, 180
Schlegel, Friedrich von, 107, 201
Schliemann, Heinrich, 194
Scholasticism, 15, 77
Schrödinger, Erwin, 206
Science, 4, 8, 9, 10, 19, 24, 25, 29, 50, 77, 177, 202; language of, 31; in the synthesis of history, 64 ff.; Herder's effort to base his *History* on, 69; Renan's *Future of*, 155 ff., 160, 161, 171; increased vogue, 191; history as science, 191 ff.; mass production: division of labor, 192; twentieth-century conceptions: causes of revolutionary changes, 203 ff.; obsolete impressions of, 206; inquiry into nature of man and society altered, 209; anthropomorphic, 216
Scienza nuova (Vico), 83 ff., 131
Scott, Walter, 48, 110, 121, 122, 126, 130, 131, 133, 134, 157, 172; romantic art of historical novels, 116, 117 f., 119; Carlyle's tribute to, 122

Scottish popular ballads, 29, 94
Seeley, Sir John Robert, 191, 198
Semitic languages, 43, 63
Shaftesbury, Lord, 27
Shakespeare, 28, 43, 45, 48, 94, 117, 184; Young's protest against Pope's apology for, 27
"Shakespeare" (Herder), 49
Short History of the English People (Green), 182-85
Simon, Richard, 52, 53, 59
Slavs, 25
Socialism, 151, 180, 213
Socrates, 28
Solon, 19
Song of Songs, 58, 60, 61, 62
Sophocles, 7, 44, 49
Spain, 16
Spengler, Oswald, 213, 215-20, 221, 222
Spenser, Edmund, 184
Spinoza, Baruch, 64; conception of the Old Testament, 52, 54, 59
Spirit of Hebrew Poetry, The (Herder), 61 ff.
Spirit of the Laws, The (Montesquieu), 9, 62
Stewart, Dugald, 131
Still Another Philosophy of History . . . (Herder), 21 ff., 47, 49, 50, 64
Strachey, Lytton, 199
Strauss, David, 164
Stubbs, Bishop, 181, 191, 197
Studies in the History of Religion (Renan), 161
Study of History, A (Toynbee), 220-22
Sullivan, J. W. N., quoted, 207
Swammerdam, Jan, 68
Swift, Jonathan, 9, 32
Swinburne, Algernon, 151

Tacitus, 8, 14
Taine, Hippolyte, 192, 195, 201; quoted, 163
Talisman, The (Scott), 80
Tasso, 16
Thackeray, William Makepeace, 152
Theoria generationis (Wolff), 68

INDEX

Theory of the Earth, A ... (Buffon), 67
Theory of the Earth (Hutton), 69
Thierry, Augustin, 118, 127, 133, 136, 138, 147, 157, 160, 180, 181, 184; style, 116, 118; early influences, 118 f.; history of Norman conquest in England, 120-22; blindness, 122; Renan's tributes to, 161
Thirty Years' War (Schiller), 123
Thoughts on History (Herder), 47, 68 ff., 79, 83, 132
Thucydides, 8
Tillemont, Louis de, 81
Toynbee, Arnold J., 220-22; his Study of History condensed to one volume, 239n
Tractatus theologico-politicus (Spinoza), 52 f.
Travels in the Alps (De Saussure), 67
Treatise of Human Nature (Hume), 206
Trevelyan, George Macaulay, 197-99
Turner, Sharon, 119

Universal History (Bossuet), 11 f., 131
Universe, conceptions about, 64 ff.
Usher, Archbishop, 13, 179

Valla, Lorenzo, 34
Verlaine, Paul, 218
Vico, Giambattista, 96, 98, 132, 133, 136, 137, 140, 157; extremely independent thinker, 83; his studies and resulting history, 83-87; style, 88; influence, 88, 131; his reputation traced, 232n
Villemain, Abel-François, 131
Virgil, 7, 94, 98
Vita nuova (Dante), 174
Voltaire, 26, 27, 32, 34, 35, 36, 52, 58, 63, 79, 80, 81, 82, 88, 96, 131, 142, 145, 169, 178, 194, 196; theological and classical versions of history assailed by, 4; impressive qualifications, 10, 18; revaluation of the past, 10 ff.; effect of his historical writing: dictum *re* the four eras, 17; how Herder mediated between Bossuet and, 49
Voss, Johann, 94

Waverly (Scott), 118
Ward, Mrs. Humphry, 178
Weierstrauss, Karl, 208
Whitehead, Alfred North, 193
Winckelmann, Johann, 35, 44, 62, 132, 173
Wolf, Friedrich August, 94, 95, 98, 106, 131, 157
Wolff, Caspar, 68
Wood, Robert, 30, 43, 98; quoted, 33, 35
Wordsworth, William, 101, 110
World wars, 212

Young, Edward, quoted, 27
Young, G. M., 81

Zola, Émile, 196
Zoology, 24